THE MYTH OF
THE MODERN

THE MYTH OF THE MODERN

A Study in British Literature

and Criticism after 1850

PERRY MEISEL

YALE UNIVERSITY PRESS

NEW HAVEN AND LONDON

Publication of this work has been supported in part by a grant from the Abraham and Rebecca Stein Faculty Publication Fund of New York University, Department of English. Grateful acknowledgment is made to the following for permission to reprint:

Macmillan Publishing Company and A. P. Watt Ltd. on behalf of Michael B. Yeats and Macmillan London Ltd., for the excerpt from W. B. Yeats, "The Tower." Reprinted with permission of Macmillan Publishing Company from *The Tower* by William Butler Yeats. Copyright 1928 by Macmillan Publishing Company, renewed 1956 by Georgie Yeats.

Alfred A. Knopf, Inc., for the excerpt from Wallace Stevens, "Credences of Summer," from *The Collected Poems of Wallace Stevens*. Copyright © 1954 by Alfred A. Knopf, Inc.

Portions of this book have appeared before, in slightly different form, in *Modern Language Studies, Structuralist Review,* and *October.*

Designed by Jo Aerne and set in Electra type by Huron Valley Graphics. Printed in the United States of America by The Alpine Press, Inc., Stoughton, Mass.

Library of Congress Cataloging-in-Publication Data
Meisel, Perry.
The myth of the modern.
Bibliography: p.
Includes index.
1. English literature—20th century—History and criticism.
2. Modernism (Literature)—Great Britain. 3. English literature—19th century—History and criticism.
4. Criticism—Great Britain—History.   I. Title.
PR478.M6P4 1987   820′.9′1   87-10617
ISBN 0-300-03946-8 (cloth)
        0-300-04560-3 (pbk.)

The paper in this book meets the guidelines for permanence and durability of the Committee on Production Guidelines for Book Longevity of the Council on Library Resources.

10   9   8   7   6   5   4   3   2

For Cynthia Ward

He did not know that it was already behind him.

—*The Great Gatsby*

Contents

A Note on Citation

A systematic form of citation has been employed throughout. For ease of reference, the list of works cited at the end of the book is divided into primary and secondary sources. After any reference or quotation from texts read at any length, the author's name (if not already mentioned) appears in parentheses, accompanied by a date, and, when necessary, page or line numbers to the text cited. Use of page or line numbers alone indicates sustained discussion.

Except in the case of essays by T. S. Eliot, Woolf, the Stracheys, and Forster, the dates of all references and citations in the list of primary works cited are from a work's first appearance in book form. Standard editions have been used when they are available; in all other cases, the text is that of the most often used American or English edition. It should also be noted that line numbers attend neither the poems of Arnold in the Edition de Luxe (*Works*, 15 vols., London: Macmillan, 1903–04) nor Eliot's *Four Quartets* in their authoritative form in either the *Collected Poems, 1909–1962* (1963; rpt. New York: Harcourt, Brace & World, 1970) or *The Complete Poems and Plays, 1909–1950* (1952; rpt. New York: Harcourt Brace Jovanovich, 1971). In the list of secondary works cited, reprint editions, both American and English, have been used throughout.

THE MYTH OF
THE MODERN

INTRODUCTION

The Will to Modernity

and the Structure of Modernism

Primitivism, formalism, alienation—these are only chief among the incongruent categories through which we try to organize what we mean when we say modernism. Despite the appearance of confusion, however, a surprisingly common and uncannily enduring assumption about the modern element in literature has persisted for more than half a century. Well before Harry Levin was inclined to seal off a period of literary history for the purposes of study in 1960 or Irving Howe to institutionalize it in 1970, the work of critics as different as Leavis (1932) and Lukács (1920) was already structured by a shared presupposition that modern literature acts out the loss of something primary that it wishes to regain. Lionel Trilling's crisp designation of the will to modernity in his 1955 essay on Freud as the redemptive search for a realm "beyond" or apart from "the reach of culture" (1955:93) remains as clear a definition as we have had of what is axiomatic in our assumptions about the modern. Despite subsequent vicissitudes in the aims and procedures of literary criticism, such a presupposition is still paradigmatic, even determining the otherwise antithetical projects of revisionist historiographers of literature such as Fredric Jameson that maintain our normative understanding of modernism simultaneous with a desire to change it (1979, 1981).

The ironies of Trilling's prose in particular, however, suggest modernism to be far different from our inherited sense of it, and certainly far more than the debatable object of belief or apprehension that it has too long been. Precise to a fault, Trilling's diction calls attention to some unlikely contingencies his otherwise classical argument detonates. Freud is an exemplary High Modernist for Trilling because he represents Trilling's central contention so fully: "This intense conviction of the existence of the self apart from culture," says Trilling, "is, as culture well knows, its noblest and most generous achievement" (1955:102). And yet the sly protestations of Trilling's rhetoric bring another factor into play. If it is "culture," in Trilling's words, that "knows," how can it know any realm "beyond" itself? By definition, culture knows through its symbols. But (or therefore?) symbols are required even to represent a world without them. Hence a rhetorical impasse. How can one be more advanced by being more primitive? How can culture get beyond itself if it can know it has done so only as a function of the systems from which it wishes to be freed? Why does Freud, for example, premise his articulation of the primary process—the unconscious—on the precariousness of the oxymoron "unconscious mind"? Why is Conrad forced into a similar kind of contradiction in the Preface to *The Nigger of the "Narcissus"* when he comes to identify "that lonely region of stress and strife" inhabited by the solitary artist with that "which binds together all humanity" (1897:xii)?

What does this paradox of liberation suggest? What aesthetic or discursive horizon does it close off or demarcate? Why the wish, and why the ironies? Why the will to modernity, and why its impossibility? Why, in short, does modern literature permit itself ideals that it disallows in practice? For Trilling, the answer is plain: Freud's exemplary will to modernity—his "need . . . ," in Trilling's words, "to believe that there was some point at which it was possible to stand beyond the reach of culture" (1955:93)—is an expression of the need to defend against the awareness of "how entirely implicated in culture we all are" (91). In fact, "the unconscious of society," says Trilling, "may be said to have been imagined before the unconscious of the individual" (90). For the artist—modernism's customary Everyman—the problem is, of course, exacerbated. The will to modernity that we commonly equate with the structure of modernism as a whole is largely a defensive response to the increasingly intolerable burdens of coming late in a tradition (Bate 1970; Bloom 1973). By the time Arnold renounces verse in 1853 or Hardy arrives in London in 1862 to write novels as well as poems, a new attitude begins to emerge in English letters, different probably more in degree than in kind from those of the past, but one in which literature has apparently taken upon itself the task of pronouncing the world grayer on the basis of its own anxieties. Hardly a direct response to the real, literature produces the inverse of the inflation of the bourgeois subject galvanized by Victorian ideology. Arnold's windless heroes or Hardy's durable but doomed travelers are reflexive emblems for the weakness and insecurity caused by a magnified riot of forms in literature proper that drives the notions of originality and self-possession to the brink of their own (im)possibility in the production of prose and verse alike. Dickens's obsession with carceration (D. A. Miller 1983) already intimates the balder but like labyrinths of Kafka in an earlier and actually more skeletal form: as the overt constraints upon the possibility of autonomy represented by law rather than as an enigma of metaphysical proportions. While it is in some measure true that Romanticism slumbers enough even in Dickens's prose to turn the Victorians "away from the sublime" (Fletcher 1983:7), constraints as such were the very center of the anxieties that produced Romanticism in the first place, both as a political ideology and as a poetic practice. Literary modernism's compulsion to repeat what Thomas McFarland calls Romanticism's "originality paradox" (1985) is really an amplification of Romanticism's own struggle with tradition; even the High Modernism of Eliot and Hulme is a "permutation" of it (1985:9). Never "a mere return to the state of nature," as Geoffrey Hartman says (1962:300–01), Romanticism augurs the start of a discursive practice whose continuity with modernism has been clear since at least 1957 (see Kermode and Langbaum). For Edmund Wilson in 1931, it was already obvious that modernism is "not merely a degeneration or an elaboration of Romanticism, but rather a counterpart to it, a second flood of the same tide" (1931:1–2).

To blame history at large for the necessity of the will to modernity is the usual justification for taking modern literature's desire to start afresh as more than a discursive phenomenon. Based as it must be on a mimetic rather than a dialogical notion of referentiality, however, any claim that literature's self-announced crisis of the modern is rooted directly in the events of the present century is based on a variety of dubious premises. Not only does Matthew Arnold repeatedly proclaim the crisis of the modern over half a century before the Great War. Even the Leavisite lament, conscience-ridden as it may be, that the democratization of learning has erased the distinctions between high art and popular (1930) ignores not only the extension rather than the contraction of the arts produced by the cinema most specifically, but also the novel's own emergence as a form in a similar way (Watt 1957). Likewise, the customary wisdom that modern statecraft and warfare have made life in this century more intolerable than it ever was before neglects both the full history of Western culture as well as the reciprocal epistemological relation between totalitarianism and human rights in the history of contemporary ideology (Arendt 1951). The present study, however, stops short of moving into the study of ideology proper, taking in fact the difference between the playful, self-accounting discourses of Hardy, Pater, Joyce, and Bloomsbury, and the rhetorically repressive, incrementally mythmaking work of Arnold, Lawrence, and Eliot as the line that distinguishes what we call art and criticism from the reifications of ideology as such. The points at which Arnold and Eliot in particular descend from the writing of art and criticism to the writing of ideology are key moments in their respective itineraries, and will serve us as a measure of our threshold of acceptance as to questions about what literature itself is or may be. Modernism is in short a calculated, if often unconscious, strategy of artists and institutions rather than of history itself.

It is, then, literary modernism's implication in the history it seems to disdain that is the reflexive counterpart and defensive impetus of what it thematizes—the desire to seek a place outside of the tradition that enables it. "What else could the writer do," asks R. P. Blackmur, "but invent a vital dogma of self-sufficiency?" (1967:8). The usual Oedipal paradox in overdrive, the will to modernity—Pound's emblematic injunction to make it new—is articulated against, and as a function of, the authority that empowers it. Hence the source of modernism's vaunted aesthetic of difficulty (Steiner 1978), a strategy of escape through hermeticism that is little more than another instance of the bondage of tradition that enables its anxiety of revolt / revolt of anxiety in the first place. Function as it is of coming late in a tradition, however, modernism proper must, of necessity, be a repetition, "the last privileged repetition," as Joseph Riddel puts it (1978:463). It is no less than the third and most overt eruption of a drive—a will to modernity—endemic to modern, that is to say, postmedieval English literature as a whole. Modernism is, in all its historical manifestations, the recurrent desire to find origins or ground despite the impossibility of ever doing so for sure (De Man 1971, 1984). As Pater theorizes it in the posthumous *Gaston De Latour*—and, not incoincidentally, as recent scholarship more scrupulously confirms an English modernism already in place in the Renaissance (e.g., Reiss 1982; Fineman 1985)—the desire to make it new is, paradoxically, the traditional impetus of the (post-)Renaissance imagination at large. We can even schematize English literary history as a sequence of three modernisms—the Renaissance, Romanticism, and High Modernism proper—punctuated only by the spectatorial luxury of eighteenth-century letters, old enough to have parentage but still young enough not to begrudge it, at least not until Dr. Johnson responds negatively to Milton. If the English Renaissance reacted reflexively to the precedent of Italy by fetishizing the image of lost Greece the Italians gave it (Giamatti 1984)—already a doubly displaced origin—the same displaced will to conquer also took the form of the Elizabethan courtier's bourgeois revenge (Javitch 1978), the explorer's (Frye 1969), and, eventually, the American's. English Romanticism reacted to the precedent of Renaissance originality by reimagining as pagan and native the lost nature that Enlightenment rationality had in the meantime required by prohibiting. High Modernism responds to both in turn by taking as its subject its own problematic status in the history of English writing, particularly its filiation to Romanticism in a line devolving from Milton to Wordsworth and Keats that bypasses precisely those Jacobean and Augustan poets upon whom Eliot seized in his curricularly influential—if not wholly warranted—rerouting of the tradition at large.

Hardly the flight toward immediate vision that we think it is, then, modernism is instead a structure of compensation, a way of adjusting to the paradox of belatedness that is its precondition. If what enables also wounds, what empowers also makes for anxiety, then we should ask how well our canonical modernists manage this dilemma that gives them life while threatening them with death. If our received notion of the modern tends to equate modernism as a structure with the will to modernity that is only one of its symptoms, then it is largely mythical, insufficiently ironic to account for the objects of its veneration. It is the purpose of the present study to ask instead how strategically our canonical modernists negotiate the implacable situation in which they find themselves as writers—this double bind in which literary endeavor seems utterly repetitive, a ghostly scene like those in Hardy's poems in which anchorless pronouns search for proper names. Which writers take the will to modernity as a straightforward quest, and which as the paradox-ridden precondition it really is? By revisiting our principal modern English classics from Hardy, Arnold, and Pater to Eliot, Joyce, and Bloomsbury, I shall attempt to elucidate the structure of modernism at large, and, in the process, perhaps reformulate some of our normative canonical arrangements as well. Yeats has, however, been excepted from the discussion given the durable comprehensiveness of Harold Bloom's study (1970) and its compatibility with the approach of the present one. Pound likewise receives no lengthy discussion given in turn the comprehensiveness of Andrew Parker's decisive essay on Pound's poetics (1982–83) and its equal compatibility—unlike Pound's own—with the approach taken here.

Beginning with the paradigmatic *Mayor of Casterbridge* in the Prologue, the present study will try to clarify the modernist problematic by attempting to gauge the irony with which the will to modernity is handled writer to writer. In Hardy's exemplary case, there is a double and prophetic possibility: on the one hand, Hardy succumbs to the will to modernity by opposing the primacy of the body and the disease of the mind, robust nature and demon culture, the kinds of oppositions that Lawrence, as we shall also see, influentially reifies in his posthumous "Study of Thomas Hardy." On the other hand, however, Hardy has also already overridden Lawrence's later misreading, offering us instead a meditation on the will to modernity as such, and suggesting a solution to the paradoxes it engenders by both thematizing belatedness and implicating the reader in its necessities. The novel narrates the conditions of its own intelligibility by narrating the condition of Henchard's unintelligibility, adequating *récit* and *histoire*, narration and story, even as their difference is maintained. In fact, narration and story are alike designed to forbid the satisfaction of the will to modernity—the discovery of recuperative origins in or by Henchard—in a compromise-formation I have elsewhere called reflexive realism (see Meisel 1984), and whose dynamic is what Freud calls deferred action or secondary revision. As we shall see, reflexive realism like Hardy's builds belatedness into its simultaneously referential and reflexive or self-accounting procedures, since it takes the tale it (re)presents, not as immediate, self-sufficient, and available to mimesis, but as a distinct and analogous function of the conventions of its own narration.

The double option presented by Hardy in 1886 represents the two sides of the debate between Arnold and Pater (usually only implicit in Pater's largely later texts) that structures English criticism in the second half of the nineteenth century. Its examination takes up part 1 of the present study. Given Arnold's overt capitulation to anxiety of influence as a poet, it is not surprising that, as a critic, he should become overtly preoccupied with the search for origins. Is there a realm beyond culture or outside language to which language and culture can alike appeal? For Arnold as critic, there is indeed respite from the crisis of modernity—of belatedness—in a realm of universal absolutes well beyond the contingencies of time and history, a realm to be found in the compensations that prose will provide him after failure as a poet. For Pater, by contrast, there is an enormous correction to be made. In "Style" in particular, Pater theorizes a mode of accommodation to belatedness that does not capitulate to the will to modernity, but that restructures our notion of it by both accounting for it and outlining an alternative mode of writing in which the dynamic of temporality—of deferred action—plays an overt rather than repressed role. Pater also puts it into practice in the imaginary portraits, not only in *Marius*, but, as we shall see rather exactly, in *Gaston De Latour* as well.

The implicit debate reappears early in the twentieth century in the striking contrast to be found between Eliot and Joyce, producing two separate lines of High British modernism proper that are the subjects of part 2. Eliot's genealogy is Arnoldean, despite the Paterian incubus he must fight off; Joyce's stance is, by contrast, consummately Paterian. Though our customary assumption is that Eliot and Joyce share a common project (largely the function of Eliot's review of *Ulysses* in 1923), the following study will attempt to show just how different their work really is. Repressing the sure evidence of Pater, Eliot will instead press an implicitly Arnoldean case against all odds in both his central essays and his poems, even against the evidence of his own strongest essay, "Tradition and the Individual Talent." Though Eliot is in plain possession of Pater's demystification of the possibility of extracultural absolutes there, he is, in his other major essays and in his two long poems, curiously bent on obscuring the pressures of belatedness in favor of inventing, like Arnold before him, a mythic literary history—an ideology rather than a mode of criticism—bequeathed to the future as truth. Joyce will instead work through Pater's recommendations, submitting Arnold's categories to a Paterian rearticulation to be seen most readily in the change in Stephen Dedalus as he moves from the world of the *Portrait* to that of *Ulysses*. With *Ulysses*, Joyce in fact makes the problematic readability of his text the reflexive emblem of the overdetermined representations of life itself that his text represents.

What alternative within High Modernism is to be found that mediates between Joyce's radical exposure of the means of literary production and Eliot's repression of it? To find it is also to find a place for a collective sensibility that has received enormous popular attention but little that situates it historically. Bloomsbury, however, is more than a minor formation with Virginia Woolf alone as its major literary figure; it is also even more than a late outcropping of aestheticism. In part 3 we shall see how the work of Forster, Woolf, and Strachey plays out a three-act accommodation to the contingencies of modern literary production—to belatedness—theorized and practiced by Pater and taken to the limit by Joyce. Forsterian and Woolfian appearances alike to the contrary, the Bloomsbury novel espouses neither the Wastelander ethic of Arnold and Eliot nor the equal extreme of Joyce's hyper-Paterianism. Instead, it finds a middle ground that will return us to the prescient Hardyesque strategy that thwarts Lawrence's reductive misreading of his master—namely, reflexive realism. Much as Hardy's novels represent the world itself as a world of representations to which any given character comes, like the writer or reader, after the fact, so the Bloomsbury novel is—quite unlike *Ulysses* in particular—not an attempt to represent our impression of reality, but only an attempt to represent our most influential notions and representations of it. With *Howards End*, we will see Arnold's and Eliot's attempts to oppose a lost plenitude and a modern emptiness disrupted as the novel's rhetoric contaminates the categories that articulate its apparent Wastelander vision, an ideology relegated, well before the publication of Eliot's poem twelve years later, to one of the novel's subjects. With *To the Lighthouse*, belatedness as such becomes the dynamic of both life as Woolf represents it and of narration as her reader experiences it. The novel overrides any distinction between form and content by making each a version of the other, both instances of the recursive, elegiac modality of the discourses that make up the real itself. With Strachey, we come at last to a sequence of texts—*Eminent Victorians, Queen Victoria,* and *Elizabeth and Essex*—that will summarize the movement of all that I will have examined beforehand: the assessment of life as a set of representations to which we come mediately and belatedly as interpretative citizens in *Eminent Victorians* (what Arnold represses and Pater expresses); the production of secret, private origins for Victoria as a function of the publicity that manages them in *Queen Victoria*; and the narration of the historical birth of the psychological categories that enable all English modernisms as they begin to unfold in the Renaissance of *Elizabeth and Essex*.

The study will conclude with a reading of Conrad's *Heart of Darkness* in the Epilogue in order to recapitulate the movement I shall have charted. The difference between the classical reading of *Heart of Darkness*—Marlow's discovery of his presumably unconscious origins in his secret sharer, Kurtz (Guerard 1958)—and a reading of the tale as a piece of reflexive realism of the highest order—as a pedagogy of reading—is the difference between our customary equation of the will to modernity with modernism as a whole and the various strategies of accommodation to the will to modernity that the present study will have traced as a supplement to our inherited view. A brief reading of *The Secret Sharer* will provide a pivot between the normative reading of *Heart of Darkness* and my own so as to suggest not only that the later Conrad may, like the later Freud, revise the earlier one; but also that, with a belated hint from the later text, even the early Conrad may already be seen to take as his subject the will to modernity that he seems only to express. *Heart of Darkness* in fact questions the possibility of Kurtz's coming to represent the primitive origin that the novel's imagery seems to assign him. The text becomes instead a mirror of the categories by which Marlow reads, and, by implication, of the categories by which we in turn read it. It requires us to discover, not a primitive origin outside language and history to which the will to modernity can once again appeal, but the naked structure of our desire to discover such a transcendent realm in the first place. The Epilogue concludes with a brief consideration of postmodernism.

As a response to literary historical conditions, then, strong modernist texts both thematize and dramatize the reality of coming too late in a tradition. They give us allegories of reading ready for our own vulgar modernist wishes—our culturally inherited will to modernity—and put the latter into question in the very act of seeming to achieve them. Strong modernist texts are inquiries into the dynamics of readerly temporality itself—how one reads and how to take one's own belated place as a reader (and as a writer) into account. The weak, if canonical, modernist text—the influential prose and poems of Arnold and Eliot in particular—is, by contrast, bent on repressing the inevitability of such a process, favoring instead an ahistoricism that refuses to address the questions it raises. Rather than frustrated attempts to probe the depths of being or to strip language of a content supposedly distinct from its form, strong—and necessarily ironic—modernism reemerges as a primer in the poetics of reading, canonization, and the formation of literary history.

The structure of thought and articulation that our modernists share is, of course, one that can only be called an unconscious epistemic configuration whose boundaries demarcate the horizon or closure of the possibility of modernism at large. Although momentary biographical remarks may at times appear (e.g., in relation to the knowledge, say, of Freud a given writer may have had, or whether he or she had read Pater), biographical considerations of the formulaic or conclusive sort have been largely avoided. Thus Eliot, socially a part of Bloomsbury, was nonetheless never really part of its aesthetics despite, for example, Leavis's remark that "Eliot was . . . completely *of* that Bloomsbury world" (1958:188). So, too, will the study bypass Woolf's own rather direct knowledge of English Freud through James and Alix Strachey, or, earlier on, refuse to fret about the lack of a direct or public debate between Arnold and Pater. As for method and procedure, then, despite occasional moments of appreciation or polemic, the concern throughout is not so much with the particular choiceness of given texts, but with a given text's position and influence or power within the larger patterns that bind discourse into the formations we call historical periods. If, at times, the style of reading is close (with Eliot, for example, or Forster), it is, at others, schematic (with Arnold, for example, or Joyce). In both such cases, however, the attempt throughout remains the tracing, in miniature or in large, of the strikingly uniform structure of modernism as a whole. The modernist problematic is, moreover, treated at times as a synchronic structure little different in Arnold or Eliot, say, than in Pater or Joyce (of course, modernism, by present definition, need in fact be prisoner to the regime from which it claims to depart). At times, too, however, it is handled as genealogical, particularly in the attempt to find relations among Arnold, Pater, Eliot, and Joyce. As a whole, then, the following pages are intended as paradigmatic rather than comprehensive, even though, with the aforementioned exception of Yeats and the exclusion of Pound (and, if you choose, of Ford and Lewis), virtually all of our canonical British modernists will have come under investigation.

Some of the inevitable methodological contradictions to which the writing of any account is necessarily subject ought to be noted here as well, especially the way the present study's dialectical organization fashions arguments that impugn its integrity as a procedural device. Such transgressions are, however, endemic to discourse itself (Derrida 1967), and to highlight its ironies is very likely the only means by which what follows may aspire to double the objects of its scrutiny.

PROLOGUE

Hardy, Lawrence, and the Disruptions of Nature

But have we a right to assume the survival of something that was originally there, alongside of what was later derived from it?

— Freud, *Civilization and Its Discontents*

"The Ache of Modernism"

It is the dour Thomas Hardy who gives us the phrase "the ache of modernism" in *Tess of the d'Urbervilles* (1891:160), a novel that takes as its premise a nostalgia for primacy dramatized by the Durbeyfields' hopelessly wishful quest for the purported ground of aristocratic origins. The resonant but ambiguous slogan has been prompted, in Angel's mind at least, by Tess's fearful sense of the trees surrounding the placid dairy as symbols of a savage nature at odds with culture. Angel's quick admiration of Tess's attitude seems to confirm the assurance with which Hardy himself appears to use the term. Assurance, however, is hard to come by in purblind Wessex. Irony clusters about "modernism" as Angel understands it, especially given his subsequent inability to welcome just the kind of natural potency in Tess herself that he admires here only abstractly. In the process, too, the almost primitive status that drives Mr. Durbeyfield to look upon his family as estranged from origins turns out to be the source of the primacy Tess's own tragic redemptiveness comes to represent by tale's end. The pattern of paradox is not, however, unfamiliar in Hardy's fiction. Its outlines already emerge in Angel's more sympathetic progenitor thirteen years before, Clym Yeobright in *The Return of the Native* (1878). The earlier novel's title is in fact a graphic instance of the will to modernity that both wounds and empowers Hardy as novelist and poet alike. The wishful return to ground or origins—to a native realm "beyond culture"—is, of course, represented by Clym's uneasy and ultimately failed romance with Eustacia, a romance that symbolizes the will to modernity compact in Hardy's celebration of the brute spirit of the Heath, that "hitherto unrecognized original" (1878:5) apparently emblematic of natural forces repressed by civilization. At the same time, however, Hardy also puts such willfulness into question in the enabling but always anxious distance that Clym's culture requires there to be between dream and satisfaction. Even Eustacia's Italianate status as a dark source of vital energy is produced by a Romantic culture that Hardy's narration not only represents but in which it is also implicated. Like Angel's, Clym's prescient "modernism" is already as historically fossilized as it is real, although it is not until the later Hardy gives us the incrementally moody sequence of *The Mayor of Casterbridge* (1886), *The Woodlanders* (1887), *Tess*

(1891), *Jude* (1896), and *The Well-Beloved* (1897) that his own modernism becomes as overtly suspect as Clym's own.

Poised as it is between two notions of the "modern" in Hardy—the early largely sympathetic (the redemptive Gabriel Oak is probably its consummate representative), the latter less so (Jude's desire for liberation becomes a cruel joke)—*The Mayor of Casterbridge* is exemplary both of Hardy's career and of the modernist imagination at large. The novel is so jammed with allusiveness both generic and figural—biblical, classical, nativist Romantic—that the very forms of literary language and structural usage that Hardy inherits begin to turn back upon themselves, as though the overdeterminations of Hardy's medium produce the tensions that structure the world of Casterbridge it represents. Such majestic, and often precarious, dialogism should alert us to the conditions of the novel as a whole, since its formal overdeterminations as a rule coincide with its representational ones. Much as Eustacia is a representation of a real aspect of the Victorian mythographies whose numerous registers produce the codes of the Wessex Hardy depicts, Casterbridge is, as a locale, also overdetermined in the kinds of organization that shape it. Besides displaying the usual rigor of Hardy's idiom-specific representation of class and regional differences in his portraiture, the world the novel represents is, archaeologically, a mirror of the sedimentation of accumulated rites, rituals, and customs that constitute it as a belated literary document. In fact, the sedimentations are sometimes almost identical—Casterbridge is ruined with both native English and classical forms from the past just as the novel itself is, whether in its generic stance as tragedy, its allusions to Rome, or in its appeal to the history of the region itself. The amphitheater, after all, is not simply a narrative symbol for a proto-Freudian unconscious and the return of its past scenes, but also, in the narrative's plot, one of the things it symbolizes: the repetitive site, for example, of the belated meetings between Henchard and Susan.

The promise of a "volcanic" core (1886:129) in Henchard that will explain everything ("Character is Fate," Hardy reminds us, quoting Novalis [131]) is, however, apparently the novel's secure psychological basis, the inward site of Henchard's innate Romantic rebelliousness that appeals to an extradiscursive essence as the source of his bluff potency (see George Levine's continuation of a tradition of interpretation [1981:238ff.]). And yet the "will" displayed by the stormy, unpredictable Henchard that is the novel's key psychological term is stained by a double meaning that makes its reliability uncertain. "Will" signifies both Henchard's "unruly volcanic stuff" (129)—the primal impulsiveness or willfulness that leads him to sell Susan in the first place—and also its direct opposite—his equally severe willfulness in the sense of the "self-control" (129) or power of choice later displayed as penance, and deployed as a means of pulling himself up from haytrusser to merchant-mayor in the years that separate the first two chapters from those subsequent. One of the novel's principal interpretative clues as to its modernism is, in short, the site of a rhetorical impasse or blown circuit rather than a tunnel to the daylight of cause or origin that Hardy's psychology may seem to promise. Modernism—or at least the will to modernity—has, by implication, been relegated to one of the novel's own objects of inquiry, less the name of its meaning than the name of a certain readerly or interpretative operation it encourages us to perform, only, as we shall see, to undercut it. The result: the paradigmatic production of the myth of the modern in tandem with its demystification.

Before Farfrae and his agronomical inventions invade Casterbridge, Hardy announces that the community is as yet "untouched by the faintest sprinkle of modernism" (30). Once, however, the outsider Farfrae arrives, a standard symbolic arrangement in Hardy's novels again emerges in which "the ache of modernism" and its attendant ills are brought on by the disruption of rural harmony by a technology that leads to the corruption of an apparently natural society wedded to the earth (see Meisel 1972). Thus, Henchard's "volcanic" willfulness is, in Trilling's sense, redemptive, since it at least seems to exist outside the border of culture, and so specifies, even requires an opposition between a lost nature and an evil civilization at the level of unconscious presupposition. In fact, Hardy goes out of his way to distinguish absolutely between town and country, urbanity and the folk, technology and nature: "Country and town," he assures us, "met at a mathematical line" (30). "Casterbridge, as has been hinted, was a place deposited in the block upon a cornfield," Hardy is sure to remind us later on. "It stood, with regard to the wide fertile land adjoining, clean-cut and distinct" (105).

How is this myth of the modern produced and sustained? By the maintenance of apparently absolute dichotomies at the level of presupposition such as those outlined above, or here, in Hardy's description of the differences between Henchard's quaint system of doing business and Farfrae's new, more efficient—and less human—one:

> Meanwhile the great corn and hay traffic conducted by
> Henchard throve under the management of Donald Farfrae
> as it had never thriven before. It had formerly moved in
> jolts; now it went on oiled castors. The old crude *vivâ voce*
> system of Henchard, in which everything depended upon his

> memory, and bargains were made by the tongue alone, was
> swept away. Letters and ledgers took the place of 'I'll do't,'
> and 'you shall hae't'; and, as in all such cases of advance,
> the rugged picturesqueness of the old method disappeared
> with its inconveniences. [103]

The differences between Henchard and Farfrae are, it seems, the very differences that set a modern world apart from an earlier, lost one. Lamenting the disruption of agrarian peace by the machine, Hardy's language appears to set up a series of interpretative oppositions whose preservation is crucial to the will to modernity as we customarily know it: the oppositions of nature and culture, soil and technology, clean and dirty, valuable and valueless, seething substance and hollow form. Even readers as discriminating as Irving Howe tend to honor such oppositions (1967:95, 99), this despite Raymond Williams's unremitting insistence that no such dichotomies are viable from the point of view of either the history of literature or of British sociology (1958:202ff., 258ff.; 1973:200ff.). And yet the novel seems bent on maintaining a modernist myth of origins in a reverential notion of an idyllic past at the source of these dualities, thereby becoming an Edenic allegory that thickens our sense of the novel as the failed "'romance'" of Henchard "'the sower'" (194), especially when his power to sow or signify comes to leave him. "Old" and "crude" as it is, Henchard's supposed lack of systematicity—his "rugged picturesqueness" and the directness commonly associated with the voice and the traditionally oral—is more natural compared to the opposing symbolizations that constitute Farfrae's traits. For all his faults, Henchard's tragic truculence is the vengeful return of the native repressed by the machine. He represents the immediate, the primitive, the original that he is. He deals with and through the hand and mouth—with apparently direct and unmediated gestures typologically consistent with his practice, for example, of relying on omens and the lower pantheism associated with them.

Farfrae, by contrast, is out of touch with the physical, a ledger-man and bookkeeper, a dynamo or machine like the one he imports into Casterbridge; not, like Henchard, a fully alive voice and presence. Good popular novelist as well as good late Romantic, Hardy satisfies the demands of both trades at once by reversing the characteristics customarily attached to the qualities he gives each of his protagonists in turn. Farfrae—considerate, delicate, conscientious in all forms of protocol and feeling—is a man without a body; even his sweet tenor voice sings tenderly of a home or origin he has departed with curious ease and about which there is virtually no discussion at all. Prophecy of bureaucratic consumerism, Farfrae surely augurs Forster's notorious "civilization of luggage" in *Howards End*, the growing estrangement of culture from nature that bodes alienation and despair for the individual and the community alike. Henchard's unpredictability—his "will" in its kaleidoscopic range of senses—arises by comparison as the satanic contrary to Farfrae's irritating tidiness.

What seems to be at issue, then, in the difference between Henchard and Farfrae is that the chill technology of Farfrae's modern culture is qualitatively different from that of Henchard's lumbering but clearly more direct and natural form of folk culture. Hence the full emergence in Hardy's novel of our already familiar atavistic modernism—the impulse to be new or advanced, the will to modernity as such, that is ironically dependent on a return to something older. How valid such distinctions may be, however, we shall wait a moment to see, at least from Hardy's own point of view. From the point of view of D. H. Lawrence, however, the meaning of Hardy's novel—indeed, of all of Hardy's fiction—lies just here.

"Modernism" Compounded

Lawrence's posthumously published "Study of Thomas Hardy" (1936) remains the most influential authorization of the kinds of oppositions that structure the canonical reading of *The Mayor of Casterbridge* adumbrated above, and that, as Lawrence shows, seem to structure Hardy's novels as a whole. Confessing the obvious in a letter of September 5, 1914 (the "Study" was actually composed during the ascendant curve of Lawrence's afflatus), Lawrence writes that the essay "will be about anything but Thomas Hardy" (1914:166n). It has to do, as Lawrence is easily willing to admit, with his own categories instead, categories, as we shall see, already put in question by the earlier Hardy, but categories that the later Lawrence wishes to reify and command as truth. With no little irony, Lawrence's own flamboyant late Romanticism is largely a product of his identification with that aspect of Hardy to be found in Henchard's representative mythology of voice and presence, a filiation that, in Lawrence's literary history, makes Henchard's dark mythology redemptive because it is at its core antinomian. For Lawrence, what is vital in Hardy is not the shell of manners in either life or literature, but, rather, what lies within. What is vital is that Wessex is, as Lawrence puts it, "always shooting suddenly out of a tight convention" (1936:410)—if, of course, we take the phrase "shooting out of" as straightforwardly militant in its expression of a resistance to "convention." For the other reading—"shooting out of" in the organic sense of a branch "shooting out of" its generative trunk—exactly contradicts Lawrence's apparently modernist intent by exposing it as a defense against the dependence upon which the desire for autonomy—Lawrence's will to modernity—is ironically propped. It is no wonder, since the problem for Lawrence is quite overtly one of the writer's relation to tradition in the first place, although it is also a reflection of any vital individual's adversary relation to society: "the individual," in Lawrence's words, "trying to break forth" (411). With narration and story usually reflexive counterparts in the fiction of Lawrence and Hardy alike—characters who wish to free themselves from conventions not unlike those the artist wishes to eschew—Lawrence's expression of what he takes to be the enduring conflict in Hardy between membership in a "community" (411) and the "natural, individual desire . . . to break the bounds of the community" (411) finds an appropriate formula in his pronouncement that Hardy's novels signify above all else the "division of a man against himself" (411). So absolute is Lawrence's judgment that it eventually grows metaphysical in its reductiveness: the "tragedy" of man against himself—of nature against human community—"is," concludes Lawrence, "the one theme of the Wessex novels" (412).

Hence Hardy's characters fall almost always, says Lawrence, into two exact and opposed groups, producing by implication a series of antinomies as familiar as the meanings they suggest, and not unlike those relational oppositions among characters and forces plotted by Lawrence himself in *Psychoanalysis and the Unconscious* (1921), retroactively clarifying the arrangement of characters in *Women in Love* (1920). Not surprisingly, *The Return of the Native* "is," argues Lawrence, "the first tragic and important novel" (413). "Dark, wild, passionate" (413), Eustacia Vye is the special vessel of what is vital in Hardy as his career moves into its mature phase. Of "Italian birth" (413), Eustacia represents a beaker full of the warm south for a frosty Wessex rigid with the cold of belatedness, of distance from the (traditionally) Mediterranean original. A reflexive emblem for the writerly desire for modernist union with the primary, or at least with its image, Eustacia prompts Lawrence's first extended specification of Hardy's strength in purely literary terms. "Romantic imagination says," remarks a Lawrence who knows, that success in life is (in a flurry of suppressed Paterian images) "to attain" oneself, to arrive at "some form of self-realization" (414)—to be natural and whole, without influence, even if passion itself must be learned. Clym Yeobright is, of course, the first full-blown case of Hardy's portrait of the sickness of conformity, unable as he is to become an "integral man" (414). Struggling "at the quick" of his "being" (414), Clym is at best a "subtle equivocation" (414) between the two dominant but opposed impulses of character and community, a symptom-formation whose pathography betokens the "final loss" of the most precious of Lawrentian gems, "his original self" (414). Clym cannot "burst the enclosure of the idea"—now separate from "feelings" (416)—because of "the system which contained him" (416). Overvaluing the symbolic status of a trope such as Henchard's viva voce system—the vital nature that struggles against the machine—Lawrence finds *The Return of the Native*'s meaning, predictably enough, to reside in Egdon Heath, "the primitive, primal earth, where the instinctive life heaves up" (415). Like the individual's innate but repressed integrity in an increasingly technological world, the Heath represents the redemptive and transcendent primary ("primal"), the original, the earliest ("primitive"), a valorization as it is of the "earth" and the "instinctive life" it signifies in Lawrence's imagination.

To be sure, Lawrence's "primitivism," as Raymond Williams reminds us, is "at times given some social or historical base" (1973:266)—in *The Rainbow*, say. Still, Lawrence's excessive primitivism—his "'revolutionary' emotionality," to use Wyndham Lewis's phrase (1929:125)—must have some reasoning behind it, and it does. The portrait of Clym is especially symptomatic, since his failings are the plain result, says Lawrence, of his being trapped by convention, a victim of "pupilage" (417). Like the late Romantic or modern writer, "he himself was not original. He was over-taught, and had become an echo . . . , his activity turned into repetition" (417). Such Shelleyan "deity chained" (417) is really a question of "blood" (417) succumbing to "mind" (417), the latter "that house" (again in a singularly Paterian metaphor) "built of extraneous knowledge" (417). Hence the establishment of Lawrence's central and enduring assertion of an original in "the primal soil," the "strong, deep root" (417), the "powerful, eternal origin," the "unfathomable womb" (418) represented by the Heath—"Egdon, the primal impulsive body" (418).

For Lawrence, then, Hardy dramatizes the struggle between the natural, the original, the primal—the sympathetic presence of Henchard's directness—and the mind's burden of "extraneous knowledge," objectified in turn by Farfrae's technology. "Like Clym," says a doggedly modernist Lawrence, "the map appears to us more real than the land" (420). For Lawrence, Clym is a tissue of representations, not an essence, not just the victim but the product of his "pupilage." From such distinctions follow the equally absolute ones between the repetition and the first or primary, the copy and the original, the representation and the thing itself—all defenses against an apparent dehumanization of life premised from the start on a series of oppositions left unquestioned. "Unfathomed nature" (419) against "the mechanical system" (420), then, is the struggle that defines Hardy's achievement for Lawrence *tout court*. Indeed, so pervasive and fundamental are Lawrence's habitual dichotomies in the "Study" that it is little wonder to recall for a moment that they also structure as central a work as *Women in Love*. Enormously porous and playful, Lawrence's language as a novelist is nonetheless calculated by like regularities in as orchestrated a fashion as the polysemy of novelistic discourse can allow. In *Women in Love* especially (*Lady Chatterley* [1928] is a late caricature of its epistemology), such didactic dichotomization proceeds by means of a rhetorical strategy in which character description changes in accord with the mode of being assigned to each protagonist, and to the romantic couplings such assignment dictates in turn. Hence Gudrun and Gerald, Ursula and Birkin have their existence, as couples, as a function of different but distinct narrative styles that mirror—in fact that are— their antagonisms. Gerald and Gundrun are regularly painted by Lawrence with unusual attention to visual detail in human portraiture (Gudrun's colored stockings come first to mind, Gerald's imposing physique next). Drawn almost entirely by figurations of visual presence, Gudrun and Gerald exude, ironically, the superficiality that Lawrence ascribes to them. Birkin and Ursula, on the other hand, are rarely articulated in visual metaphors, lacking the plain density of physical presence assigned to their counterparts in accord with the disembodied, transpersonal knowledge that their contrastingly successful relationship is meant to signify.

Although Lawrence has strangely little to say about *The Mayor* itself at any length in the "Study," its reiterative position in his view of Hardy is nonetheless plain and predictable. "In *The Mayor of Casterbridge* the dark villain is," says Lawrence, "already almost the hero" (437). With Henchard a more brooding version of Clym before and Jude after, Lawrence takes "the moral conclusion" (438) of the Wessex novels to be the attempt to fulfill one's "own individual nature" (439) in its struggle with that "extraneous knowledge," as he puts it earlier, with which culture has invaded the natural house of the soul. So emerges the inevitable formulation of man ". . . against himself" (439) as the enduring agon that structures Hardy in particular and modernism at large. As he surveys Hardy's achievement entire, Lawrence unleashes his oppositions with particular fury and with some stress as well: "Always he must start from the earth, from the great source of the Law" (480). Suddenly, Lawrence's categories begin to show traces of the rhetorical contamination they have managed to avoid in other articulations. How can "the Law" be the "source" of "the earth" that is usually otherwise opposed to it? And with an aforementioned "antinomy between Law and Love" (476), how can the subsequent formulation, the "law of the womb" (482), not be read as an unintentional contradiction despite the apparent harmony of Lawrence's litany of oppositions within the "Study" itself? While "Law" and "earth" may not be a clash for Lawrence on his own terms—the "earth" is the female principle that generates "Law" in his sense—such binarisms eventually flood one another in any extended elaboration of their semantic inventories, resulting in self-erasure rather than in reasonable representation. Nonetheless, continues Lawrence—despite the rhetorical precipice his language has reached—Hardy invites us to privilege the modernist original, the man "full of blood" (491) like Henchard rather than the "mechanical, automatic" Farfrae (491).

The oppositions are doubtless clearest, if not simply redundant, in Lawrence's reading of *Jude the Obscure* as the "Study" concludes. Hobbled though he may be, Jude is sensuously vital, Sue Bridehead barren, devoid of "experience in the senses" and wishing only "to know" (496). Indeed, Sue's frigidity is, for Lawrence, representative of "northern civilization" (496) and its late Romantic struggle to regain the Eustacian warmth of the south (a struggle Lawrence himself topographically frustrates in *Women in Love* when, ironically, his four principals journey, not to the Mediterranean, but the Tyrol). Had Jude been lucky, even his studies "would have burned down his thick blood as fuel," and thus would have brought him "to the true light of himself" (500). The Paterian tropes alone ("burned," "light") ought to inhibit Lawrence's conviction of his own originality by revealing how traditionally coded his representation of it is. But it is just such bondage to culture, fathers, "repetition" (501)—in this case, Pater directly—that Lawrence's investment in what is natural and passionate is designed to overcome, or at least to repress. Jude's problem and Lawrence's own are, like Clym's, versions one of the other. Vexed by Sue as by himself, "all" of Jude's "study was," like Clym's, a study "of what had been"—a barren unoriginality that is but "a mechanical, functional process" (501). The dread opposition between vitality and mechanism, passion and dynamo, originality and repetition—between Henchard's viva voce and Farfrae's machines—returns still again, and, with it, the recognition that Jude's will to modernity is, like Hardy's own such imputed will, woefully premised on the knowledge of its impossibility. Jude "must go back deep into" what Sue finally cannot give him—"the primal, unshown, unknown life of the blood, the thick source-stream of life in her" (503). "Unknown" and "unshown," the "primal," even for Lawrence, must remain beyond the horizon despite his wish to possess it.

Lawrence's organizing categories nonetheless remain a direct function of the kinds of dualities that seem to structure *The Mayor of Casterbridge*, and, from Lawrence's point of view, Hardy's imagination as a whole. It is the desire to find "the Originator" (514) that prompts Lawrence's aggressive, even impatient, modernism, whether in prose, poetry, or fiction. As a description of Lawrence's own priorities as a writer, it is probably accurate enough. How accurate it is in relation to British modernism in general and Hardy's writing in particular, however, remains to be seen.

Hardy's Reflexive Realism: Deferred Action in *The Mayor of Casterbridge*

Lawrence, of course, underestimates Hardy. He has fallen into the precise epistemological trap Hardy's novels prepare for their reductive readers. There are larger contingencies in both the structure and matter of *The Mayor* in particular, casting suspicion on the seriousness with which Hardy pursues the uniform ideals that Lawrence finds across the bulk of his fiction. Lawrence has in fact failed to heed his own caution in the "Study": that any work of art must contain, as he puts it, "the essential criticism on the morality to which it adheres" (1936:476). If any novel meets Lawrence's injunction that a text do what it says, it is *The Mayor of Casterbridge*. Having noted how quickly the novel's realism turns simultaneously reflexive in, for example, the amphitheater's symbolization of the past at the level of the novel's narration as well as its actual participation in it at the level of plot or story, it is easy to see that chief also among its numerous reflexive possibilities is the extent to which it takes as one of its principal concerns the tacit identity of its depiction of how Henchard acts and knows with its own behavior as a text.

Let us return to the passage from *The Mayor* with which we began and see just how absolute Hardy's oppositions may be. Not one but at least two interpretations are possible. The novel's Edenic parable, the promise of a nature beyond technology—a prior state of poetic and existential plenitude in which more was sacred than domestic(ated)—rests upon a series of inflated Romantic oppositions that may be true for Lawrence alone. Instead of opposing Farfrae and Henchard, then, let us ask what they share despite the passage's manifest distinction between them as representatives each in turn of natural vitality (Henchard's viva voce) and the coldly efficient machinations of modern business (Farfrae's protosuburban cheeriness in handling letters and ledgers).

A common factor unites rather than divides the two. The mode of each is the same—the enabling mode of "memory" that joins rather than distinguishes between speech and writing. Voice and writing—symbols of the opposition between nature and culture that structures "the ache of modernism"— are, from another point of view, little different in either system—memory—or precondition—temporality. What both share technologically despite their merely technical difference is their common inherence in narrative form as such, one that joins the structure of subjectivity with that of the novel itself. By asking what Henchard and Farfrae share rather than what divides them, even the distinction between Henchard's system as moving "in jolts" compared to Farfrae's "oiled castors" (instead, presumably, of the quainter castor oil) redounds upon itself as "will" does, at least if we read "jolts" with electrical rather than manual connotations, and so mechanize, as it were, the very system opposed to the machine. Indeed, so easily do such reflexive mockeries emerge in Hardy's language that we are led to suspect the text not only regularly to contaminate the modernist oppositions that appear to organize it, but also to include such categories among the notions it submits to demystification. In fact, "modernism" means both the invasion of the country by the city and the sanctity of the nature it violates—both terms of the opposition are, it seems, required to articulate either one. Williams even points out the extent to which the etymology and history of usage of the word "organic" in English puts into question its fixity as one pole in the presumed dichotomy in Hardy between nature and culture. The Greek root means "tool" or "instrument," the kind of "mechanism" to which the "organic" eventually comes to be opposed (1958:263). We might also note a similar destiny for the word "technology," whose Greek root means the "art" to which such otherwise identical "technology" will also come to be opposed later on in the history of its usage.

What, then, does Hardy's novel offer in place of its Edenic allegory? Once the Lawrentian dualities that seem to organize it begin to dissolve, what order of interpretation takes their place? Handled as reflexive realism, the novel emerges instead as a text designed to identify narrative form with the forms of life as it is lived. *The Mayor* implicates Henchard and the reader alike in a common problematic of reading that erases the distinction between the novel's form and content as the necessary implication of the collapse of the symbolic distinction between Henchard's primitivism and Farfrae's technology. The world of Casterbridge is largely a world of texts or representations in the first place. Hardy's metaphorical identification of systems of living with systems of textuality is habitual, especially given the attention he calls to the double meaning of the figure "character"—a crucial word in the book's ironically psychologistic subtitle ("A Story of A Man of Character") that is etymologically grafted alongside the meaning "letter" as well. As it turns out, "character" is quite plainly legible in Casterbridge. Lucetta's desire for Farfrae, for example, is explicitly readable for whomever has the key to the code of her nonverbal gestures: "The fact was," says Hardy, "printed large all over Lucetta's cheeks and eyes to any one who could read her as Elizabeth-Jane," for example, is now "beginning to do" (1886:196). In fact, Elizabeth-Jane learns to read manners and letters alike as her social education proceeds through Lucetta, while her own physiognomy is in turn given the same telltale semiology assigned to the novel's ruins: "In sleep," says Hardy of the girl, "there come to the surface buried genealogical facts, ancestral curves, dead men's traits, which the mobility of daytime animation screens and overwhelms" (144).

Such metaphors are, however, only local examples of the extent to which the novel is, as we briefly began to see earlier, the site of an enormously efficient rapprochement between Hardy's narration and the plot of his story. The life of narrative representation is the life of signs and the life of signs the life that narrative represents even in the first instance. The content of the novel is a set of forms in play, both in its overt referential drama (is Henchard a gentleman or laborer? what is Elizabeth-Jane's social status? what codes instantiate the different judgments we might be inclined to make?), and in the incongruent comparisons to which Henchard is subject—as Faust at one point (131) and as Job at another (90); as Cain (361), as Samson (373), as Adam ("he pursued his solitary way eastward" [366]), even as the "Prince of Darkness" himself (315). Bursting its skin with all the tricks of the Victorian novelist's trade, the novel's notorious coincidences, overplottings, and editorial interventions are themselves the setting of forms—social, moral, novelistic, mythic—into garish collision. Having violated the manners of marriage even as he exposes its material status in selling Susan to Newson (a premonition of Sue's famous definition of marriage in *Jude* as being "licensed to be loved on the premises"), Henchard's ritual oath not to drink so as to discipline himself nonetheless coincides with his frank liaison with Lucetta. The latter transgression is checked in turn by Susan's reappearance and the acting out of another ritual drama of discipline also in the ironic service of Henchard's willful dissimulations. The collision of conventions at the level of the novel's story is thereby a version of the collision of literary forms, and other forms of English usage, to which Hardy the latecomer is subject as a narrator—

biblical, tragedic, romance, *Bildungsroman*, the structure of Romantic land-scape imagery, and so on. The novel's negotiation of the larger forcefields of local, literary, and official English usage—of the wake of influence and convention in which it comes into being from the start—is the reflexive counterpart of the jarring polyglot of Henchard's own social and allusive inscriptions. As a subject, Henchard represents, not the revenge of the dark side, but rather the novel's own unstable situation within the vortex of precedent and presumption that saturates Hardy's decidedly decadent prose, overlearned in the craft of its melodramatic pathos to the point of turning its uses almost pedagogical.

What is the virtually tragic problem in Hardy's universe, and in what ways do the novel's reading and its hero reflect it in turn? A central, though again apparently marginal, text here is the moment of consternation that Henchard experiences as he gazes upon the Elizabeth-Jane whom Susan has apparently restored to him upon her return to Casterbridge. Henchard is, of course, puzzled after Susan reappears with an older Elizabeth-Jane whose hair is lighter than he remembers it to have been when she was a baby (101–02). Nervous, Susan hurriedly argues that children's hair can turn lighter as well as darker. "And the same uneasy expression came out on her face," says the narrator, "to which the future held the key" (102). As Hardy's musical metaphor suggests, Susan shares with the narrator a piece of knowledge that both Henchard and the reader still lack: the truth of Newson's paternity in the case of the second or belated Elizabeth-Jane. As it happens, the reader, too, is in exactly Henchard's position, not knowing a first time until something else happens later on to call it into play retrospectively. Like the reader's, Henchard's frustrated desire to satisfy his curiosity about his daughter's hair is quickly dismissed as an irrelevant (not merely forgotten) item.

For Henchard, in other words, the scene is, in a very real sense, not itself present to him at the time of its chronological occurrence. He still believes Elizabeth-Jane to be his own, and so represses the evidence that would contradict what he wishes to be true. This is Henchard's central moment of misrecognition, since a question here would foreclose all the misguided actions, and their consequences, that follow on his certitude that the girl is still his child. The scene in question doesn't really even happen so far as Henchard is concerned until later on, when the wishful thinking that has prevented it from being remarked has been removed by virtue of a later piece of knowledge—in this case, the discovery of Susan's letter, disclosing Newson as Elizabeth-Jane's real father (143–44). Only in the temporality or narrative of Henchard's mind, and in the reader's that constitutes the narrative at large, can the original event come into being. (Ford Madox Ford's *The Good Soldier*

[1915] notoriously features this precise procedure in its unreliable first-person narration at the parallel levels of real and readerly desire.) And in the case of the original clue to Elizabeth-Jane's nonidentity with her earlier incarnation—Henchard's puzzlement and subsequent forgetting of the unlikely color of her hair—the origin comes into being only after the fact, belatedly. Even the truth itself is, strictly speaking, a mistaken one as well, since Henchard must be dishonest to Susan's memory—opening her letter before Elizabeth-Jane is married—in order to find out, without expecting it, the real facts of the girl's paternity (139–46). The unexpected truth is a function of an unintended error—a double paradox by which the origin in question is painfully produced retroactively.

There is hardly a more exact formulation of the operation of both Henchard's and the reader's mind than Freud's notion of *Nachträglichkeit*, or deferred action. Theorized at greatest length in the case history of the Wolf Man (Freud 1918), deferred action describes rather precisely the curious nature of this (non)event in Hardy's narrative and its paradigmatic status as the inherently belated dynamic of all vision, both in Hardy and, as we shall see, in modernism at large. Freud derives what will become the inescapable precondition of all discursive production from what his patient both declares and describes. The Wolf Man's dream of the frosty white wolves in the tree outside his window as a four-year-old—the childhood dream around which the analysis centers, and whose interpretation is its driving desire or primitivist/positivist grail-object—is, Freud tells us, the deferred and disguised memory of an event (the primal scene proper) that the patient experienced, or could have experienced, at the age of one and a half—that of witnessing his parents in the act of copulation. But because a child of one and a half does not yet possess the knowledge of sex required to interpret, or even to register, such a scene, it cannot properly be said to exist for him at the moment of its "real" or chronological occurrence. It is only when the dreamer gains a knowledge of sex that the memory—the primal—may come into being at all. This "sexualization after the event" (1918:17:103n) is to be accounted for, says Freud, as follows: "He received the impressions when he was one and a half; his understanding of them was deferred, but became possible at the time of the dream owing to his development, his sexual excitations, and his sexual researches" (17:37–38n). They are, in short, "the products of construction" (17:51).

Such a structure is a miniature of the structure of psychoanalytic knowledge/production as a whole, the rhetorical means by which Freud fashions the phantasms of his imaginative universe and the categories that define it. Deferred action's counterpart in *The Interpretation of Dreams* (1900), for example, is secondary revision (before that, it is the notion of "screen memories" in 1899), the mechanism whereby the dream as such—the original—is produced only retroactively, by the dreamer's distorted report of it. The figure "unconscious mind," of course, is Freud's enabling oxymoron, and, like Milton's "darkness visible" or Lévi-Strauss's *la pensée sauvage*, it is an educative or pedagogic oxymoron, a symptomatic and parabolic error required of rhetoric when it is asked to do unusual or inventive things. A mixed metaphor whose own transgressions according to accepted Cartesian usage ("mind" equals "consciousness") are what produce the newish space of Freudian hyperinteriority, "unconscious mind" signals that Freud's project is posited on the self-contradictory implications of such oxymora. In the *Three Essays on the Theory of Sexuality* (1905), for example, Freud begins with a familiar kind of psychoanalytic paradox: how can one know what happens in early childhood if one of early childhood's principal characteristics is that we regularly forget its history? Similarly, Freud assures us in *The Interpretation of Dreams* that "nothing but a wish can set our mental apparatus at work" (1900:5:567), even though such a statement requires us to ask whether psychoanalytic thought itself is therefore no more than wish-fulfillment.

The deferred action of the Wolf Man, then, assumes the presence of the primal as the analeptically logical referent of what succeeds it. "Light is thrown," says Freud, "from the later stages of his history upon these earlier ones" (17:47). Like the goddess Psyche, Freud's psyche, too, is—like all Romantic idealities—produced after the fact, the seat of an ambiguous primacy, simultaneously deferred and present. Trace of a desire endemic to modernism at large, the unconscious and the primal scene are symptoms of the late Romantic Freud's desire to reach for the warmth and immediacy of beginnings in the face of his later position in history. Testimony to a particularly northern European desire for parity with the southerly priority of the ancients, the Hebrews, even the Renaissance, and one presumably to be fulfilled by the search for the bedrock of drive ("instinct" in Strachey's bluntly Romantic English), it is a search that serves as Freud's particular version of a realm, to use Trilling's definition of the will to modernity, "beyond" or "apart from culture."

In Freud's dark and ironic modernism, however, such primacy or origins emerge only belatedly, culture or symbol situating a nature preexistent to it as Keats does in the nightingale ode, or history situating its own beginnings ("Who himself beginning knew?") as Milton does in *Paradise Lost*. Indeed, in a paradigm equal to Freud's own, the early Romantic Milton rejects the truth of classical mythology (the best example is the early *Nativity Ode*) only to resurrect it with apparent unwillingness in the later poem. For without pagan representations, "erring" as they are, no such Christian poem can speak. The price of the poem's readability: that we know origins or primal scenes only through the belated technologies that obstruct our view of them, and, in so doing, construct whatever view we have. Much as the Wolf Man's primal scene emerges as a function of his later knowledge of sex, so Milton's Christian truth can only be articulated by means of pagan error (on the emergence of a "diachronic semantics" with Milton, see Hollander 1981:113–15). The primary event is known not despite but because of the distortion through which it appears afterward. There is, properly speaking, no objective or original event as such (it is, to recall Freud's words, the "product . . . of a construction"), only its (re)construction through the rhetoric of narrative or memory.

Nor is deferred action or secondary revision simply a microscopic event in the world of Hardy's Casterbridge. If it is the precondition of Henchard's vision—the source of his sense that everything is "too late" (166)—it is also the precondition of the novel's own illusionism or means of production as a text. Like the belatedly produced primal scene of Elizabeth-Jane's (non)recognition by Henchard, the novel's recursive movement toward its official primal scene of causative original sin in Henchard's sale of Susan at the novel's beginning is also the means of its movement forward to disclose Henchard's secret and ruin him. The novel can adduce its own origin or primal scene as causative only after the events that precipitate it/it precipitates have occurred. The novel's psychological "key," that is, comes from the "future" it seems only to predict. It is actually just the reverse, with future events bearing out the truth of their origination in this self-announced study of, again in the words Hardy quotes from Novalis, the wager that "Character is Fate." The "dramatic glare of the original act" (251) is not a property of the "original act" itself, but of the subsequent course of events that so centers it belatedly. Indeed, the novel's apparent promise of the book's organization as a quest centered on "the search for his wife and child" (18) the moment Henchard sells them is aborted just moments later: "A certain shyness of revealing his conduct," says not just an equivocating, but a downright duplicitous, narrator, "prevented Michael Henchard from following up the investigation with the loud hue-and-cry such a pursuit demanded to render it effectual" (19). Neither quest nor discovery, the novel is bent instead on dismantling both linear causation and origins in favor of studying the belated dynamic that produces such twin illusions in life and literature alike. Even the way Hardy turns the romance components of his story into tragic ones reflexively enacts his thematic, too. With far more scrupulosity than, say, Dickens, Hardy removes from the structure of quest-romance the one element that represents redemption, satisfaction of the quest, proper return to origins: the discovery of the lost child's aristocratic or wellborn lineage. Not only not highborn, Elizabeth-Jane corresponds to neither of her proper names—she is neither a Henchard nor the original little girl whose first name she still bears.

Hardy goes so far as to thematize the belatedness that defines the dynamic of character in both life and letters by returning us overtly to the novel's primal scene toward its end only to frustrate the search for specifying origins in any exact way. Henchard physically acts out the impossible desire to return to the primary by revisiting the original spot or place of the tent in which he sold Susan. But, of course, he "walked to another spot" (367) instead; indeed, this is "not really where the tent had stood" at all, says the narrator, though "it seemed so to him" (367). As if to emphasize how great a role repetition plays in his version of subjectivity, Hardy even reminds us that, on the first morning after the sale, Henchard requires not just one verification of what has transpired the night before (Susan's "ring" and Newson's "bank-notes" [15]), but, given the enormity of the event, a "second verification of his dim memories" as well (15).

If the primary is a function of the secondary, the origin a function of what succeeds it, then the organizing oppositions upon which the book appears to pivot turn out to be, not mimetic or empirically available oppositions, but rhetorical ones put into play by a modernist desire for the primal that installs origins retroactively. Even Henchard's nature as opposed to Farfrae's technology emerges as a dichotomy only after Farfrae's appearance, the former a function of its newly ordained difference from the latter. The novel's apparently organizing oppositions are in fact categories whose proper identities the narration elides as the price of establishing them. The viva voce system needs the lack represented by the fall into writing in order to maintain the plenitude supplied it by virtue of the contrast. Similarly, the secondariness of writing needs the fullness of rude speech from which it has fallen in order to be its distant echo. The possibility of being present at the origin at the time of its supposed occurrence—whether the scene of (non)recognition with the sleeping child or the primal scene proper when Henchard sells Susan—is simply out of the question. It is the fate of Henchard and the reader alike to know only belatedly because all the novel's causative terms—will, character, nature—are articulated relationally, as a function of their differences from themselves. Hence knowledge as such is gained retrospectively rather than immediately and absolutely.

Producing its litany of organizing categories differentially, then, even the novel's central notion of "character" itself—the seeming center of a text that is, as Hardy puts it in the preface, "more particularly a study of one man's deeds and character than, perhaps, any other" (viii)—is an effect of just that narrative mechanism most opposed to it in the criticism and practice of fiction in the 1860s, when Hardy began: the plot (see Kendrick 1977). Apprentice author of "sensationalist," or plot-centered, novels such as *Desperate Remedies* (1871) and early successful author of the contrasting "portrait," or character-centered, ones such as *Under the Greenwood Tree* (1872), the mature Hardy frustrates not just Lawrence's later influential categories, but also those of his own time. After all, we come to know Henchard only through what he does, and what he does has a recurrent pattern that tells us about the nature of his character, which unfolds in time. Hence character is a narrative rather than a self-sufficient, atemporal essence. Like the oppositions between nature and culture that dissolve through the form of narrative that equates them, the opposition between character and plot in Victorian criticism becomes another of Hardy's own narrative subjects in a text that is as much an allegory of reading as it is a modern tragedy—indeed, the former may well help to explain the latter.

With *récit* and *histoire* counterparts one of the other in Hardy's reflexive realism, then, Henchard's psychic mechanisms at the level of *histoire* are doubled by the textual mechanisms that manipulate Hardy's reader at the level of *récit*. It is almost as though misrecognition and belated coherence are the price of subjectivity and readership alike. Henchard, acting for us all, cannot receive love because he must first produce his need of it. And to do so, he must drive off his loved ones, unconsciously or not, so as to feel the palpability of their absence, hence the presence of his own desire for their return. Desire itself must reject its objects in order to produce them, oscillating by design in a viciously incessant self-production by rejection or negation. Hence Hardy's description of Henchard as "self-alienated" (380) is a self-evident redundancy, calling attention tactfully, backhandedly, to the inevitable implication that it is precisely an individual's alienation—his distance from what is socially given—that gives him that uniqueness we call subjectivity or individuality. Indeed, alienation may well be the very structure of subjectivity, not its greatest burden to overcome. As a dynamic structural principle, subjectivity is in fact the structure of alienation, since the retroactive situation of an origin or plenitude from which it is estranged is the product or profit of its discourse rather than its price. Thus, too, our three modernist keywords—primitivism, formalism, alienation—all have very different roles from what is customarily assumed. The primitive or primary is, as it turns out, a function of what succeeds it; the formal is also the thematic, the thematic also structurally identical with the formal; and alienation is not the burden of subjectivity but its precondition.

Hardy's reflexive realism and the belatedness that is both its form and its content provide, then, a dramatic solution to the apparently insuperable difficulties that the modernist problematic presents for the writer. What advantages does reflexive realism offer as a form? How does it relieve the modernist dilemma or rhetorical impasse of seeking primacy within the terms of the secondary? In his representation of the world itself as a set of representations, Hardy takes the belated emergence of the supposedly "original" subject into life as both inevitable and constitutive. With *récit* and *histoire* seen as twins— as analogical reflections one of the other—the lives of Hardy's characters, inscribed as they are in a tangle of rival customs, are the precise counterpart of the novel's own profound implication in a set of literary systems to which it comes late as well. Like Freud's, Hardy's text is, in a more restricted sense, an overdetermined discourse about an overdetermined discourse. "Trenched with the remains of prehistoric forts" (16), the landscape of Wessex is a reflection, not so much of Dorset, but of the deep furrows of literary precedent that line Hardy's text with a precocious anxiety that it both displays and dispels. One could even say that the novel's story is a reflection, not of a self-sufficient object-world mimetically apprehended, but of the anxious conditions of the narration that produces it. Indeed, if the novel reverses customary priorities—if culture produces nature, form produces content, plot produces character—then it follows that *récit* also produces *histoire*: the story is a reflection of the language that assembles it.

Like Flaubert across the Channel just before him, Hardy (and, as we shall see in the Epilogue, Conrad just after him) is a critical figure in the history of the novel. Nor is it for the usual (and dubious) reason that he presages the psychology of High Modernism proper. Instead, Hardy at last establishes English fiction, as Dostoyevsky's contemporaneous dialogism does Russian, as a fully reflexive project, and, ironically, as a direct function of its realism. The history of the novel as a whole is in fact the history of a search for organization at the level of plot or story itself; its enduring quest-motif in particular persists, as in Pynchon, well after any possible reality can any longer be said to come of it. The representative movement from picaresque to *Bildungsroman* in the novel's brief history itself reflects an incremental movement toward the kind of progressively organized structure whose immanent formalization finds its thematic counterpart in the growing institutionality in which the desire of its heroes must be played out. Hence the movement from an enabling concern about the breakup of codes in Cervantes to the highly systematized worlds of ambition in which we find Julien Sorel or Dickens's Pip. That it is Hardy who cruelly dramatizes such decisive systematicity in Jude's inability (like Flaubert's Emma) to enter such machinations comfortably and with success should come as no surprise.

It is also appropriate that a novelist who is also a poet of the first rank puts such a reflexive realism in place. Poetry has, of course, been reflexive in its representationalism all along. The walls of Troy are the walls of *The Iliad*; the anxious quests of *The Faerie Queene*'s allegories are likewise versions of Spenser's own as a writer, with both also versions of the coherent society that epic (at least until Milton) programmatically projects rather than expresses. Dante even casts Virgil in the role he assumes anyway in the later poem's narration, chief among its genealogical components as he already is. In such exemplary cases, the poem's representationalism or mythmaking powers are customarily analogous with its rhetorical ones, its realism and its reflexivity always implicitly the same even in—indeed, as the signal result of—the salutary difference that maintains them as distinct. Hardy's inscription of belatedness in the novel's very form suggests that, popular in its genealogy until the time of Flaubert, it has by now, in England, too, gathered into itself the official genealogical conditions of poetic tradition as well, particularly its customary tropologies such as those Romantic ones that the exemplary Flaubert deploys in his insinuation of literary codes into the depiction of daily life itself. The description of Emma's birthday cake in *Madame Bovary* (1857), for example, is done in a variegated rhetoric that is a deliberately fitful montage of poetic and quotidian vocabularies. But, as in Hardy, it is the clash between those codes in their imaginary or ideological state in the subject and their contrasting configuration within the real that is the engine of both Emma's experience and the narrative's relation to its representation. In Leo Bersani's persuasive reading of the novel (1976), Emma "contributes" to the history of "literary romance" because she "skillfully dismisses art by trying to separate the romance from the literature . . . thereby ignor[ing] the work—the effort and the product—of the writer." Flaubert's writing thereby becomes "a continuous correction, through stylistic example, of Emma's confusions" (1976:102). Hence the "heaviness" of Flaubert's writing, concludes Bersani, "could therefore be thought of as pedagogically useful: he is constantly demonstrating the extent to which literature renounces the immediacy of sensations in order to express them" (1976:104). Emma and Flaubert's narration, in other words, are inverse versions one of the other.

Nor is it therefore surprising to say that the novel finds its reflexivity in its very realism. Emma, like Jude to come, is a legendary locus of precisely those romantic images that form life itself in the arrangements it makes with us case to case. Like Flaubert's, Hardy's narration grows reflexive not because he finds the world he writes about inexpressible, but because the world he means to represent already turns out to be a tissue of signs, texts, codes, traditions—a species of the same medium by which its apparent immediacy or reality is to be described in a literary language supposedly different from it. The daily world itself, in other words, is no more immediate than the images out of which its reality is made. Much as the poet is belated because the tools he inherits are no more his own than the sculptor's marble, so the characters who people the world of Hardy's novels are alike belated in relation to the secondariness—and overdeterminations—of those forms in which life itself is to be experienced. Like the poet in relation to tradition, the citizen, too, is inscribed as a function of the (im)possibility of his genuine originality or newness in a world to which he comes, by invariable definition, too late. Hence Hardy's raw materials are social instances of the conditions that have governed the entire career of poetry. Such a stance thickens even more the genealogical density of the late nineteenth-century novelistic text by overtly adding to its new reflexivity not only the entire system and history of poetic usage, but also the poetic potential of the paraliterary—the colloquial vernacular as well as the popular, historical, and devotional texts out of which it emerges—that is its chief subject to begin with.

Hence Farfrae's new "horse-drill" (191) or sowing machine—what Lucetta calls his "'agricultural piano'" (192)—adds a grim logic to the already unsettling claim that the enigmatic restoring "process" he introduces earlier turns overripe or bad wheat back into good or fresh—almost "restore[s]" it (53). If the restoring process may be read as the narrative's oblique though summary metaphor for the modernist's will to make it new despite the decadent or overripe literary conditions that threaten its future growth with extinction, the machine is a far more elaborate device by which the novel may be said to describe itself. Sending Henchard into a chaos of contradictory impulses much as it sends its figurations into an equivalent chaos of oscillating possibilities of meaning ("will," "character"), the novel also wishes to recontain the reverberations it has unleashed in both life and literature at the level of its language. Farfrae's machine accounts for both possibilities at once, even though its aim is to repress the former at the expense of the latter. Indeed, in describing the purpose and function of his "piano," Farfrae must also describe the kinds of oscillation that he wishes to control: "'It will revolutionize sowing heerabout! No more sowers flinging their seed about broadcast, so that some falls by the wayside and some among thorns, and all that. Each grain will go straight to its intended place, and nowhere else whatever!'" (194). Farfrae's clearly symbolic machine, in other words, is designed to enforce the orderliness with which rows of seeds are planted. It is a semantic or semiotic device, a reading or writing machine, since the word "seed" is, in its Greek root *sème*, identical with the word "sign." Farfrae wishes to maintain the seeds in a field in a rowlike fashion that limits their spillage (the latter a purely random contingency, the function of the wind or of careless sowing, much as semantic spillage is an equally random effect of the overdetermined structure of language); he wishes to keep them disciplined rather than allow their potential overflow to give rise to alien or contradictory associations. The machine is designed, in short, to eliminate the play inherent in the "sowing" of seeds and signs alike, to inhibit the migration or "'broadcast'" of *sèmes* in both senses of the word. Indeed, it is precisely such double possibilities in signification (is a seed a grain or a sign?) that the machine is designed to repress.

Despite her lament that the machine means "'the romance of the sower is gone for good'" (194), even Elizabeth-Jane agrees with the machine's principle of clarity because it corresponds to her own painfully learned sense of protocol and coherence at the level of life and manners:

> Any suspicion of impropriety was to Elizabeth-Jane like a red rag to a bull. Her craving for correctness of procedure was, indeed, almost vicious. Owing to her early troubles with regard to her mother a semblance of irregularity had terrors for her which those whose names are safeguarded from suspicion know nothing of. [248]

No stranger to the effects of spillage in life itself (she is, it is hard to forget, mistaken by Henchard as the sign of his own originating seed), Elizabeth-Jane's admittedly problematic proper names suggest still another level of semiotic "'broadcast'" in the novel that the machine—like her own dedication to protocol—symbolically represses. Henchard, one remembers, doesn't just confuse the semic or signifying properties of his seed with Newson's. He also has two women, two sites for the deposit of his seed, doubling in turn his two modes of willfulness, the one impulsive (selling Susan, taking up with Lucetta), the other ruling (equivocating with Lucetta, taking care of Susan). He is not like Faust or Job, but like Faust and Job simultaneously. Even Farfrae, Henchard's supposed opposite, coherent as he seems, also needs the symbolic discipline of such a machine to keep his own subjectivity in citizenly place. With a strange contrast of nostalgia and indifference marking his undecidable feelings about his native Scotland, it is no surprise that Hardy famously describes him as a "variegated cord" whose "contrasts could be seen intertwisted" ("not mingling") in "the curious double strands" in his "thread of life" (183). Farfrae is, as his coolness suggests, composed of incongruous elements despite the appearance of harmony. Again like his supposed antagonist, Farfrae also quite graphically spills his seed in two women—Lucetta and Elizabeth-Jane—acting out the same semiotic instability customarily assigned to Henchard alone.

If promiscuous sowing is unacceptable in manners, Hardy's propensity to double the extravagance of Henchard's—and Farfrae's—desire in his own language must also be checked. Potentially a Joycean schizo-narrative in its jolting reflexivity and decided agglutination of figures, *The Mayor* is nonetheless also a coherent representation of certain modes of incoherence, whether of Henchard's belated mode of knowledge or of the novel's own tendency to produce colliding metaphors or warring systems of figuration. Unlike Henchard, however, Farfrae is still repressive, not because he represents a technology less natural than Henchard's own, but because his machine aims for the kinds of (impossible) unity to which characters and texts alike must yield in the face of social restraints both real and novelistic. The semantic oscillations in key terms such as "will" or "character" are, on the one hand, the kinds of reflexive spillage that the novel calls upon so as to heighten its poeticity and put into question its apparent modernist meanings. On the other hand, however, such spillage is also what the novel must repress so as to get on with its story, psychologistic causation and all. Hardy's reflexive realism is a balancing act that allows for both Lawrence's reading and our subsequent one, neither excluded by the other, each in fact required by the other so as to allow each to be what it is. Resolutely realistic, the novel also maintains its reflexivity against the repression Farfrae's machine represents by making its story a version of the narration that constructs it. Much as Susan gets Henchard to believe that Elizabeth-Jane is his own despite the contrary evidences that must be repressed, so too does the novel get its reader to believe in Casterbridge despite the linguistic irregularities that undercut the stability of Hardy's mimesis.

The Mayor of Casterbridge, then, does not repress but makes thematic the means of its own production as a text. Reflexive realism's adequation of *récit* and *histoire* means that no recontainment or repression of a narrative's operation can ever be possible—the balance of a work fully, and ironically, depends upon it. Hence the job of the modern writer is not that of idealizing a lost life or nature that was never present to begin with, but to find a way to simulate it even as it accounts for its impossibility. The sequence of our double reading of

Hardy—from Lawrence's privileging of Hardy's will to modernity to Hardy's own reflexive realism—will in fact serve to measure our view of the history of British writing from Arnold to Bloomsbury. Beginning with Arnold, we will see the will to modernity in all its rawness, together with the accompanying desire to repress the means of discursive production that makes the modernist wish to return to origins impossible to satisfy. Pater, by contrast, will return us to the implacability of belatedness—of deferred action—that frustrates all modernisms, and that will prepare us for our readings of Eliot and Joyce in part 2 before our discussion of Forster, Woolf, and Strachey in part 3.

ONE

The Belated Reader

. . . thou breath of Autumn's being,
Thou, from whose unseen presence the leaves dead
Are driven, like ghosts from an enchanter fleeing,

Yellow, and black, and pale, and hectic red,
Pestilence-stricken multitudes: O thou,
Who chariotest to their dark wintry bed

The winged seeds, where they lie cold and low,
Each like a corpse within its grave, until
Thine azure sister of the Spring shall blow

Her clarion o'er the dreaming earth, and fill
(Driving sweet buds like flocks to feed in air)
With living hues and odours plain and hill:

Wild Spirit, which art moving everywhere;
Destroyer and preserver; hear, oh, hear!

—Shelley, "Ode to the West Wind"

Matthew Arnold and the Deliberate
Compensations of Prose

Let us turn to Matthew Arnold first for an exposition of both the conditions under which the early modernist must work and the ideals that he produces in order to withstand them. It is nothing less than tradition that weighs Arnold down, a poet who rightly puts aside the Muse in 1853 in favor of an empiricist criticism, both literary and cultural, that does for Arnold in prose what Arnold the poet can never accomplish—the production of a strong and influential myth of the modern. Although Arnold's reputation as a poet will always be subject to some dispute, as an essayist he remains among the principals of English nonfiction prose, and among the principals, too, in the history of the intellectual's self-definition in modern culture. To Herbert Paul in 1902, Arnold still appeared, as he would to T. S. Eliot in 1930, a trifle radical and even rowdy—his range is too wide, his manner, despite himself, slangy, like the leader writers whose prose and thought he decries. Paul goes perhaps too far the other way to suggest just how aristocratic Arnold's values really are, although it allows us to measure our present distance from Paul's apprehension by showing us how far we are today from that orthodox sense of Arnold, which now looms too purely polemical in its certain defense of classical models. Arnold is, at his most characteristic, the poet of "Dover Beach," holding the line of culture at the flood tide of anarchy. Eliot was to try to hold it under even greater pressures, blaming Arnold for initiating a breakdown in the compartmentalization of learning that lay at the problem's root, and finding its consummate expression in Pater (1930). But if Arnold defends against anarchy, he also fathers it, although to say so suggests a more exemplary status for Arnold than Eliot is usually willing to concede. If we are less concerned today with the reality of either the threat of Arnold's anarchy or the defense of his culture against it, it is largely because we can thank Arnold the prose-poet, masquerading as empiricist, for inventing our official modern crisis rather than for discovering it. Arnold's career, discontinuous as it is in the rupture between verse and prose, is nonetheless regular, even lawful, in the preoccupations that unite the early poet and the late religious renegade. But Arnold's shift from poetry to prose is designed to solve a problem that oppresses the poems even as it structures them, and one that leads Arnold to his real power as a writer, the power to create an imaginative world and bequeath it to us under the guise of fact.

Baldly reflexive in their representations, Arnold's poems provide a superb introduction to the plight of the modern writer drained of inspiration. Counterparts one of the other, Arnold's dreary heroes are the plaintive personations of Arnold's own plight as a late Romantic poet, judging at least by the uniformly sad, measured demeanor of the imaginary heroes of his poems, who fear the collapse of laws and the confusion of boundaries. As early as "Mycerinus" (1849), Arnold's hero grows "pale and weak" like the cooling firmament he beholds, since, in such a landscape of loss, "the barrier" that keeps "past and future" separate now "dies away," allowing "past and future" to "intertwine." Like the exemplary strayed reveller (1849), the Arnoldean hero is a "Wavetoss'd Wanderer" who asks "Who can stand still?" in this universe of sea change. The capitulation of the strayed reveller to the anteriority that engulfs him largely summarizes the fate of all Arnold's poet-heroes. Like Arnold himself as poet, he gives himself up to "the wild, thronging train" of "eddying forms" that represents influence or tradition, an image that prefigures both Pater's flux and Hardy's procession of the dead in "Wessex Heights" (1896), and an image as compelling as any in Arnold's verse for what, in an anticipation of Pound, he will call, in a slightly different context in "The Function of Criticism at the Present Time," the "vortex" (1865:3:27), or, prefiguring Stevens in "The Study of Poetry," the "burning ground" (1888:4:40).

Empedocles is the most explicit of Arnold's heroes in voicing the exact problem: "we are strangers here; the world is from of old" (1852). We bring a "bias" with us into life—or, rather, the "bias" brings us—because "To tunes we did not call our being must keep chime." "Like a sea," such influence "soaks all-effacing in," and robs us of uniqueness even as it gives us relative identities predetermined by the rules and figures of custom, belief, and poetry itself. To speak of originality is beside the point, since even "our wants have all been felt, our errors made before." Our "settled trouble" is, in short, that we come "too late," "ere quite the being of man, ere quite the world/Be disarray'd of their divinity." Divinity, as we also know from Arnold's later writings, marks the real and authentic, that source or origin in the past and that clarity and directness of original perception in the present that between them adumbrate the ideal of exact or literal meaning, linking the vision of empirical science with the style of perception idealized in Arnold's verse, and preserving the notion of a real and unsullied world before or behind the "bias" of figure.

Arnold's poetry suffers from the precise ailment that sickens his heroes: the overabundance of influence, the overdeterminations of an inherited figurative language that sap the possibility of original voice by preparing one's place—or lack of it—beforehand. Against the frustration of the flux that washes the new in the blood of the old emerge the lost ideals: the notion of an origin before the birth of custom in both life and poetry, and the notion of originality in the present that would allow the latecomer the freshness and directness denied him by the determinations of culture and its prefiguring of identity. If, in Empedocles' words, "each succeeding age . . . will have more peril for us than the last," "we shall," he says, "fly for refuge to past times, / The . . . soul of unworn youth." The vision of the ideal is, in one register, a notion of an absolute human nature beyond culture: "man's one nature, queen-like," which, in the sonnet on Butler's sermons, "sits alone, / Centred in a majestic unity" (1849). In the cosmic register, it is the proposition of the opening of "In Utrumque Paratus": "If, in the silent mind of One all-pure, / At first imagined lay / The sacred world" (1849). It is the desire for a time before figure, the myth of "the freshness of the early world," as Arnold puts it in the "Memorial Verses," the myth of direct touch with nature, at once classicist and primitivist in the ironic authority of its wish for "birth / On the cool flowery lap of earth" (1852).

Love is another figure for the ideal of a world beyond or before figure or culture, even though the form and history of the love poem already preclude the possibility of the speaker's union with his object. Marguerite is the Laura of Arnold's Lucy sequence, the impossible ideal of real touch: "arms reach to clasp thee! / . . . in vain" (1853a). Love also signifies the "promise of control" (1854), since the presence of the beloved, like the dream of an origin or of original vision, provides a bulwark against "the boundless ocean-plain" (1867) that is Europe's present figurative condition, and the sign of its bondage to flux, figure, influence.

The pressures mount as Arnold's career as poet proceeds, reaching its emotional culmination in the pathos of "Sohrab and Rustum" (1853a), in which son capitulates to father in a bitter reversal of normally achieved power. It is a logical finale to a series of laments by failed or stricken nobilities throughout the verse, for whom even Empedocles' suicide is obfuscating next to the rank admission of failure in the later poem that links the vocabulary of flux and sea change ("all strength was ebb'd") to capitulation to the enduring authority of the father's face and voice.

These accents are, understandably, especially acute in "Rugby Chapel" (1867), Arnold's official paternal elegy or autobiographical "Sohrab and

Rustum." Like the growing Romantic gloom of the "autumnal evening" in "Stanzas from the Grande Chartreuse" (1867), its "autumn-evening" setting bespeaks the sapping of original strength in which—and as a result of which—even "the nobleness of grief," as he puts it in the "Stanzas," "is gone." Dr. Arnold manages (at least in the nostalgic haze of retrospect) what his son cannot, a knowledge of where the border of the law is, since the law and his own identity are linked, much as the law's fluctuation is linked to the son's failure to achieve such a mooring for himself. If the father "Tread the border-land dim /'Twixt vice and virtue" with a sure step, sure of what separates one thing from another, his son, by contrast—like all the failed questers of his early poems—passes from secure paths to perilous ones, becoming "lost in the storm" which "boils o'er" the "borders" of the pathways left open to him, and so confuses the road in a virtual parody of Romantic quest-romance on the heights. The son's path is at best "A feeble, wavering line"; Arnold's job is to locate and secure what of it he can, to travel in his father's footsteps to "the bound of the waste."

Arnold's most celebrated poems, "The Scholar-Gipsy" (1853) and "Thyrsis" (1867), know precisely what ails the poet, and situate ideals and contingencies alike with a self-consciousness that begins to prepare us for the salutary shift to prose. In "The Scholar-Gipsy," the topography of Arnold's predicament grows exact as the poet wishes to "again begin the quest!" The beginning, the origin, is no beginning at all, but a repetition, like those that characterize Arnold's legion attempts at original voice as poet on the burning ground. Indeed, it is suddenly clear that origin and repetition require one another for their mutual coherence, each term unique or separate only in what distinguishes it from the other. Much as the "white sheep . . . /Cross and recross the strips of moon-blanch'd green" here in the first stanza—pastoral made pale and decadent by repetition, Eden illuminated by no more than secondary light—so it is by the crossing into a sheeply innocence about the possibility of voice that Arnold violates the law of figure and so discovers it to be judging him, binding him to its rule in the making of poems. By following the scholar-gipsy's "trace," Arnold traverses not so much the countryside proper as an imaginative or figurative landscape already mapped by the crossings and recrossings of Greek and Christian romance, and of Wordsworthian Romanticism.

Indeed, the spirit of the scholar-gipsy (the name itself is a paradox or contradiction, while its life emanates from the pages of "Glanvil's book") is a paradigmatic form of the success denied Arnold as a poet in his own right—at least the rhetorical simulacrum if not the reality of an "early" or direct presence, girded by "powers/Fresh," "Free from the sick fatigue" of belatedness, from what

Arnold calls a bit earlier in the poem "repeated shocks, again, again" that "Exhaust the energy of strongest souls / And numb the elastic powers." For even the scholar-gipsy, despite his apparent freshness, "waitest for the spark from heaven," just as Arnold himself must await it, only to find that it "still delays" (even the Wordsworthianism of Arnold's diction, like his other feats of Miltonic and Romantic ventriloquism, is the reflexive counterpart of the burden). Despite his claim that the scholar-gipsy was "born in days when wits were fresh and clear," here the early ideal, too, is poised at a Keatsian lip of frustration and delay equivalent to Arnold's own. Like the "trace" of the scholar-gipsy's path, which indicates his presence by the sign of his absence, the "spark" is always deferred because it, too, is a figure; not a possibility of real or literal redemption, but a phantom object produced by desire in the difference between expectation and impossibility engendered by the figurations inherent in language itself. It is this necessary confinement by figure that Arnold resists—indeed, will come overtly to repress—and that asserts itself with renewed vigor when the line of its rule is crossed by Arnold's willfully modernist wish for a direct language of literal truth.

Hence the ideal itself is a relative fiction in "The Scholar-Gipsy" as Arnold suggests his representation of native freshness to be a kind of belated and displaced repetition, not just of Wordsworth's heroes and Glanvill's myth, but also of the still earlier Mediterranean or classical myths of freshness, warmth, closeness to origins that lie behind them, and that the poem tries to retrieve in its sudden and curious swerve to an epic simile in its penultimate stanza. But even Arnold's "Tyrian trader" with "southward-facing brow" sights, not land, but another barge, "freighted" with fruits to be sure, but still (like his own position) only a bark on the flood no matter that the flood in this case is the Aegean itself. Much as the scholar-gipsy awaits the spark along with Arnold the contemporary, so the ancient image of Greek surfeit also remains afloat; moreover, it can only be located by its relation to something else.

Like "The Scholar-Gipsy," "Thyrsis" retraces the pastoral mythologies that embody the ideal of freshness and original voice, and in the same reverse order that betokens their unpacking in the earlier poem. Neither "English fields" (native, Wordsworthian Romanticism) nor "that lone, sky-pointing tree" (Christianity) suit Clough's spirit, and so he flies instead to the promised land behind them both, "a boon southern country" representative of classical earliness proper, and of which Christianity, much less Romanticism, is a repetition from Arnold's point of view. This refreshing retreat to origins is made, of course, in the name of the departed Clough's promise of direct and original apprehension—"by his own heart inspired." But because Arnold must express his ideal originality by recourse to the series of myths that produce the notion, it is already little more than a fiction, a rhetorical illusion complicit with the fading mythologies against which—but also through which—it tries to identify itself. What enables is also cause for anxiety—in Arnold, it is a standoff. Hence the sheer ritualism necessary to elegy—"see him come back"—with Clough's redemptive return no sweeter than any other requirement of form in Arnold's universe. What is "changed," then, in the opening of "Thyrsis" is not the hills themselves, but their earlier state in relation to their later one. Arnold measures a difference of states in time, each of which requires the other in order to gain the separation that in fact unites them. Thus the "spot" or ground, resonant with the charged spirit of an earlier age, acquires its spirit—as the scholar-gipsy acquires his—not by the indwelling of a real divinity now lost, but by a measurement that installs the ideal as a means by which the present can establish itself at a sorrowful distance from it. Arnold's key terms, that is, turn out to be part of a regular rhetorical structure toward whose recognition his career as poet moves. Origin and repetition, freshness and belatedness, power and weakness, stability and flux; each emerges in relation to the other, power emerging only in relation to its lack, presence as an ideal only in relation to the reality of its absence. Binding and unravelling, law and violation, are linked in a single structure that requires each antinomy to insure the existence of the other. Reflecting on the gipsies, the speaker of "Resignation" (1849) contrasts their wildness with civilization's stability, and so provides an exact example of the interdependence of Arnold's contraries:

> It seems as if, in their decay,
> The law grew stronger every day.
> So might they reason, so compare . . . .

It is by comparing that Arnold and his heroes establish the states between which their beings oscillate, fully part of neither one side nor the other—neither altogether fresh nor altogether repetitive—because always part of both at once.

Arnold's late lyrics—"Calais Sands," "Carnac," "A Southern Night," "Dover Beach" (1867)—are explicit "boundary" poems, concerned as they are with how the lines or borders that separate realms and produce identities are fashioned. The sea metaphor is precise for Arnold's purposes, and is a preoccupation for good reason: the figure of the verge of land and sea, of stability and flux, of the line of the law as such, makes it clear that sea and shore require one another for a boundary to be drawn between them, and for each side to receive its customary definition. Thus Arnold takes a central tropological strand of the earlier, fallen-nobility pieces—the ebb and flow of sea and strength—and makes it the overt critical subject of verses already tormented by being public languages for private despair. The "intellectual deliverance" (1857:1:19) that the Arnold of "On the Modern Element in Literature" will seek as a critic is designed to overcome precisely this tyranny of figure in the situation of poetic voice.

The categories of Arnold's literary criticism reconstitute those of the poems, although there has been a strategic displacement in what they signify and a more aggressive repression of the belated means of production of the still-familiar ideals. As the young Trilling remarked, "the poet's vision gave the prose writer his goal" (1939: Introduction). The ideals of power and self-definition have been transformed into the ideal of accuracy, the language of forces into the language of a transparent empiricism. The poet's desire for clarity and directness of imagination is converted into Arnold the critic's desire for clarity and directness of perception. The difference between them transforms the problematic difference between figurative and literal meaning in the poems into the salutary and enabling difference for the critic between the luxury of fancy and the scrupulosity of fact. Arnold reimagines the language of forces in a language of exactitudes, the rhetoric of empiricism and mimesis repressing the language of poetic figure, reconstituting the agon of forces in contention as measurement on an apparently absolute and permanent scale.

Arnold's notion of Homer is the overwhelming symptom and cipher in his criticism for the late Romantic pressures under which he labors as a poet, making explicit the epistemological presuppositions under which he functions as poet and essayist alike. Like his appeal in the 1853 Preface to "the empire of facts" (1853b:11:289), to that which is "independent of the language current" (11:289), to "what is permanent in the human soul" (11:290), Arnold's appeal to Homer as a kind of ultimate touchstone resides in what he calls Homer's "directness" (1861:5:164) and "plain naturalness" (5:172), overdetermined signs for that desire for earliness, freshness, closeness to origins that is the major lament of the poems. Like the critic's job in "The Function of Criticism" to "'see the object as in itself it really is'" (1865:3:1), the job of translating Homer requires an exact "union of the translator with his original" (1861:5:162–63), the translator reduplicating in relation to Homer's text Homer's own exact relation to language, and that of his language to its objects.

Even in the later lectures, the same picture of Homer is maintained. In the second, for example, "the translator is to reproduce Homer"—as though he were already there—"and the scholar alone has the means of knowing that Homer who is to be reproduced" (1861:5:182–83). Arnold's scholar, it should also be noted, is the very reverse of the one Pater will go on to imagine in "Style," a believer as he must be in Arnold's assumption that language is a transparent conveyor of something outside itself. In the third lecture, Arnold scowls at "the artificial character" of Pope's "rapidity" in translating Homer's own "plainness" (1861:5:218), this because Pope's "rapidity" is, according to Arnold, "not of the same sort as Homer's" own (1861:5:218). Despite such nascent contradiction, the lectures conclude with an enduring, even redundant portrait of Homer's "absolute plainness of speech" (1861:5:247) as Arnold attempts to translate some scraps of Homer for himself (for the results, see Strachey 1914).

Of course, the ideal is not only and not really Homer (nor even Jesus, who takes Homer's place in Arnold's later religious phase), but also and above all Wordsworth. At moments Keats and Maurice de Guérin come close to the Wordsworthian ideal, since "they speak like Adam naming by divine inspiration the creatures; their expression corresponds with the thing's essential reality" (1865:3:122). Wordsworth's own consummate and "enduring freshness" (1888:4:97), however, is signified by the fact that, in Arnold's words, "he has no style" (1888:4:114): "It might seem that Nature not only gave him the matter for his poem, but wrote his poem for him" (1888: 4:114). It is a judgment repeated with Byron ("Nature herself seems to take the pen from him as she took it from Wordsworth" [1888:4:146]), though this formulaic repetition already identifies its status as a trope in Arnold's linguistic arsenal, and not as a claim—despite Arnold's manifest values—to be evaluated in terms of its accuracy.

Arnold praises Wordsworth and Byron, then, because, from his point of view at least, they have apparently burned away all figurative language. They are the exact reverse of Homer's translators, who have superadded the ornament of figure to a Homeric language that simply wraps itself around its object. Such language is at one with what it describes, a literal language that is merely instrumental, a transparent vehicle through which the world itself may be said to speak. Much as there is an original Homer whose essence may be accurately retrieved, so there is, according to Arnold's poetics, a world as such beyond or outside language that language—even poetic language—merely transcribes. The best writing, says Arnold in the 1853 Preface, "subordinates expression to that which it is designed to express" (11:285); says a thing "plainly" in "the very directest language" (286) instead of being "artificial," "tortured," possessed of "an irritability of fancy" (286). Like Wordsworth's, good writing must be written with "no style" at all. Arnold here subordinates figurative meaning to literal meaning as a question of literary value, in the process repressing the inevitability of the former in his constant attempt to maintain the possibility of the latter. In so proceeding, however, Arnold veins his criticism with a structure of contradiction so regular that it has the virtual force of law in the constitution of his rhetoric. Though Geoffrey Tillotson reminds us in an essay on Arnold that "surely a literary critic is always aware of words as words" (1968:75), Arnold himself apparently wishes to forget the exigencies of language altogether in a Romantic zeal that is really the symptom of something else.

If we look again at the "pure transparency" in Homer that his translators ought to duplicate, the problem of originary repetition—of "again begin"—recurs, the problem that Arnold is at particular pains to repress in the criticism. For suddenly the freshness that is the virtue of returning to Homer as he (supposedly) is turns out to be a freshness that must be derived through repetition of his privileged earliness. To keep the vision of the present as clear as that of Homer himself requires so perfect an identification with him, such peerless sympathy, that clarity itself begins to turn into its opposite, the lack of freshness ironically entailed by repeating the past to the letter. One grows clear and original in apprehension by repeating an earlier style of apprehension, each term soiling or tainting the other as the price of their mutual coherence. In the "union of the translator with his original," we should query the possessive pronoun for its proper referent, which necessarily shifts between Homer and the latecomer, neither of whose proper realms can be said to be available as such in the project of translation, which threatens to disassemble the ideals its symbolic role is supposed to grant it. Rhetoric inevitably intrudes whenever Arnold wishes it away.

Like his Homeric Jesus or Homeric Wordsworth, Arnold's Wordsworthian Homer is no simple and naive invention, but the pivot of a series of internal dissonances in his criticism that reveal the kind of strategic rhetoric that Arnold means to eschew or repress as a manifest empiricist. The 1853 Preface provides an adequate formulation of it: the "feelings" (1853b:11:275) touched by the best poetry are "permanent and the same" (275) no matter the historical moment at which they arise. They represent the "inherent qualities" (275) a great or noble action has, connected as it is with what is "permanent" and abiding in man regardless of time and place. And yet how do we measure what is "permanent" or "inherent," heralding as Arnold does here the argument of *Culture and Anarchy?* Why, "solely in proportion to its greatness and to its passion" (275). That is, what is absolute outside of language, history, society is to be apprehended in the proportions among its terms, on a scale that weighs the differences between one action and another, and so derives their qualities by means of the relations they maintain. A similar kind of contradiction or crossing-over is required when Arnold inspects the status of law itself in "The Function of Criticism" (1865): "What is law in one place is not law in another," says an Arnold who looks ahead to an analysis of rights in his later political essays; "what is binding on one man's conscience is not binding on another's" (1865:3:11). And yet "the prescriptions of reasons are," in the same paragraph, "absolute, unchanging, of universal validity" (3:11), appealing, as great spiritual events like the French Revolution do, "to an order of ideas which are universal, certain, permanent" (1865:3:11). Even the "touchstone" method in "The Study of Poetry" is a comparative or proportional one at bottom: "to have always in one's mind lines and expressions of the great masters, and to apply them as a touchstone"—as a basis for comparison—"to other poetry" (1888:4:12–13). Again, the repressed strategy of deriving the "absolute" or "inherent" from the relative. The best or "highest" (1888:4:15) gives away its real status as a comparative by the form of its articulation. No touch with origins can be unmediated, since it is always produced as a belated effect of the differences by which langu~ge retroactively installs whatever ground it has.

To be sure, Arnold acknowledges his yardstick to be a proportional one: If this "order" (1865:3:6), says Arnold, is to lead to man's "perfection, by making his mind dwell upon what is excellent in itself, and the absolute beauty and fitness of things" (3:23), yet this "order of ideas, if not absolutely true," is "yet true by comparison with that which it displaces" (3:6). The "absolute," as Arnold well knows, is derived "by comparison." And yet the assertion of the permanent ideal persists despite its contamination by—and of—this equally decisive logic of the purely relational status of the phantom objects language signifies in the crossings and comparisons among its component figures. If, for example, criticism must be "disinterested," engaged in "a free play of the mind on all subjects, for its own sake" (3:18) and "leave alone all questions of practical consequences and application" (3:20), still—and quite unlike the Pater to come, despite Eliot's judgment in 1930—it must "establish an order of ideas" (3:6); it must, like the French Academy, "give the law" (3:49). What aim could be worth the cost in so regular and problematic a rhetorical discordance? That power is at issue—the strength of "order," the "promise of control"—is clear enough, though how Arnold seizes it in the essays—how he belatedly survives himself as a poet—lies in the precise advantage his bluff empiricism grants him as a critic. Arnold's misreading of the status of the very medium of prose is what allows him to secure the power he lacks in his poems, where medium surrounds and victimizes him by making him the creature of figure rather than its master. The situation in prose is, according to Arnold the strategic idealist, a different one. The poet, he says in "Maurice de Guérin" (1865), must "accept his vehicle ready-made" (3:90). "In prose," by contrast, "the character of the vehicle for the composer's thoughts is not determined beforehand; every composer has to make his own vehicle" (3:90).

Surely Arnold is being disingenuous, since every composer must at least work with the medium of music itself, much as any writer must work with language, even if he rejects particular handlings of it. The willful blindness, however, representative as it is of the blind ideals of Arnold's verse and criticism alike, is obviously useful, since it allows Arnold to find a place free, at least in his successful imagination of it, from the numbing, and far more overt, repetitions endemic to the practice of poetry. Arnold's essays win the ground of prose by defining language as being without figure, the more literal the better because the closer to the thing it expresses or describes. As a critic with such overt presuppositions, Arnold can thus use figure exorbitantly but covertly as the structuring device of the world he means to fashion. In this way, Arnold's witting misprision as to the status of his new medium releases his power by allowing him to write poetry under the guise of prose, figurative language, that is, masquerading as literal. It also allows him to distinguish prose from poetry even as he contaminates the difference between them.

If Arnold's ideal as a poet is the fiction of the literal—of the origin, of a clear and direct apprehension of the world as it is—he achieves the ideal in the fiction of his criticism, which disguises itself as a language of frank simplicity and accurate assessment even as it deploys a figurative strategy to produce and canonize a world of literature it claims only to see clearly, as it is. Once Arnold crosses out of literature into social criticism, he extends this movement by crossing into a political discourse whose enabling fiction of strict correspondence to the age seems to place it entirely in the service of the world as it is, not as poets or literary critics imagine it to be. If Arnold contaminates the difference between poetry and prose even as he distinguishes between them as a critic of literature, he contaminates the difference between language and "the empire of facts" even as he distinguishes between them as a social critic. If his literary criticism is founded on an empirical accuracy and a direct relation to things as they are, his social criticism reifies such ideals in the ironic ideal of culture itself as it seeks to win the appearance of a Homeric project so transparent that it seems to enact the pattern of virtue it describes even as—even though—it erases its putative naturalness by virtue of its identification with the culture normally opposed to it.

If Arnold's organizing categories in the literary criticism duplicate and displace those in the poems, the social criticism duplicates and displaces them once again. Like the Homeric and Wordsworthian ideals in the criticism, and like the ideal of the real Jesus in *Literature and Dogma* (1873), the ideal of culture in *Culture and Anarchy* (1869) is one of "fixing standards of perception that are real" (1869:6:16). The "desire for clearness" (6:82) insures objective sight, as does the premise of "a common basis of human nature" (6:89), since both are meant to represent that freedom from contemporary bias required in estimating what is permanent and true for all people at all times. Arnold expresses these ideals through the figure of men "disentangling themselves from machinery" (92)—from the ideologies of the moment—and finding behind or apart from the engines of custom and belief that which is genuinely human, "something original and heaven-bestowed" (92), or, in the equally authoritative scientific metaphor, "the force of . . . original instinct" (94), identical in both cases with man's "best" (94). Hence the notion of culture, like the centering notions of the State and the exemplary French Academy, means "a certain ideal centre of correct information" (95), "the sheer truth as reason sees it" (103), "an unclouded clearness of mind" (124).

These ideals are as impossible here as they are in the criticism proper, and yet they serve Arnold's productive economy as an essayist in fashioning the successful illusion of a new, imaginative world denied him as a poet. The claim that culture alone of all the discourses of society stands outside the "machinery" of custom and contemporary ideology not only puts itself into question once again in the problematic and utterly contradictory identification of what is most natural or original with culture as such. It also recalls the similar claim in the literary criticism that the vehicle of poetry comes to the writer ready-made, part of a machinery, full of precedent and protocol, while that of prose is open to free use, somehow outside the machinery of custom or precedent. In both cases, Arnold privileges one side of a distinction between nature and culture, truth and language, each of whose terms nonetheless requires the other for its sense. Arnold invokes the machinery of custom—of the supplementary ornaments of society to man's essential nature—in order to curry the opposite it brings into being—eternal human nature. The similarity between prose and human nature in Arnold's rhetoric is all the more outrageous for the sudden and unsettling structural identity it also draws between the two things most separate in Arnold's imagination—poetry and the culture of the masses. Much as his insistence that the ideal of high culture represents what is permanent or original and so leads him into the incalculable contradiction of identifying nature with the culture it normally opposes, so the symptomatic ramifications of Arnold's rhetoric also lead to the epistemological likeness of the unlikely companions of high culture—poetry—and mass culture on the ground of their shared habituation and paralysis at the hands of the machinery common to both.

But the rhetoric of Arnold's formulations is designed—no matter the contradictory tendencies to which they give rise—not to tell an innocent objective truth, but to elevate prose and culture alike by endowing both with an alinguistic, asocial status, thereby allowing them to come down to Arnold himself as clean, unspotted, natural, fresh. And yet Arnold can only gain the clarity of culture by virtue of its difference from the anarchy or impropriety that threatens it, and that calls it into being as a defense against it. Like the speaker in the Marguerite sequence who longs for the flood so as to identify himself as the one who stands against it, Arnold the social critic champions the flux he names anarchy so that he can defend against it by producing culture.

Arnold himself is clear that culture and anarchy arise only in relation to one another; indeed, that we become aware of what order there is only at the moment that it is violated, that it threatens to depart. With the "increase" in "anarchy and social disintegration," he says in chapter 2, "that profound sense of settled order and security, without which a society like ours cannot live and grow at all, sometimes seems to be beginning to threaten us with taking its departure" (1869:6:57). What threatens, ironically, is order, at least as it threatens to absent itself; to fill or defend against its absence, then, Arnold invokes the presence of culture proper: "We have got a much wanted principle, a principle of authority, to counteract the tendency to anarchy which seems to be threatening us" (58). But now it is suddenly the threat that is couched in terms of a presence instead of the promised presence of culture, whose name remains absent here—it is the presence of anarchy that emerges in the place vacated by the departure of order. Culture and anarchy, in other words, stain one another because they are interdependent, terms whose crossings-over situate each side of their supposed antinomy and reveal their complicity.

Hebraism and Hellenism are, of course, Arnold's master tropes in *Culture and Anarchy* for the rival notions of language at work in his prose. If Hellenism is clarity, originality, spontaneity, Hebraism is law, repetition, tradition; if Hellenism is delight, Hebraism is "the impossibility of being at ease in

Zion" (128); if Hellenism is directness, primariness, literal language, Hebraism is belatedness, exile, figurative language. Even more, however, these rival qualities emerge differentially, only as phantom products of the figurative language that puts the terms that constitute them into play. They are "rivals not by the necessity of their own nature" (of which, properly speaking, they have none), "but as exhibited in man and his history" (121; as the qualities derived from their effects). What distinguishes them, says Arnold, is only an "ineffaceable difference" (123) as such, a term that grasps the very mechanism or principle that produces the mutually contaminating referents of Arnold's prose at the level of the figurative strategies it pretends to ignore.

Arnold's fearful recognition in the poems that human culture as a whole is a figurative formation—a complex of discourses whose rhetoric produces whatever rights, law, and nature there may be—is central to his stance as a political democrat, even though it presents problems for his poetics. Here in fact he must tamper with the central democratic notion that citizenship is itself a legal fiction in order to maintain the manifestly empirical status of his prose. Although one feels "instinctively," as Arnold puts it in "Equality," such a thing as a "high standard of civilisation" (1879:10:58) and so may endow it with natural and eternal qualities, yet, in contradistinction to the assertion of "instinct" or "nature," Arnold admits that the very notion of "natural right," whether in democracy or feudalism, is "baseless" (10:59). "All rights are created by law," based on "expediency," "alterable" by the circumstances of history (59). As he puts it in the companion essay, "Democracy," "those who have grown up amidst a certain state of things, those whose habits, and interests, and affections are closely concerned with its continuance, are slow to believe that it is not a part of the order of nature" (10:21). And yet earlier in the essay, Arnold has himself asserted that the "vital impulse of democracy" is "identical with the ceaseless vital effort of human nature itself" (9). Is democracy based on nature or culture? on instinct or on law? Clearly Arnold's argument partakes of both sides, each one tainting the other.

Arnold's eternalizing empiricism and idealization of an object-world of nature and truth collide as a rule with his notion of right and law as the figurative production of ideology, much as his desire for a literal vision free from figure in the poems collides there with the inevitability of figure in voicing desire itself. At the same time, however, the poetic and cultural ideals converge with the later religious ones, linked by a rhetoric that suggests a common desire for literal truth in all facets of Arnold's imagination. Christianity has a "natural truth" because "the *fact* is with Jesus," as he puts it in the preface to *Last Essays* (1877:9:193). Jesus "reverted to the solid, authentic, universal fact of experience . . ." (9:185). Like Homer or Wordsworth, or like Arnold himself, Jesus is an empiricist: "The natural experimental truth of his explanations is their one claim upon us" (1877:9:192).

The convergence of poetic, religious, and cultural ideals does not, however, serve Arnold as an argument for demonstrating the discursive status of the world and its truths—that is left to Pater. For Arnold to do so would mean exposing the means of production of his strategically empirical argument as well as the ideal of the literal truth that organizes his desire throughout his career. No, the Bible is literature for Arnold not because it is fiction but because it is true. It is in fact a religious standard that is being maintained along with the scientific one, although Arnold maintains it by granting the status of truth, not to religion as such, but to literature. If the notion of inherent truth is gone from religion, it can still be displaced onto high culture, and so establish the priority of a new class of clerks at the same time that it secures Arnold's own imaginative achievement in prose. Although Arnold produces the discursive space of the modern intellectual, he does so by resisting exactly what the Eliot of 1930 claims him to have won: the breakdown of cultural boundaries. Eliot, however inadvertently, apprehends Arnold as rhetorician, as secret producer of the crisis he bewails. To secure the notion of a theological culture, Arnold must also endanger its possibility: to assert the ideal of such a center means to locate it against the decentering anarchy such culture requires for its coherence, for its status as such. Thus Arnold produces not a transparent social criticism but a discursive matrix that fashions a world it claims only to describe. Here Arnold at last achieves that primary act of imagination denied him as a poet. As social critic Arnold not only survives himself as poet and even literary critic, but also reconstitutes poetry in the midst of the world; indeed, he reconstitutes the world in the image of a successfully resolved will to modernity that can produce the image of the new in social criticism denied to it by the far more visible contingencies of verse.

Does All Art Aspire to the Condition of Music?

Pater's enduring neglect as a central figure within his own tradition continues apace despite Harold Bloom (1967, 1970, 1974) and despite the quite obvious and decisive influence Pater has upon High Modernism at large on both sides of the Atlantic. If Pater's most overt response to Arnold's will to modernity comes in the second paragraph of the Preface to *The Renaissance* (1873), in which he directly impugns the attempt " 'to see the object as in itself it really is' " (viii), his most precise—and also implicit—response to Arnold's desire for a transparent language devoid of figure comes in the late "Style" (1889). "He will not," says Pater of the writer, "treat coloured glass as if it were clear" (1889:20), plainly questioning the possibility of transparent, literal, or original meaning in the use of language. Sign, too, of the legendary realist claim that mimesis is indeed its operative mode, the notion that language is transparent is in fact Pater's frequent critical target. It is also the signal of a larger project in Pater's variegated language that theorizes what is problematic in Arnold's will to modernity by calling attention to the rhetoric of temporality that Arnold tries to erase, and that eventually turns the problem itself into a solution.

Pater can criticize Arnold the immediatist—the vulgar modernist—because Pater, too, has his Arnoldean side. Like Arnold's, Pater's rhetoric is also marked by (at least) two competing systems, one a rhetoric, like Arnold's manifest one, of originality and presence; the other, like Arnold's repressed one, a rhetoric of comparisons and differentiation (see Meisel 1980). Let us for a moment, then, assess the Arnold in Pater before we see how Pater puts his own Arnoldean modernism into question (Eliot is right, up to a point) despite his complicity in expressing it, too. It is nowhere clearer than in Pater's celebrated dictum that "all art," as he puts it in the essay on Giorgione added to *The Renaissance* in 1888, "constantly aspires to the condition of music" (1888:135). The ironies of constancy in change aside, Pater's contention well conveys just the kinds of assumptions about art and what it should be held by Arnold. Music is, for the Arnoldean side of Pater, queen, exemplary because it is pure form, absolutely perfect since it is altogether without semantic content—at least when not socially encoded by titles, program notes, lyrics, and so on. Music is therefore in a position to objectify the ideal of unity—of an exact harmony of sound and sense, for example, in literature—that renders the work of art transparent and whole. How succinctly, how cleanly, how efficiently Pater's metaphor presents Arnold's ideals, this despite the temporal unfolding that really structures such an otherwise immediate process. Glossed retrospectively from Arnold's point of view, Pater's musical metaphor is at one with Arnold's modernist desire to see with "plainness and clearness without shadow of stain," as Arnold puts it in "A Summer Night"; to see, in short, with a "clear transparency" of vision, "free from dust and soil" (1852). Indeed, Arnold's metaphors for representing the ideal of purity, for the harmony of form and content, have the overcompensatory energy of a plea when we compare him to the more hesitant, cautious Pater. For the modernist Arnold, what is plain and direct about Homer, say, is an example of what Arnold calls in the 1853 Preface the "wholesome regulative laws" (11:293) that culture as a whole should obey. Arnold even provocatively likens his own wish in the lectures on Homer for "that union of the translator with his original" (1861:5:162–63)—a wish that would remove the "mist" (163) between them—to one of Coleridge's poetic figures, "'the mist,'" as the earlier poet puts it, "'which stands 'twixt God and thee,'" and "'Defecates to a pure transparency'" (1861:5:162).

By contrast with Pater's, Arnold's modernist metaphors form a kind of pathological complex—the identification of cleanliness and regularity with originality itself. As it turns out, Arnold's familiar desire for originality is filiated etymologically to an anal figuration latent in his customary rhetoric, the precise system that Pater—and Joyce—will go on to reverse. As the French *propre* suggests, a desire for the clean is synonymous with the "proper," with what is original, with what is one's own. Hence originality and immediacy have their defensive impetus in an anxiety about waste, a fastidiousness about the purity of the ideal of the origin or of ground (property, to extend the semantic broadcast) that sharpens our sense of what it is that makes Arnold— and one aspect of Pater—the mythographer of the modern par excellence. Arnold's desire to scour or clean away the haze or mist that distorts, for example, the Homeric origin in order to produce a new but wishful freshness leads us to something quite unexpected: that the metaphor of excretion, of waste and dirt, is etymologically grafted to the notion of influence or precedent itself. As the *Oxford English Dictionary* tells us, the term "fundament"— that which is basic or primary, the latter one of Arnold's favorite terms for the origin—also means "anus." The fundamental, the primary, is, alas, etymologically akin to the dirt it wishes to clean away. The site of dirt and cleansing is, in short, the same.

We are brought, in other words, face-to-face with an acute version of the kind of rhetorical defile that programmatically thwarts the will to modernity. What Arnold wants—and what Pater will forbid no matter his similar desires—is what defines the will to modernity in all its aspects and all its eras: the clearing away of that inescapable wake of precedent or influence—of waste or "surplusage," the latter figure one of Pater's recurrent formulations for it— that *Gaston De Latour* in particular will disallow (1896). Before proceeding to *Gaston* itself, however, let us see how Pater directly accommodates Arnold's fear of waste—of influence—by building its necessity into the structure of all signification. If Pater represents a more cautious version of the Arnoldean desire for original expression in the celebrated musical metaphor, he also takes just such desire to task elsewhere in his rhetoric.

The best gloss on the musical metaphor from Pater's own antithetical point of view—the one paramount in *Gaston* and the one that criticizes his own manifest Arnoldean ideals throughout his work, early and late—is Lucian's diacritical, rather than essentialist, semiotics in *Marius the Epicurean* (1885). Lucian puts in question Pater's musical metaphor in *The Renaissance* by arguing that there can be no such thing as pure or original signification, since signification as such emerges only differentially—by the contrast and comparison of one thing with another, and, in the process, the production of each thing in turn:

> —And we too, Lucian! if we have found the holy vessel in possession of the Stoics, shall no longer have need to search other philosophers, having attained that we were seeking. Why trouble ourselves further?
> —No need, if something had indeed been found, and you knew it to be that lost thing: if, at the least, you could recognise the sacred object when you saw it. But truly, as the matter now stands, not two persons only have entered the temple, one or the other of whom must needs have taken the golden cup, but a whole crowd of persons. And then, it is not clear what the lost object really is—cup, or flagon, or diadem; for one of the priests avers this, another that; they are not even in agreement as to its material: some will have it to be of brass, others of silver, or gold. It thus becomes necessary to search the garments of all persons who have entered the temple, if the lost vessel is to be recovered. And if you find a golden cup on the first of them, it will still be necessary to proceed in searching the garments of the others; for it is not certain that this cup really belonged to the temple. Might there not be many such golden vessels?— No! we must go on to every one of them, placing all that we find in the midst together, and then make our guess which of all those things may fairly be supposed to be the property of the god. For, again, this circumstance adds greatly to our difficulty, that without exception every one searched is found to have something upon him—cup, or flagon, or diadem, of

brass, of silver, of gold: and still, all the while, it is not
ascertained which of all these is the sacred thing. And you
must still hesitate to pronounce any one of them guilty of
the sacrilege—those objects may be their own lawful property: one cause of all this obscurity being, as I think, that
there was no inscription on the lost cup, if cup it was. Had
the name of the god, or even that of the donor, been upon
it, at least we should have had less trouble, and having de-
tected the inscription, should have ceased to trouble any one
else by our search. [1885:2:158–60]

As it turns out—and here emerges the central paradox of Pater's vision—the
very "surplusage" or residue that Pater's vaunted *ascesis* wishes to burn away in
the special example of music is precisely what is necessary for signification to
occur in the first place. Like Henchard's inability to recognize Elizabeth-
Jane's true status until the future provides him the key with which to organize
his impressions in retrospect, Lucian's analysis here suggests recognition of
the grail-vessel to be dependent upon a set of relations that unfold in time or
futurity, thereby requiring the grail to emerge only belatedly, if, indeed, at all.
To return, then, to the musical metaphor, it becomes clear that, without
residue, there would be no harmony, no first note against which to compare a
second—in short, no means of measurement by which harmony can be
established. In "The Child in the House," Pater labels such a semiotics "a
difference for the sense" (1895b:175). The waste or surplus that Arnold and
Pater—at least the Pater of the musical model—want to purge is in fact
necessary to music or meaning from the start, much as language is necessary
to speech, or tradition to individual talent.

If it is Arnold who retrospectively mimes Pater's musical ideal of visionary
clarity and the unity of the work of art, then it is Virginia Woolf—from the
later point of view of High Modernism rather than Victorianism—who glosses
the musical model from the angle of Pater's own antithetical vision. For in
Between the Acts, Woolf translates the exact terms of Lucian's argument in
Marius back into readily musical terms, representing music's tonality (or
atonality) as a temporal sequence rather than as a static or synchronic given:

The tune began; the first note meant a second; the second a
third. Then down beneath a force was born in opposition;
then another. On different levels they diverged. On different
levels ourselves went forward; flower gathering some on the
surface; others descending to wrestle with the meaning; but

all comprehending; all enlisted. The whole population of the
mind's immeasurable profundity came flocking; from the un-
protected, the unskinned; and dawn rose; and azure; from
chaos and cacophony measure; but not the melody of surface sound alone controlled it; but also the warring battle-
plumed warriors straining asunder: To part? No. Compelled
from the ends of the horizon; recalled from the edge of ap-
palling crevasses; they crashed; solved; united. And some re-
laxed their fingers; and others uncrossed their legs.
[1941:189]

Just as Lucian's grail-object emerges only by comparison with other objects, so
for Woolf one note cannot exist without its difference from another, a process,
like Lucian's—and like Henchard's—strictly temporal as well.

What obstructs vision, then, is, ironically, that which constitutes it. Pater
negotiates the seemingly implacable paradox engendered by the will to modernity by offering us an alternative to its wish for unmediated contact with
absolutes, a model of differential signification that explains and accounts for
the precondition of belatedness in all knowledge. Much as Freud's primal
scene emerges as the deferred function of a later knowledge that situates it as
an origin retroactively, so, too, does the Paterian original—the "first" note in
the sound of music, the grail-object in *Marius*—emerge only as a function of
what follows it, thereby situating it even harmonically as a product of the
unavoidable retrospect of temporality. For the unironic Arnold, of course, the
modern is, as it will be for the young Gaston, the fresh and self-sufficient
emergence of the universal. For Pater, by contrast, modernism is the haze,
the obstructions, the relics or vestiges of precedent by means of which we
(re)constitute what past we have. For Pater, in other words, the will to modernity is a plainly symptomatic outbreak in a larger problematic called modernism, the latter best handled as a means of accounting for the will to modernity
itself, and, optimally, as a means of accommodating it, of resolving the
anxieties that motivate it through the use of an ironic mode of discourse of the
kind we have already seen at work in Hardy's reflexive realism.

"A writer," says Pater, again in "Style," "may think of those laws, the
limitations of vocabulary, structure, and the like, as a restriction, but if a real
artist will find in them an opportunity" (1889:12–13). This is, for Pater,
"scholarship" (12)—the dutiful acceptance of belated inscription in a set of
laws, and an attempt to exploit belatedness itself as a means of accommodating the sense of loss or lack it engenders in writers like Arnold. A scholarship

of belatedness is one of heightened "broadcast," as Pater (presaging Hardy) puts it in the conclusion to *The Renaissance* (1873:234), the kind of signifying or semic display that Farfrae's machine in *The Mayor* tells us about in detail by trying to repress. Indeed, Pater's injunction in "Style" that the belated, scholarly writer abet the broadcast of the language he inherits and even promote the "quite alien associations" (1889:18) to which the "latent figurative texture in speech" (20) inevitably leads is realized most plainly in *Ulysses*, in the riot of what Woolf calls the "shuffle" of "sunken meanings" in her own rewriting of "Style," "Craftsmanship" (1937:246–47). Pater himself, of course, remains more hesitant in such practice than his most audacious disciple, Joyce (even next to Yeats), and in the posthumously published—and provocatively unfinished—*Gaston De Latour*, he both theorizes and practices a mode of reflexive realism not unlike Hardy's that both describes and demonstrates belatedness, identifying form and content in a subdued but proleptically Joycean logic of language.

Pater's Necropolis

If we have traced Arnold's ideal through the length and breadth of his production, let us, in Pater's case, look closely at a single work instead, the neglected but decidedly crucial *Gaston De Latour* (1896). *Gaston* is a central text for any Paterian speculations on the notion of modernity, preoccupied as the book is with the term itself and with the mistaken usage to which it has fallen prey. Conceived and begun after, and on the model of, *Marius the Epicurean*, *Gaston* is, like so many of Pater's imaginary portraits, witness to the history of the Renaissance and its characteristic freshness, disciplining its imaginary hero to a sequence of three Renaissance masters—Ronsard, Montaigne, and the rather more enigmatic Giordano Bruno. But if Pater's theme will be the impossibility of the "modernity" for which Gaston yearns, it is already compact in the book's narrative method. As in *Marius* (see Meisel 1980:144–46), *Gaston*'s language is a working example of its thematic, blending form and content, to use Pater's terminology, to the point of virtual identity. If the book addresses the problem of the belatedness that stifles any desire for freshness at the level of the story it tells, it also does so, actively, at the level of its narration.

Although we shall turn directly to theme in a moment, the rhetorical ingenuity of Pater's historical fiction ought not to be overlooked, especially since it provides us with a superb working instance of the dynamic of belatedness—of deferred action or secondary revision—as well as a means of defending against its inevitability by its use rather than its repression. The problem of precedent will itself become the medium of a solution to the apparent loss such belatedness seems normally to engender. In the narrative devices of *Gaston*, the temporal difference between Pater's language and the Renaissance it relates becomes, not the measure of a mournful belatedness on Pater's part, but, rather, the sudden emergence of a field of narrative opportunity inhering in the very distance that seems a restriction. As in *Marius*, after all, Pater's narrator habitually explains early by means of late, describing, for example, the government of Chartres at the time of the story told in the belated light of its coming, in the retrospective temporality of Pater's modern narration, "more than three centuries before the States-General of 1789" (1896:33). In the case of the St. Bartholomew massacre that provides the book its dramatic core, Pater's method is overtly one of narrating things according to his own frank perspective as a latecomer—"as men looked back afterwards" (118). Thus Bruno, too, is measured in relation to later figures that this narration knows about and Bruno does not: "Already Bruno had measured the space which Bacon would fill, with room, perhaps, for Darwin also. . . . To Dutch Spinosa, in the next century . . . the theorem that God was in all things . . . suggested a somewhat chilly withdrawal from the contact of all alike" (149–50). And Bruno himself, of course, is subject to the same deferred action within the coordinates of his own historical situation: "For if Bruno must needs look forward to the future, to Bacon, for adequate knowledge of the earth . . . he could look backwards also gratefully to another daring mind"—presumably Galileo's—"which had already put that earth into its modest place, and opened the full view of the heavens" (150).

Such direct narrative use of secondary revision is also often true of Pater's descriptions of Gaston himself. Indeed, when applied to Gaston, it can create an extremely complex array of implied temporalities. Some of Gaston's experiences are, for example, given to us by Pater only at the time of their recollection in Gaston's memory (e.g., "looking back long afterwards" [36]), thus creating not just the usual division in narrative between *récit* and *histoire*, but also showing *histoire* itself (Gaston's anyway) to be itself compounded of two levels of *récit*. Gaston even reads Montaigne's essays only after he has known the man who wrote them, obtaining "the key we lack to their surprises" (87) in decidedly retrospective fashion, and so boldly reversing Arnold's scheme in a Hardyesque manner by showing the "key" or origin to be the consequence of its effects rather than its cause. Secondary revision or deferred action in life as well as in literature—the evocation of the earlier by means of the later—is even on full display in Pater's description of a religious representation at Saint Taurin "only lately set in its place": the biblical "incidents" were "innocently," but nonetheless effectively, "adapted," says Pater, "to the actual habits and associations of the [later] age which had produced them" (7).

But *Gaston* is also quite overt about its readerly mechanisms, elaborating their necessity in a variety of ways. The place of Gaston's origin—his ground or property—is graphically split or bifurcated, denied any claim to absolute or univocal origination because of a double history in the history of his family that accounts for "the Château of Deux-manoirs" (1) at the start of the tale. Home has an acknowledged "irregularity of ground-plan" (2), a function, as any home or origin must be, of the kinds of later misreadings that produce it retroactively. Pater calls attention to it in such phrases as "Once, in the beginning" (13), thereby assuring us that the origin is never fixed because it is a product of any number of later derivations. Even the apparently anchoring figure of Chartres early in the novel is another graphic instance of a center that is already divided at its origin, "its one landmark the twin spires" (19).

Such preconditions at the level of the book's very ground should prepare us for both the "lately attained key" (21) by which Gaston gains entrance to the ongoing Renaissance, and to the anxiety it produces by making him feel estranged from the freshness he sees growing up in his midst. As chapter 1 concludes, the newly troubled—and suddenly modernist—Gaston wishes "to feel at one with himself again" (25). And early in chapter 2, we get as precise an emblem of Gaston's problem as we could expect: "His earlier vision was a thing he could never precisely recover, or disentangle from the supervening reality" (27). His "first" (27) visit to the often dreamed-of Chartres is "not in summer" (27)—not in freshness—but in the belated element of "frost" (28). Reinforced by the suffusion of late Romantic images of autumn and twilight—the "last handfuls of the harvest" (6), the "late August afternoon" (12), "the autumn fields at evening" (26), even the ominous "August sunshine" (121) just before the massacre—Gaston's "preference for darkness" or "dimness" (31) suggests that the soul itself lives in a "perpetual twilight" (31), making of Gaston himself a kind of Stephen Dedalus to the Paterian Joyce: an ironically pictured Arnoldean modernist who will learn Pater's lessons of temporality and belatedness slowly and with reluctance.

In order to move beyond family and tradition (for Pater's hero is, predictably, a renegade by temperament), Gaston will now turn to the "present" (32) as he approaches the state that Pater's chapter on Ronsard, Gaston's first hero, calls, simply, "Modernity." "Modernity," of course, is the desire to wipe away the belated "world of echoes and shadows" (38) in favor of "a rival new religion" that preaches "liberty of heart" and the "solid matter of human experience" (38). Indeed, just after the desire arises, Gaston is given a momentary epiphany as he ascends (in classic Romantic fashion, and consonant with his surname) the tower of Jean de Beauce and stands "at last amid the unimpeded light" (41), associated not just with "peach-blossom and wine" (41), but with the "new world of the Indies" as well (41). The price of revelation, however, is the forgetting of the ineluctable "coil of perplexity" (41) he leaves below. Hence, too, Ronsard's exemplary verse predictably betokens the "fervent" "intellectual springtide" that "was" to be (the narrator's retrospection is again overt) "unique in Gaston's memory" (50). Ronsard is an earlier version of the myth of Wordsworth, apparently liberating verse from its history "in a dead language" (51) in order to express instead "the wakeful soul of present time consciously in possession" (52), "close at hand, with the effectiveness of a personal presence" (52). This is Renaissance "modernity" in all its rawness, pivoting on a desire that is the mirror of Arnold's late Romanticism: "Gaston's demand . . . was for a poetry, as veritable, as intimately near, as corporeal, as the new faces of the hour, the flowers of the actual season" (52).

But haunting all such desires for modernity are the familiar—and now thematic—obstacles. In search of freshness, Gaston finds the idealized Chartres to be, as Pater's figuration has already suggested, no more than a collection of "reliquaries" (31) that only "seemed to bring the distant, the impossible . . . close to one's side" (30). Indeed, the "relic-worship" (30) for which Chartres is famous both reconfirms Gaston's sense of burden as well as his growing desire for newness or freshness that the Renaissance seems to offer him. Thus Gaston as modernist turns his attention, not just to the "present," but to "the uncalculated present" (32), "uncalculated" because, like Pater's hero, it still lacks the future that will allow it to come into being later on. Of course, "retrospective minds," says Pater, tend to see the "irony" of their condition "throughout" (122), an irony that Gaston soon experiences in the fever of his will to modernity. By taking up the new "classical enthusiasm," for example, Gaston now knows that his present time takes place "sixteen hundred years after Cicero was dead," and that when in turn "they played Terence, . . . it was but a play within a play" (37). Even Renaissance freshness is, it seems, a defensive reaction to the originals of a golden age whose achievements enable the future by making it anxious about the past that empowers it.

If Ronsard's representative poetry is a reflection "of contemporary life"—"at once more deeply sensuous and more deeply ideal" (54) than the verse of the past—its equally representative irony of discipleship lies in its ability to teach or bequeath to Gaston a "freshness" (56) that is patently learned. Nonetheless, says Pater, "it was the power of 'modernity' as renewed" (ironically) "in every successive age for genial youth, protesting, defiant of all sanction in these matters, that the true 'classic' must be of the present" (57). For "poetry need no longer mask itself in the habit of a bygone day" (57) when the present has what it at least believes to be "a privileged apprehension" (57). Before "Modernity" can be attained, however, Gaston himself realizes his own error: "the power of the old classic poetry itself"—at once inspiration and villainy—"was explained by the reflex action of the new" (58). Such deferred action is especially evident when a "novel accent" in contemporary verse can awaken "long-slumbering associations" (56) only belatedly apprehended in an earlier text. Ronsard himself has, by Gaston's reckoning, tried for no more than "the naturalisation of Greek beauty in the brown cloud-lands of the North" (67). The haggard though still young Ronsard is a personal emblem, not for an Arnoldean will to modernity, but for the impossibility of such a stance. So ghoulish does Ronsard in fact become that Gaston can only exclaim, "The dead!—he was coming to be on their side. The fact came home to Gaston that this evocator of 'the eternally youthful'"—a handsome contradiction in terms—"was visibly old before his time" (68). The paradoxes no longer signal failure but now a form of necessity in which the modernist becomes a "scholar" or archaeologist, a denizen of the necropolis of tradition. Rearranging the bones of his ancestors as Marius actively does, the Paterian artist surrenders his will to modernity—and the impossible notions of originality associated with it—to his undeniable complicity in both the genealogy of tradition and the temporal situation that determines his unstable relation to it. A notion of the work of art as criticism or interpretation replaces the Arnoldean desire for a notion of creation ex nihilo. The self-originating artist is a myth that is, in strong modernism, dead on arrival. Gaston even realizes that the new poetry of Ronsard is the work, not of individuals—"the product not of one or more individual writers" (70)—but of a larger, transubjective impetus that gives real credence here to the name of the Pleiad as a collectivity: "the actual authorship belonged not so much to a star as to a constellation" (70). Or, as Pater will remark of Montaigne later, "the work, by its own force . . . outstrips the workman" (100).

Victim, then, of the "incompatibility" of Ronsard's "ideals" (71), Gaston moves on to Montaigne next in an attempt to "harmonise" (72) himself once again—a project more and more destined to failure as the narrative proceeds.

Traveling "south-west" (76), then directly "southwards" (77) to find Montaigne, Gaston once again proleptically (re)traces such Romantic steps at the level of plot, though so represented because of Pater's belated narration—all this, at the same moment, Pater reminds us, "as popular imagination just now"—then—"set thither also, in a vision of French ships going forth . . . to the Indies" (77). After all, northerly France—like northerly England—feels "mentally enfranchised by the sprightlier genius of Italy" (78), closer as it seems to be to the warmth of origins reconstituted by the mythology of the New World, although each ideality is an ironic effect of the system from which it wishes to be freed. To be sure, the southern region really does seem to offer "light here in the earth itself" (78) and "a novel freshness in the air" (80). The possibility of modernity has once again been raised as the approach to Montaigne begins.

Unlike Ronsard, however, Montaigne's modernism is more straightforward than ghostly, happier and far less painful. While Pater tells us that Renaissance enjoyment of the "present . . . needed, retrospectively, a theoretic justification" (83) given to it by Montaigne's "emancipating ethic" (83), Montaigne himself seems to flourish without lingering, as Ronsard and Pater themselves do, among the ironies inherent in a belief in modernity as such. For Montaigne, it is more a question of "sincerities" (90) than of the "genius of second thoughts" (88). Nonetheless, Montaigne's otherwise straightforward endorsement of "native original predilection" or "the remote origin of . . . native soil" (92) is—at least in Pater's rendering—balanced by an equivalent caution that there is in fact, as Pater quotes him, "'nothing pure'" (93) despite the ideals we erect. Montaigne is even willing to forgo the Renaissance fetishization of antiquity by claiming, similarly to Eliot in "Tradition and the Individual Talent," that the present at least has more "'vigour'" (98) than the past because it has the perpetual advantage of already being in possession of it. Despite Montaigne's manifestly Paterian claim that "One's own experience" (107) is all one has, he is also, and also like Pater, one who suspects the originality to which he seems to aspire. No wonder, since "'every piece [is] playing every moment its own game,'" in Montaigne's own words, "'with as much difference between us and ourselves as between ourselves and others'" (106). A "double philosophy" from a "two-sided thinker" (113), Montaigne's duplicitous logic is, like Pater's own, too cautionary for what turns out to be Gaston's enduringly Arnoldean quest for self-harmony despite the ironies Ronsard and Montaigne alike have offered in order to assuage the will to modernity that continues to assail him.

Having reached Paris as this apparently unfinished tale moves toward a rather plain conclusion, Gaston will also reach its apparently summary figure there in the form of his third hero, Giordano Bruno. By now, of course, Gaston should be largely rid of his early will to modernity, but there is one last attempt to reignite the "theories of inspiration" (135) that Ronsard and Montaigne have put in doubt. It comes, of course, in the form of Bruno's seductive madness. Himself an Italian, Bruno is "in fact" (138) what the North only dreams of—a genuinely "heady southern imagination" (140). Despite his attractiveness, however, Bruno is reckless compared to Gaston's earlier heroes, and one who restores the possibility of a modernity that Gaston has twice seen debunked. Believing the pre-Socratics, for example, to have been "nearer the original sense of things," "like some hardy growth out of the very heart of nature" (141), Bruno will assert his "lower pantheism," as Pater calls it (132–61), despite the overt odds against it, a pantheism in which "integrity and fulness"—those lost ideals or even possibilities—are "present" "within all things" (142). " 'Nature' " is "a sacred term" (144) for Bruno all over again, as though Gaston's journey is ready to conclude, wishfully, where it began. While, like all power, Bruno's is one of "borrowed fire and wings" (147), he still believes "actual 'union' " (147) with the universe to be possible no matter the difficulties that await such tactless modernity.

Surely Bruno's belief in "the indwelling spirit" (152) and "God literally everywhere" (153) is an overwhelming example of the extent to which the book as a whole actually moves backward as it moves forward, giving us a descending brand of modernity rather than an ascending one. Pater even suggests the ending to be shrouded in "an ambiguous atmosphere" (160), and it is only fitting that a text that theorizes and enacts deferred action should itself be the reverse of what its manifest trajectory seems to be. If we take the sequence of Gaston's heroes straightforwardly, we find a movement from the ghostly Ronsard to the comparatively complacent Montaigne to the Arnoldean Bruno that is the very reverse of Pater's own theorization of a modernity that cannot—contra Bruno—ever be fully realized. Unexpectedly overdetermined in structure for an unfinished text (only local polishing and perhaps a revision of the final paragraphs seem necessary in any case), *Gaston* frustrates what appears to be a dialectical unfolding in its hero's development as he moves from Ronsard to Montaigne to Bruno. The narrative's expected movement toward resolution is really one of regression. Viewed retrospectively, it is the nagging ghostliness of Ronsard that first pushes Gaston away, reminiscent as it is of the necropolitan fears that Gaston's own modernity was invented to repress; it is, more gently, the irony of Montaigne that drives Gaston away again, still in search of the assertion of modernity that his Arnoldean quest has required him to find. With Bruno, we return full circle to the myth of the modern in a narrative that, as we well know, takes the questioning of the myth as its principal subject. Not only does the sequence of Gaston's heroes present him with a sequence of less and less decisive accommodations to the will to modernity that all three share with Pater's young hero. It also identifies the resolving movement of quest-romance as a whole with the perennially impossible desires of modernity in all its (apparently equivalent) historical manifestations. Resolution and closure in writing or experience are no more available than are immediacy and originality. If Pater calls the latter pair into question thematically, he calls the former into question in the deliberate structure of his text.

Shadwell's belated (and seemingly nugatory) subtitle, "An Unfinished Romance," helps to explain or account for this curious double movement that *Gaston* enacts as a whole. A romance cannot, by definition, be unfinished, since it is the genre of recuperating origins. The ironic Pater therefore finishes his romance by presenting us with the kind of madly innocent figure of Bruno that makes the impossibility of successful romance or modernity clear to the point of deadpan absurdity. Pater, in short, resolves his narrative with a portrait of the kind of stance the entire narrative has been at pains to undercut. The book is thereby incomplete by virtue of its apparent completion, and also incomplete by virtue of completing itself against the impossibility of doing so. The balancing act is reminiscent of Hardy's reflexive realism, though articulated perhaps more efficiently if not as richly. It gives its readership the illusion that a renewed will to modernity is actually plausible even as it takes such wishful thinking away in the design by which it articulates it. Like Hardy, Pater adequates narration and story by making, as we have seen, deferred action not only the theme of his text but also its structure. Pater thus gives *récit* and *histoire* an inverse rather than a parallel relation such as they enjoy in Hardy, making his text equally reflexive in its realism, but far more wickedly so. If Hardy at least identifies the manifest psychic action of his hero with that of his reader, no matter how painful the experience of coming too late may be, Pater goes even further. Cautioned as he is, Gaston is nonetheless sent on a fool's journey by the time he seeks out Bruno. Unlike Henchard, he remains expectant rather than being ready—as Pater's reader also ought to be—for an end of pure negation. Although it is only by virtue of belatedness that signification can occur at all, Bruno apparently completes the narrative by telling us that the immediate, the modern, is indeed available to us after all. Like Arnold, such a character wishes to repress the waste or contamination of prior influence that perpetually undoes his will to modernity, and Pater is duplicitous enough to end his book on the note he forbids.

With the difference between Arnold and Pater clear, we can now begin to suggest the extent to which their largely implicit debate produces two divergent lines of High Modernism at large, Arnold's devolving upon Eliot, Pater's upon Joyce. If there is a uniquely Joycean solution to belatedness that emerges through the genealogy of Pater, there is a more customary Eliotic modernism that emerges through the contrasting line of Arnold. Since Arnold's line represents the ideal—the will to modernity as such—to which Joyce, like Pater, will not submit, let us turn first to an examination of the fate of its fixed principles in the major prose and poems of Arnold's most influential, though largely unacknowledged, High Modernist heir, T. S. Eliot.

TWO

Two Versions of High British Modernism

Thou who didst waken from his summer dreams
The blue Mediterranean, where he lay,
Lulled by the coil of his crystalline streams,

Beside a pumice isle in Baiae's bay,
And saw in sleep old palaces and towers
Quivering within the wave's intenser day,

All overgrown with azure moss and flowers
So sweet, the sense faints picturing them! Thou
For whose path the Atlantic's level powers

Cleave themselves into chasms, while far below
The sea-blooms and the oozy woods which wear
The sapless foliage of the ocean, know

Thy voice, and suddenly grow gray with fear,
And tremble and despoil themselves: oh, hear!

—Shelley, "Ode to the West Wind"

I pace upon the battlements and stare
On the foundations of a house, or where
Tree, like a sooty finger, starts from the earth;
And send imagination forth
Under the day's declining beam, and call
Images and memories
From ruin or from ancient trees,
For I would ask a question of them all.

—Yeats, "The Tower"

. . . fill the foliage with arrested peace,
Joy of such permanence, right ignorance
Of change still possible. Exile desire
For what is not. This is the barrenness
Of the fertile thing that can attain no more. . . .

It is the natural tower of all the world,
The point of survey, green's green apogee,
But a tower more precious than the view beyond,
A point of survey squatting like a throne,
Axis of everything, green's apogee

And happiest folk-land, mostly marriage-hymns.
It is the mountain on which the tower stands,
It is the final mountain. Here the sun,
Sleepless, inhales his proper air, and rests.
This is the refuge that the end creates.

—Stevens, "Credences of Summer"

Repression and the Individual Talent

"What makes Arnold seem all the more remarkable," says Eliot in the introduction to *The Sacred Wood* (1920), "is, that if he were our exact contemporary, he would find all his labour to perform again" (xi). Although Eliot again reverses his position on Arnold in 1930 by making him responsible for the dread Pater, here, at the imaginative center of his career, Eliot finds Arnold a "contemporary" because he prophesies, wittingly or not for Eliot himself, Eliot's own later movement from literature proper to the cold embrace of a theology that even Arnold manifestly eschews. "Arnold, in his destruction," says a famous.v troubled Eliot, "went for the game outside of the literary preserve altogether" (xiii). So, too, does Eliot, making his own career a repetition of Arnold's in a higher key. But while Eliot's project as both critic and poet is firmly in Arnold's line (Ian Gregor soldered the link in 1970), it is a genealogy that also includes a knowing repression of Pater's criticism of Arnold in order to salvage, quite intentionally, the ideals Pater forbids. The result is the production of a myth of the modern probably more influential than Arnold's own. We can therefore chart, especially in the principal prose, an early use of Pater in Eliot's most significant essay, "Tradition and the Individual Talent" (1919), followed by a violent repression of both Pater himself and the earlier essay in the subsequent "Metaphysical Poets" (1921) and "The Function of Criticism" (1923a), a trend that Eliot finally addresses directly in 1933. Pater also plays a major role in Eliot's two long poems, *The Waste Land* (1922) and the *Four Quartets* (1944), although it is a role that must be equally repressed in order for Eliot to solidify and sustain his dubious strength. As we have with Arnold, then, let us examine Eliot's canonical works in both the poems and the prose, even though chronology requires us to do so in reverse, since Eliot's criticism prepares the ground—or lack of it—for his poems much as Arnold's poems prepare the ground for his prose.

"Tradition and the Individual Talent" is a lancet against what Eliot calls the primacy of "personality" in the analysis of poetry and in the assessment of poetic achievement as a whole. Like the Objectivist movement at large, it is no less than an attempt to bleed criticism of a Paterian impressionism based on the category of temperament in order to replace it with the standard of

Impersonality instead. Even more overtly Paterian—and also an intimation of anxiety-of-influence criticism—in its earlier form (quoted in Bloom 1982:18), "Tradition and the Individual Talent" is plainly symptomatic of the extent to which the supposedly anti-Romantic projects of Eliot, Hulme, and Pound all alike are in fact defensive reactions to Pater that try to undo Pater's influence by using Pater's own logic to counter their misrepresentation of him (on Hulme as Romantic, see Kermode 1957; see also Levenson 1984). Already a reflexive emblem for the belatedness that nervously impels them, Eliot and his school—and the New Criticism to which it eventually gives rise—prove themselves silent disciples of their paternal precursor both in the vociferousness of their rejection of aestheticism and in the exactitude with which they employ Pater's own secondary, nonsubjectivist profile in order to undo the plainer Paterian stance that seems to endorse the personality they bewail as a causative and explanatory category.

Despite Eliot's exemplary polemical bias against personality in "Tradition and the Individual Talent," then, his working definition of criticism is decidedly Paterian, down to the delicacies of his rhetoric: "articulating what passes in our minds when we read a book and feel an emotion about it" (1919:13). Not only does Eliot need Paterian personality as the factor that impels his own antithetical criticism; he also relies, as he makes plain here, on the reader-centered, impression-oriented stance he is out to demote. Eliot is even forced to use the term "aesthetic" to distinguish his own criticism from the merely "historical" kind (the Paterian word for the latter is "antiquarianism"), the kind that fails to see the active role of the past in the formation of any poem in the present, and, conversely, the active role of the present in the constitution of the past retrospectively. This is a considerable lapse in Eliot's defenses, since it allows us to see just how exact a misreading of Pater Eliot's is, recalling as it does how in Pater himself personality is not finally to be understood as the simple identification of man and artist Eliot implies it to be. For Pater, personality is instead something fashioned, something aesthetic from the start, precisely the notion of the artist that Eliot himself will go on to recommend. Much as the mythological figure of Demeter, for example, has "no single author" in Pater's *Greek Studies* (1895a:101), even the Mona Lisa in the "Leonardo" essay is the "sweeping together" of "ten thousand experiences" (1873:125) rather than the direct expression of Leonardo's personality that a more superficial reading of Pater might suggest it to be. Art is "the receptacle" of "powers at work in the common air" (1873:116), necessarily the impersonal product of a sensibility that inherits and broadcasts rather than simply expresses a self whose stability as a category is questioned by Pater, too, especially in the Conclusion to *The Renaissance*. Like art, personality itself—its supposed source—is an ironically impersonal construction analogous to a text rather than its prior cause. Even "our common ideas," says Pater in *Plato and Platonism* (1893), "are not the consequence, not the products, but the cause of our reason in us: we did not make them; but they make us what we are, as reasonable beings" (168). If, says the Eliot of 1919, "the poet's mind is in fact a receptacle for seizing and storing up numberless feelings, phrases, images, which remain there until all the particles which can unite to form a new compound are present together" (19), Eliot's own mind is, by implication, itself a reflexive receptacle here for what Pater has already called the "particles" of language in "Style" (1889:14, 20).

What we mean by uniqueness or personality, then, argues Eliot, following Pater rather than rejecting him, is not the self-engendered emergence of creative originality ex nihilo, but a rearrangement of tradition in a new work that simply gives it the appearance of being new. Such rearrangement is not only the best definition we can offer for originality; it also compels us to reorder the past whenever a new work enters the language as the price of its readability. Eliot has suddenly—and silently—made an enormous and irreparable claim: that the sensibility of the artist is structurally equivalent to that of the reader or critic. The work itself is perforce an act of belated interpretation like the one that grasps it. Neither writers nor readers are originals, nor are their materials; each is constituted in a vortex of tradition in which belatedness is both the precondition and the acknowledged dynamic of writing and reading alike. (Walter Benn Michaels shows the same epistemology at work in the dissertation on Bradley [1981:170–202]; for the more conventional view, see Materer 1979, 147ff.). In trying to unseat Pater, Eliot recalls the Pater for whom *ascesis*, or "self-restraint" (1889:17), is the basis, as it is for Eliot himself, of artistic success. "What happens," says Eliot of the best poets, is a "continual self-sacrifice, a continual extinction of personality" (17). Indeed, Eliot's summary of his argument late in the essay is an almost exact repetition of Pater himself as he argues, say, in "The School of Giorgione," that the artist is not a personality but a node or function of influence, already putting in question the validity of his proper authority when construed as a direct function of a discrete personal sensibility. Says Eliot, following Pater,

> the poet has, not a "personality" to express, but a particular
> medium, which is only a medium and not a personality, in
> which impressions and experiences combine in peculiar and
> unexpected ways. Impressions and experiences which are im-

> portant for the man may take no place in the poetry, and
> those which become important in the poetry may play quite
> a negligible part in the man, the personality. [19–20]

Thus Eliot's wishful image of the chemical apparatus designed to absorb influence in the name of shedding it—leaving "no trace" of it (18)—is an apt
representation of what Eliot tries to do in separating himself from the Pater
upon whom he secretly relies. Another reflexive emblem for the will to modernity, Eliot's apparatus is a figuration taken from the past designed to repress it,
and one that thereby hints at the Arnoldean values that will, as we shall see,
eventually emerge in Eliot's argument despite their logical impossibility. As if
to explain its own necessity, however unconsciously, Eliot's apparatus for the
erasure of influence is itself an example of the influence it pretends to erase.
Borrowing at peril throughout the essay, Eliot describes how the "greatest
poetry" gains its peculiar strength not from "the intensity of the emotions"
involved (as the Arnold of the 1853 Preface might well argue), but from "the
intensity of the artistic process, the pressure, so to speak, under which the fusion
takes place" (19). But while the "fusion of elements" (19), as Eliot puts it, that
takes place in a great poem is, in its scientific and impersonal language, supposed to distinguish Eliot's Objectivist sensibility from Pater's apparent indul-
gence in an emotive, subjectivist one, Eliot's language ("fusion" in particular)
only reconstitutes Pater by drawing the majority of its terminology from the
Preface, and especially the Conclusion, to *The Renaissance*—ironically, from
those passages that already put the self in question in Pater's own text. Even in
his complaint that Wordsworth's notion of poetry as " 'emotion recollected in
tranquillity' " is an "inexact formula" (21), Eliot echoes the Preface to *The
Renaissance* in which Pater himself seeks a more exact "formula" (vii) for art
than those of the past despite his apparent desire to reject the term. Eliot's
attempt, moreover, to correct Wordsworth's notion turns out to be the exactly
Paterian contention that it is the concentration and "refinement" (16) of forces
the artist represents, not the unmediated expression of a personality whose fixity
as a category is always questionable in Pater himself (any temptation to catalogue the Pater in Eliot ought also to require the recognition that the notion of
the "objective correlative" in the essay on Hamlet is derived rather directly from
Pater's "Style" [1889:30]).

But despite the reflexive "trace" of Pater's particular influence and the
belated or deferred status of artistic production theorized throughout the essay,
Eliot will nonetheless try simultaneously to recontain all that he has unleashed by asserting that the tradition of which he speaks constitutes "an ideal

order" (15), not the more flexible idea of order it suggests instead. No matter the essay's plain theorization of the writer's/reader's temporal location in a relationally structured vortex as well as the necropolitan Paterianism that attends it ("No poet, no artist of any art, has his complete meaning alone. . . . [Y]ou must set him, for contrast and comparison, among the dead" [15]), Eliot oddly renounces such historicism by implying that the heritage of tradition is not temporal at all, but, as his later essays and poems will fully show, absolute and eternal. Eliot, in other words, willfully misreads his own temporally inflected notion of the vortex as a synchronic whole, as a perpetual "ideal order" despite the constant flux that threatens, even generates, its coherence moment to moment in history. "It is," says Leavis, "a most significant defeat of intelligence that presents itself to us in Eliot's essay" (1958:181). It is also, says a punning Blackmur, "a special blinding light of his own" (1952:288). Like Arnold, Eliot quite plainly renounces the mechanics of temporality (of "contrast" and "comparison" in particular) that he has so eloquently described. Indeed, the nascent duplicity of "Tradition and the Individual Talent" will translate itself into the willful repressions that result in so many of Eliot's most famous ideals, whether his misreading of French Symbolism as the production of static, concrete objects on the order of Pound's "medallions," or his later vision of literature and culture as a whole. And yet the possibility of such absolutes is, far more clearly than in Arnold, already impugned by the temporal and belated status of writing and reading alike as "Tradition and the Individual Talent" actually describes it. "For Yeats," in direct contrast, "an image becomes symbolic," says David Perkins, "within a tradition" (1976:149). One of the most candid accounts of secondary revision within literature proper, Eliot's essay cannot, however, preserve its frankness because the imagination behind it has another, incompatible goal to fulfill.

It is precisely the temporal emergence of all phenomena in "Tradition and the Individual Talent" that Eliot—like Arnold—wishes to repress, not just with the notion of an "ideal order" in the 1919 piece, but also throughout his subsequent work, essays and poems alike. If the Paterian vein in "Tradition and the Individual Talent" is easily exposed, the equally famous "Metaphysical Poets" goes on to expose the Arnoldean scheme that replaces it in Eliot's literary values. Prior to the essay's greatest and most influential mythic establishment—the "dissociation of sensibility" (1921:288) put in question by Kermode in 1957—Eliot begins to adumbrate his goal by setting up falsely dichotomous terms that will end up recoiling upon the system that produces them, but that are necessary if Eliot is to produce the kind of

Arnoldean myth he desires. In trying to define what the "metaphysical" (obviously a misnomer) really is in poetry, Eliot contrasts two supposedly different modes of poetical conceit, the "metaphysical" proper—"elaboration" (282)—as "contrasted with" what Eliot deems the more customary "condensation" (282) of images in a poem. The difference between elaboration and condensation is, as we know from Freud, finally no difference at all, of course, since each one is an inversion of the other. Indeed, Eliot himself, quite inadvertently, shows how little real difference there is between them. On the one hand—as in Donne's "Valediction: Forbidding Mourning"—we have only "condensation," "the mere explication of the content of a comparison," "the comparison of two lovers to a pair of compasses." On the other—as in Cowley's "To Destiny"—we have "instead," says Eliot, "elaboration," "a development by rapid association of thought which requires considerable agility on the part of the reader" (282). Is there really a difference to be drawn? Eliot admits about the second instance what he has repressed about the first. Both act in fundamentally equivalent ways. "Here," says Eliot of his second passage, "we find at least two connexions which are not implicit in the first figure, but are forced upon it by the poet" (282). But is not this "rapid association" or "elaboration" simply an extension of the same kind of reading required to follow a plainer "condensation"? It is a difference in degree rather than kind—"rapid association" is required of the reader as much by "condensation" as by "elaboration"; the latter only makes what is otherwise automatic in its temporal unfolding foregrounded and overt.

From this problematic distinction follow a series of claims as unstable as the one upon which they rest. To be sure, "the sudden contrast of associations" in Donne's "The Relique" involves a "telescoping of images and multiplied associations" (again see Pater's "Style" for Eliot's technical and evaluative source) that is indeed "characteristic" of the poets in question (283). Despite Eliot's momentary agreement with Dr. Johnson's own rather biased judgment that the best explanatory reason for the canonical "impeachment" of the Metaphysicals "lies in the failure of the conjunction" in their verse ("the fact that often the ideas are yoked but not united"), Eliot goes on to reject the claim, not only by noting such failure in Johnson's own verse, but also by claiming that "a degree of heterogeneity of material compelled into unity by the operation of the poet's mind is," simply, "omnipresent in poetry" as a whole (283). And having "compelled" the Metaphysicals into "unity" by force of his own claim that "unity" is an "omnipresent" principle of verse, Eliot goes on to hint at the garden-spot the essay will eventually elevate to the status of a lost ideal: that, despite Johnson's judgment, Metaphysical "language"—exactly like Arnold's ideal notion of Homer's language—"is as a rule simple and pure," especially in Herbert (285). Even when it is "far from simple," it exemplifies "a fidelity to thought and feeling" (285). In fact, Eliot's idea of "perfect success" (284) in verse is suspiciously like that of the Pater of personality he rejects (and the side of Pater that is most like Arnold)—that, in a work of art, "the idea and the simile" (284)—the thought or feeling and its verbal representation, the tenor and the vehicle— "become one" (284).

With Dr. Johnson having "failed to define metaphysical poetry by its faults" (285) because of his low estimation of Donne and his school, Eliot can now produce one of the most famous examples of recanonization in the history of English poetry. "By adopting the opposite method"—that "the poets of the seventeenth century (up to the Revolution) were the direct and normal development of the precedent age" (285), the Renaissance proper—Eliot can now give us the exact reason for the value of an "ideal" or finally static "order" that "Tradition and the Individual Talent" asserts even as it lames in its theorization of temporality: that the "virtue" of the Metaphysicals is the result of their possession of "something permanently valuable which subsequently disappeared, but ought not to have disappeared" (285). The prescriptivism is obvious, but the strategy of the claim less so. Not unlike the Johnson who characteristically refers to the Renaissance (if not the school of Donne) as one of the lost golden ages, Eliot has decided—and will bequeath his decision to us with one of his more memorable terms—that the age of Donne was the last age of English poetry able to express itself with full-throated ease. The Elizabethans, the Jacobeans, and the Metaphysicals all alike easily "incorporated their erudition into their sensibility": "their mode of feeling was directly and freshly altered," claims an Arnoldean Eliot, "by their reading and thought. In Chapman especially"—the choice is particularly odd—"there is a direct sensuous apprehension of thought or a recreation of thought into feeling, which is exactly what we find in Donne" (286).

Unlike Pater, Eliot is apparently dead serious in his Arnoldean erection of a lost golden age in the Renaissance, a golden age little different in sensibility from that of an antiquity with which the eighteenth century also readily identified the Renaissance, too—although behind Eliot's praise of such lost "erudition" lies, of course, Pater's notion of the artist as "scholar" in "Style." It is a myth so central and necessary to Eliot's project, however, that it provides the essay with its famous crescendo. "Something . . . happened to the mind of England," declaims Eliot, "between the time of Donne or Lord Herbert of Cherbury and the time of Tennyson and Browning; it is the difference between the intellectual poet and the reflective poet" (287). Thus emerges the crucial myth of the modern, familiar already in Arnold, Hardy, and Lawrence: that thought and feeling are now disjoined compared to their former oneness in a happier age whose primacy we have lost. Tennyson and Browning, says Eliot, "do not feel their thought as immediately as the odour of a rose" (287), although it is of course unlikely that Shakespeare or Milton do either. Eliot nonetheless has, like the Arnold of 1853 and after, increasingly absolute notions of what the poet should be, and must rewrite literary history accordingly. The lost fullness to be lamented in *The Waste Land* is therefore the lost fullness of an earlier literature to which Eliot is a latecomer, and whose imagination—rather than the world—is, paradoxically, barren because of the waste of influence rather than despite it. Most astonishing is that Eliot has already articulated a Paterian theory of rearrangement of the dead, a mode of recontextualization that would advantageously exploit the additional knowledge granted the latecomer rather than lament it as a burden. And yet it is not temporality that Eliot theorizes here, but rather static "new wholes" (287).

Strangely avoiding all the latecomer tactics provided by Pater's recommendation in "Style" that the modern writer attend to the "alien associations" of language and so reject the ideal of unity from the start, Eliot will also ignore the obvious historical fact that poets of a different age "possessed a mechanism of sensibility" different from his—or our—own in order to insist, like the classicizing Arnold, on the absolute standards of something "fundamentally valuable" because it is "direct" in its apprehension. Behind this is Eliot's implicit assumption that language is transparent, a fact first pointed out by Leslie Brisman in 1977, and one whose structural necessity for Eliot will become clearer once we move into the poems. Despite, then, the constitutive dimension of temporality adduced in "Tradition and the Individual Talent," Eliot reifies his early poets as modernist ideals of an immediacy that "could devour any kind of experience" (287). The reason for the myth of such a lost golden age becomes obvious enough with the famous pronouncement: "In the seventeenth century a dissociation of sensibility set in, from which we have never recovered" (288). Moreover, the "disassociation, as is natural, was aggravated by the influence of the two most powerful poets of the century, Milton and Dryden" (288).

Eliot's hatred for Milton aside, the logical contradiction of a "natural" sort of "dissociation" puts in question the lack of naturalness the dissociation is supposed to effect. In fact, the logical difficulties into which Eliot is led in order to provide and preserve his modernist myth of a lost, "fundamental" origin from which we are estranged are staggering when compared to their discarded Paterian alternative in the earlier "Tradition and the Individual

Talent." Perhaps most ironic in Eliot's argument, however, is his failure to account for the contamination of his own enabling terms by the argument to which they have led. Although it is easy to say that Eliot maintains the oppositions between, say, thought and feeling that his argument cancels because he is, as a modern, a victim of the dissociation he describes, it is also clear that Eliot actually provides himself such disjunction in order to install, not empirically but rhetorically and retroactively, a prior, ideal conjunction evidenced by no more than the positing of its later lack in—and as a function of—his own ostentatiously fallen or corrupted modern categories.

Such non-negotiable impasses in Eliot's almost reckless contentions in the light of "Tradition and the Individual Talent" lead to all sorts of subsequent problems as the essay winds down. Trying to maintain his myth at all costs, Eliot must engage in almost scandalous contradictions. "While the language became more refined" in eighteenth-century verse, he argues, "the feeling became more crude" (288). Gray's sensibility in the "Elegy in a Country Churchyard" (to say nothing of Tennyson's and Browning's) is "cruder than that in the *Coy Mistress*" (288). The result: the inadvertent though telltale formulation that comes in the form of self-contradiction: belated, nonfresh poets are "cruder" (288), while earlier, fresher ones are "more mature" (289). Though such contradictions are by now familiar to us in Eliot as well as in Arnold, they remain repressed, pushed aside, like the temporal logic of "Tradition and the Individual Talent," in order for Eliot to reconstitute an Arnoldean surrender to the conditions of belatedness with the invention of a myth that sustains modernity as a state of crisis.

"The Metaphysical Poets" concludes by engaging in a kind of wish-fulfillment unparalleled for its sheer opportunism, especially given its shaky logical base. The wish-fulfillment—a famous one—is that of rewriting the canon of English poetry so as to draw a straight line from the Metaphysicals to Eliot himself. Accompanying the mythmaking is the enabling but increasingly unacknowledged presupposition that the role of the poet is a Romantic, even a Paterian one: it is, as Eliot puts it, "to find the verbal equivalent for states of mind and feeling" (289); "of transmuting ideas into sensations" (notice the allusion to the terms at work in the subtitle of *Marius*), "of transforming an observation into a state of mind" (290)—all such ideals revisitations of the overtly Arnoldean, late Romantic wish that poets make a profession of retrieving a mythical "direct sensuous apprehension of thought" (286). Again Eliot relies on a vulgar Paterian (and decidedly Arnoldean) aesthetic that judges art on the basis of its ability to make "thought" and "feeling," like "translator" and "original" in Arnold, coincide. The formulation is simultaneously a symptom of his own "dissociation" as a latecomer that proves his use of such distinctions to be inevitable and so renders him blameless in their sale; but also a symptom of his willful installation of a lost golden age so as to give his own poetic project a calculated protective advantage: if his disadvantaged status as a latecomer is evidenced by a vocabulary corrupted by the dichotomy between thought and feeling that is itself evidence of a poetic fall from grace (a disjunction successfully used, it should be noted, by Milton under similar circumstances), such originary wounding by precedent is also a guarantee that will allow Eliot the poet whatever excuses he may need if he too exhibits the same dissociation without healing it.

That literary history must be rerouted from Donne to Eliot himself, thereby swerving from Milton, Romanticism, and Pater alike, suggests that such Romanticism, early and late, must contain the historical—and therefore inadmissible—evidence that tells us why Eliot is up to his duplicitous game in the first place. It is because Eliot, too, is a product of Romanticism, and so must repress it in his new literary history because it is what traditionally, and so ironically, impels him to make it new in the first place. Like the "ideal order" of "Tradition and the Individual Talent," such a rewriting of English literary history in "The Metaphysical Poets" allows Eliot both the establishing fiction of his own most significant poem as well as an instant defense against any charge as to the impossibility of its fragments being brought into an absolute unity in their own right. If Eliot fails, it is history to blame; if Eliot succeeds, only Eliot can take the credit.

"The Function of Criticism" (1923a) is almost as Arnoldean in its poetics as its title might suggest, although it also polemically asserts its priority over Arnold's "Function of Criticism at the Present Time" by silently noting its own lack of need for a "present time." Its principles are, after all, more frankly and absolutely universal than Arnold's own. Eliot begins by quoting from "Tradition and the Individual Talent," if only to show that, in the four years that separate the two essays, what is only a latent desire in the earlier work— the Arnoldean desire for a rekindled primacy or "ideal order" finally realized in the myth of the modern produced by the transitional "Metaphysical Poets"—has now become the overriding intent of the later. Once again, too, however, Eliot is, like Arnold, required to repress the temporality by which such ideals are articulated. Indeed, the ideals "The Function of Criticism" proposes are put directly into question by the means of their production. The "problem of order" (23), says a retrospective Eliot, is the real and neglected theme of "Tradition and the Individual Talent"—a surprisingly candid assessment of how malleable the earlier essay makes literary history, and, in turn, a hint as to how unwelcome the exposure of such malleability has already become as Eliot grows only a little older. With "order" a perpetually shifting idea in the earlier essay, subject as it always is to the secondary revision of later poets in relation to past ones, the increasingly Arnoldean Eliot now wishes to freeze the process altogether by reifying the notions of "ideal order" and "new wholes" in order to repress the temporality that produces either one. Admitting again that it is by means of relations that every new poet necessarily reorders the old that makes for an "idea" of "order," not a fixed or "ideal" one—and one always subject to later revision—Eliot goes on to concede that "the function of criticism seems," as Arnold has already suggested, "to be essentially a problem of order too" (23). It is, to be blunt, a problem of influence, and Eliot, taking full advantage of his secret status as belated Paterian scholar, will repress the Paterian means by which he will fashion his own influence by constructing instead another, ironically refreshed, Arnoldean myth of absolute value.

By the essay's second paragraph, Eliot even recapitulates Arnold's strategic expressions and repressions as he makes the case for his emerging ideal. "Literature," he says, actually echoing Pater, is "not . . . a collection of the writings of individuals, but . . . 'organic wholes' . . . systems in relation to which, and only in relation to which, individual works of literary art, and the works of individual artists, have their significance" (23–24). Although contrast and comparison—"relations"—are the only ways in which a given work of art may come into being (one is reminded of Bloom's later remark that there are no poems, only relations among them [1975]), the temporal and differential products of these "systems" are, in a shift of vocabulary epistemologically scandalous, "'organic wholes.'" But can the deferred results of impersonal systems become either "whole" or "organic"? The rhetorical problem is, as it is in Arnold, repressed rather than treated. To compound matters, Eliot also borrows again, and again secretly, from Pater when he speaks of the "surrender and sacrifice" (24)—the *ascesis*—tine artist must exercise in relation to tradition. The tradition is, of course, "outside" the artist (24), but also (though it is an irony that Eliot himself must miss in order to proceed with his argument) the stuff out of which the artist's purported interiority or "inside" is already constructed. Almost miming Arnold, it is, says Eliot, "our instincts of tidiness" (24)—of what is proper, clean, wholesome, regulated, orderly—that "command us" to make a fixed and ideal sense out of the flux of the "unconscious community" of literature as a whole (24). And yet, as in Arnold, it is precisely "tidiness" and wholeness—those metonymies of an impossible primacy—that the relational terms that produce them as ideals forbid. How can there be proper and organic features to a work of art when the dynamic that produces them is belated, systematic, and impersonal, perpetually unable to discover a primacy that is mythical to begin with?

Like Arnold, Eliot waxes Hellenic at moments of particular stress, and the Arnoldean—even Johnsonian—cadences at the close of the essay's first section suggest the eventual commitment to classical, that is to say universal, standards in both art and judgment that will soon become Eliot's overriding theme—the modernist attempt to produce the illusion of a world of value external to culture but dominant in its building. Criticism, after all, is in the service of "the correction of taste" (24), this despite the autotelism and the (Paterian) "indifference" (24) of the work itself. The assertion that criticism is the correction of taste is also put into question by the terms that articulate it: the apparently "clearly cut" "task" of the critic, says Eliot, is "comparatively easy" (23–24)—the colloquialism is exact. Like poetry, criticism requires the same kind of "comparison" or proportionality that even Arnold confesses to be the measure of its judgments. And yet, again like Arnold before him, Eliot goes on to repress the relational structure that produces his absolute ideals. Despite the readerly (and writerly) preconditions of temporality and belatedness as "Tradition and the Individual Talent" lays them out, Eliot will nonetheless claim the role of criticism to be "the common pursuit of true judgment" (25) no matter the plain differences in history that make criticism necessarily different in the aim and assessment of truth age to age.

Eliot acknowledges rather openly at the start of the second section of the essay that the question of canon-formation and the principles it entails are points at which no more than "a definite and final choice" is "involved" (25)—points, moreover, at which the critic's rage for "order" seems, in Eliot's case as in Arnold's, to require that choice to assert itself as absolute. Of course, the Paterian reality of choice forbids its results from ever pretending to be absolute in fact, much as the belated constitution of any past order forbids its status as universal. With Eliot's guard down for a moment, perhaps we can also see the reason for his use of John Middleton Murry, through whom he introduces the essay's major trajectory. Despite the banter with an otherwise adversarial Murry, both Murry and Eliot agree, it seems, that any defense of what both call Classicism rests on the assumption that what sustains the Classical stance is the belief that there is an " 'outside' " (26) different from the " 'inside' " (26), the latter to become the late Romantic's condemnable " 'inner voice' " (27) further on in the essay. Unlike Murry, Eliot endorses such Classicism over Romanticism because it subjugates the individual to the "outside," while

Romanticism pays all homage to the "inside" alone. Eliot is quite right to worry aloud that the terms "inside" and "outside" can provide for substantial quibbling (26–27), since the distinction loses its force the moment we recall Eliot's own earlier contention that what is individual or, by implication, inside is already a function of what is outside it—the "systems" or tradition that constitute it relationally.

The difference between inside and outside, however, is a summary and emblematic kind of distinction for Eliot the critic, and it is on the reality of its difference that, as his prose knows if he does not, his arguments must either rest or fall. As usual, Eliot's use of such dichotomous terms—as "Tradition and the Individual Talent" has already made plain, and as Eliot has already reminded us earlier here—turns out to be self-contaminating because rhetorically interdependent. Nonetheless, Eliot maintains their discreteness for polemical reasons. Eliot's repressed, Arnoldean Romanticism—like Pound's or Hulme's as well—makes him champion a Classicism supposedly distinct from it. And since Romanticism also means Protestant interiority (no mediation of godhead by an institution, whether of church or poetic tradition), Eliot's attack on the "'inner voice'" (27), then, is anti-Protestant as well as anti-Romantic (that these are also anti-American tendencies goes without saying). Murry's remark describing the modern is a grossly symptomatic expression of the anxiety of influence that makes modernism itself a late Romanticism, and which Eliot, as a victim of it, must go on to repress: the desire to have "inherit[ed] no rules" (27). Indeed, Romanticism is Eliot's primary fear because it is not simply his own enabling vocabulary as a poet, but also a second modernism in its own anxiety to make it new compared to the Renaissance. Eliot's own touted newness thereby becomes the repetition of a repetition that exposes the crisis it asserts as imaginative rather than empirical.

Unable, then, to escape the desire himself, Eliot calls upon the mythology of Classicism instead, and, as we shall see in their structural homology in the poems, upon Christianity as well, as though both were truth rather than the supreme historical fictions that even Arnold admits them to be (hence, too, Eliot's mild slap at Arnold's Whiggery [29–30]). Most problematic perhaps is the silent identity drawn between the manifest distinctions of Classical and Romantic when Eliot recalls that Murry admits that an absolute fealty to the inner voice is also a belief in the quest for "a self that is universal" (27). Whether it resides "inside" or "outside," what unites them is the belief that, in either case, a vessel has been found to contain something "universal" at all. Though this surely sullies the differences between Classicism and Romanticism—both in search of a "universal"—and shows Eliot's own Classicism to be but another kind of Romantic recuperation, Eliot uses it, not to call into question the notion of universality as such that binds him epistemologically to Murry (for that will be his own Romantic Classicism), but once again to attack the Protestant—or really Gnostic and antiquely Romantic—belief that "God and [one]self [are] identical" (28). Eliot again and again admits the mediation that forbids his ideals, although his criticism—and his poems—will programmatically repress it in order to gain for themselves a revisited set of impossible Arnoldean goals. If Eliot's range of prejudices is clear in the first two sections of the essay, the third makes the implications overt and, mercifully, rather brief. Eliot's snobbery here is a function of his elevation of Murry's earlier opposition between inner and outer to one between "the Inner Voice" (29) and "Outside Authority" (29). "Why," asks Eliot, "have principles when one has the inner voice?" (29) The necessary interdependence between the two is again elided, even though Eliot knows better.

The essay's fourth and final section opens with a strategically negative use of certain weaknesses in Arnold to further Eliot's otherwise Arnoldean point of view. The weakness is that Arnold "overlooks," according to a briefly pellucid Eliot, "the capital importance of criticism in the work of creation itself" (30). Though Eliot will condemn Arnold seven years later for doing precisely the reverse—blurring the distinctions among the disciplines (1930)—here he condemns Arnold for being the frankly idealistic, and therefore failed, late Romantic that he is. Arnold is, especially as a poet, woefully burdened by what Eliot calls the "critical labour" (30) required of the artist: "the labour," as a Paterian Eliot puts it, "of sifting, combining, constructing, expunging, correcting, testing: this frightful toil is as much critical as creative" (30). If Pater, like the Eliot of "Tradition and the Individual Talent," discovers a way of accommodating this "critical labour" through the notion of "scholarship," Arnold, as we have seen, sees such labor as a restraint rather than as a challenge, forcing him to erect repressive myths of a lost primacy to account for his own failures. "No writer is completely self-sufficient" (31), says Eliot as he returns to the arguments of "Tradition and the Individual Talent." Frowning upon the Arnold who recoils at the critical labor required of him, Eliot again wishes to attack the impressionism that is the polemical target of "Tradition and the Individual Talent," now represented as the new ideology of spontaneity, the neo-Wordsworthianism of a vulgar modernism that is as untenable as it is un-Paterian. Eliot still sounds like the Pater of "Style" when he reminds us that "we do not assume that because works have been composed without apparent critical labour, no critical labour has been done" (30).

With all the shifting of gears, Eliot fluctuates quite desperately as the essay moves toward its close. For while he insists upon the element of criticism in creation, he now also insists that there is, logic be damned, no creation in criticism: "there is no equation" (30). Given all that Eliot has said and done in both "Tradition and the Individual Talent" and "The Function of Criticism," this simply cannot be true. Eliot even recapitulates the customary distinction upon which his "no equation" clause is based by reminding us that the work of art itself is "autotelic" (30)—self-referential—and "that criticism, by definition, is *about* something other than itself" (30). But, of course, Eliot's own practice as a critic as well as a poet makes it abundantly clear that art and criticism alike are about art and criticism—neither is purely autotelic nor purely referential. How can the work of "creation" have relations with tradition unless it, too, is, like the criticism to which it is opposed, "about something other than itself" called tradition?

Given these latent difficulties, Eliot grows conciliatory late in the essay, as though to air his guilt and to recall the truth of "Tradition and the Individual Talent" to which the beginning of the essay has already alluded, and with whose hitherto repressed implications it will, at least penultimately, end. But as soon as Eliot seems to acknowledge his hidden Paterian side by speaking again of the need for a "formula" (31) in criticism, he abruptly confronts us with the very term Pater himself is so suspicious of when seen as an absolute: the word "fact" (31). Good critics, says Eliot, "must have a very highly developed sense of fact" (31). What, however, does this sudden and apparently digressive introduction of the necessity of "fact" in criticism have to do with the terms of any of the problems Eliot has raised? The appeal to the self-evidence of "fact" as a category, we soon find out, amounts to nothing less than the discouragement of "'interpretation'" (32) in criticism itself. Though Eliot puts the term in quotation marks so as to devalue it, "'interpretation'" is, despite Eliot's earlier attempt to disguise the fact, the working principle of criticism as well as of literature proper. Eliot is now quite clear about what he wishes to stifle: "'interpretation' . . . is only legitimate when it is not interpretation at all, but merely putting the reader in possession of facts which he would otherwise have missed" (32). By endorsing just that kind of antiquarian criticism rejected in "Tradition and the Individual Talent," Eliot manages to preserve the same kind of distinction as that preserved by Arnold between poetry and prose. If, for Arnold, poetry is figure and prose is literal, Arnold's own figural strategies as a writer of prose may be left unnoticed. And if, for Eliot, literature is interpretation and criticism is not, then Eliot's more athletic interpretations as a mythmaking critic will go equally unnoticed, too. Moreover, "fact" in the critic's domain is, of course, epistemologically identical with the pristine Arnoldean category of "the original" (32) work of art in the artist's equally sequestered domain. Once again, however, both idealities crumble, since their mutual contamination is the price of their articulation: if the artist's original is the critic's fact, then the distinction between art and criticism the opposition means to voice is, alas, enabled by the cancellation required by their epistemological identity as tokens of truth.

But why this protectionism, this defense, this desire to maintain the modernist categories that Eliot himself has put into question throughout his principal early essays? Eliot even goes on to expose again the proportional makeup of his ideals of "fact" or "ideal order" as the essay comes to a close. "Comparison and analysis," he admits, "are the chief tools of the critic" (33). Much as Arnold (only inadvertently) demonstrates, especially in the Homer lectures and in his theory of touchstones, that his ineffable and transcendent classical absolutes are in fact produced by comparison and contrast, Eliot too continues to show us, far more frankly than Arnold himself, the temporal conditions under which his putative fixities are secured. "You must," says Eliot, "know what to compare and what to analyse" (33), implying in turn the forever earlier contrasts and comparisons that situate critics and artists alike throughout history, and that place them both in the like role of interpreter that Eliot ordinarily reserves for the artist alone in order to have his contrastingly factual way with us as a critic.

Of course, all this sobering talk of fact is, in the final analysis, a question of power. Eliot's condemnation of interpretation in or as criticism in his own criticism is itself an act of powerful interpretation par excellence. Eliot's critical project is to produce a myth of the modern that allows him to defend against belatedness, even if it turns out to be a far less efficient and convincing defense than the Paterian one to be managed by Joyce. The claim that "we must ourselves decide what is useful to us" (32) is as clear a statement of criticism's own decided will to interpretation as is its search for "order" or "the correction of taste." Like the social criticism of Arnold, Eliot's criticism is itself an act of interpretation that claims to eschew interpretation in favor of fact, or, as Eliot puts it at the essay's close, "truth" (34)—that is, of a strong myth that insists on the reality rather than the rhetoricity of the retroactively derived origins it desires. Like Arnold, Eliot must thereby constantly assert values whose articulation puts them into question. As Eliot admits, even "truth" can be said to exist only when it is possible "to find a scheme into which, whatever they are," the necessary facts "will fit . . ." (34).

The Waste Land: The Flight from Lucifer

Eliot's centrality as a poet rests very largely on the assent with which we continue to maintain *The Waste Land* as a document crucial to the mythology of modernism. To read the poem in the light of the frightening clarity and motivation of Eliot's criticism is, however, to become perhaps as disingenuous as the poet himself in recognizing the mannerisms of his verse to be in the service of a project different from the one we normally grant him. As Stephen Spender attests, Eliot's poetry is "given its ideals by the prose" (1953:155); indeed, it epitomizes its principles to a fault.

In general strategy, of course, *The Waste Land* means to show that daily life in any era—even in the supposed dessication of modern civilization—recapitulates the eternal rhythms of being in its ancient epic dimensions, when the world was full and men were happy; that, despite the apparent meaninglessness of modern experience, man lives according to fixed and universal ideals that once made—and can once again make—life as sacred and orderly as it is meant to be. This is the famous "mythical method," belatedly (and implicitly) bestowed upon the poem by Eliot's review of *Ulysses* the year following the publication of both works (1923b), a strategy that met, not surprisingly, with Yeats's disapproval (see Sultan 1977:31). Hence the same kind of willful neglect of history and contingency as in the essays, and one that degenerates in the poem's intentional praxis into a universal archetypalism on the order of Jung's (see Drew 1949). The poem's five-part division betokens a dialectical structure that will resolve its apparent fragments into an isomorphic symbolism that yokes all myths, all religions, all literatures in a serene and pacifying conclusion. Like Joyce and Schliemann in Jackson Cope's reading (1981), Eliot's romance with contemporary anthropology acts out a literal version of the modernist nostalgia for origins, sometimes by means of a repaganization of Christianity itself in an attempt to homologize Weston and the Bible (for a summary, see Perkins 1976:505ff.).

And yet the poem's organizing strategy is already self-divided from the start. After all, to mount a thematic of dessication amid the actuality of such eternal returns at every moment in the text of the poem is already to cancel the loss it expresses. What is lost must not in fact be lost at all if it can be filled by the very thing it lacks. Why, then, does the poem—like the essays—produce a myth of the modern unparalleled in English if its mode of articulation suggests such a myth to be both profoundly unstable and insufficiently ironic or self-accounting? "A poem that is to contain all myths," remarks Leavis, "cannot construct itself upon one" (1932:81). Our real argument must, to be sure, come in some confrontation with Eliot's poetic language, even in the brief symptomatic reading of *The Waste Land* that follows. What exemplary presuppositions does the poem's opening make, and at what boundaries do its contradictions eventually tire, collapse from the weight of their convictions? The legendary opening line of the poem already admits its secret—and surely unintentional—double purpose, that of giving us a project at odds with the operation that produces it. The operation here is the obviously temporal one of allusion to and *renversement* of Chaucer, a turning about that signifies a reverse condition in English poetry since its first official efflorescence. And yet such an assertion is put instantly into question by the dialogism or allusiveness that allows the line to signify. For to be in touch with Chaucer enough to read—or write—Eliot's opening line as a reversal of the earlier poet's is already to have shown a connection with tradition, past customs, and so on, that the line necessarily proves at the level of narration even as it denies it at the level of what it narrates. How can there be a break if it is the continuity of our readership that lets us see it? It is a patent contradiction, and sums up in miniature what the poem will display at large—a repression of the readerly continuity it implicitly presumes despite the claim that it is no longer available.

Let us, then, read *The Waste Land* for what it is—a late Romantic quest-romance—rather than as the mimetic jeremiad that it is usually taken to be. In its overt references to the history of English poetry, surely the poem's manifest field of reference is, as Eliot says any poem's must be in "Tradition and the Individual Talent," tradition itself. And yet it is just this continuous field that the poem, astonishingly enough, wishes to repress in order to resurrect it in a mock crisis in which all glory will fall to the poet for restoring it. Presuming itself to be formally "autotelic," *The Waste Land* is, like any poem, in fact "about" something else—the tradition it claims it lacks and the tradition it uses both to simulate the lack and then to repair it. The poem's celebrated fragmentation depicts not a world in pieces, but the belated imagination sitting among the metonymies of a tradition so rich in its overdeterminations that literary language visibly cracks in response to the sheer weight of accumulated poetic usages that burden it. "The literary past," said Conrad Aiken in his review of the poem in 1923, "has become so overmastering as almost to constitute the motive of the work" (1923; rpt. 1968:54). As Richard Poirier has remarked more recently, "Against the tendency to believe in the wasteland as an historical fact, it has to be consciously remembered that the fragmentation which is [the poem's] principal characteristic is a condition of Eliot's mind even when he is not addressing cultural issues" (1967/1971:58).

Hence "the assumption," in Denis Donoghue's words, "of the burden of history," although in the final instance "martyrdom is Eliot's favourite version of the Sublime" (1974:186–87). So much may we give to the poem's formal "innovations" so long as we recognize them to be a defensive and almost entirely reflexive response to its own belatedness rather than to a condition in the modern world as such. Eliot's vaunted fragmentation, sharpened by Pound's editing, is, moreover, less an invention than simply a heightening of the necessity of montage as the functional procedure of all forms of discourse, according to Eisenstein himself (note especially his demonstration of montage in *Paradise Lost* in *The Film Sense* [1947:58ff.]). Even more—as the Paterian undercurrent in the wishful title of part I, "The Burial of the Dead," suggests—such a poetic condition confirms what Eliot otherwise denies: his status as a late Romantic poet, implicating him in a tropology of ruin and waste far older than the twentieth century (one recalls, for example, the "waste" of the landscape of Tennyson's *Idylls* that Arthur, poet-surrogate, proleptically disposes of well beforehand), and directly in the line of a Romanticism that Eliot will, like Arnold before him, eventually reject in favor of an extra- or paraliterary mode of authority instead.

Eliot engages in such duplicity in order to insure his own apparent originality by constructing the most influential modernist myth of all—that modern life is itself a wasteland, projecting onto the world a state that really inheres largely in the history of imagination alone. Pound's superb editing of the text confirms as much (1971). Scrupulous in removing any Romantic allusion, echo, setting, or mood locally, Pound ended up making of an otherwise shapeless mass, most of it Browningesque satire by comparison with the final product, an efficient and coherent Romantic quest poem of a high order. Thus the deeper logic of the marginal note "*Blake* too . . . often used" (1971:9) next to lines that Eliot almost exactly retained (1922:66–68), together with the predictable removal of a reference to "Walter Pater" (1971:27). Perhaps most remarkable is Pound's excision (and Eliot's assent) of an inversion of the opening of Keats's first *Hyperion* as the original start to "The Fire Sermon." Though followed immediately by a series of mock-heroic couplets also deleted, Eliot's "admonished by the sun's inclining ray, / And swift approaches of the thievish day" (1971:23) tries to turn Keats on his head ("Deep in the shady sadness of a vale / Far sunken from the healthy breath of morn"). Pound had also wanted to remove the phrase "At the violet hour" (1922:215; 1971:43), probably because of its too blunt an evocation of formulaic Romantic landscape of the kind that Pound, like Eliot, wished to put behind him. Indeed, Eliot himself appears to have substituted the phrase "the arid plain" late in the poem (1922:425) for "a desolate sunset" (1971:79), as though to remove the poem still again from the Romantic tropologies that constitute the particular burdens of his tradition. As the price of the myth, then, Eliot represses not only the fact that it is really his late Romantic imagination that is in ruins instead of the world; he also represses the connectedness he needs (and has) in order to succeed as redeemer of the modernist fragmentation he only projects.

The end of *The Waste Land*'s first line and the start of the second describe the poem's real conditions of emergence quite candidly: "breeding / Lilacs" (1922:1–2) means, according to conventional symbolism at least, the generation of signs of death, a contradiction that, even from a mimetic point of view, suggests the kind of implacability the poem encounters because of its belatedness (i.e., the past means death to regeneration); from a dialogical point of view, however, the contradiction suggests the conditions of poetic production as such: that one must breed by means of the signs of the dead that this poem—unlike, say, one by Hardy—wishes to bury or repress. Indeed, to call this opening section "The Burial of the Dead" is to get it backward, though such distortion is Eliot's obvious intention as poet much as it is as a critic: for the dead are hardly buried. Rather, Pater-like, their graves are perpetually open. The skeletons among whom we walk here are not those of our supposedly lifeless contemporaries, but the bones of tradition itself.

To say, then, that the poem is a mixture of "Memory and desire" (3) is to say what is already plain—that the two terms are the poles of Eliot's own poetics, one the desire for immediacy, the other the inevitable precondition of memory, poetic memory in particular, the kind that inhibits the wish for immediacy in poetic practice and that makes it so burdensome a pursuit. The ideality in question is, of course, a paradisiacal one. The desire for primacy is clear enough in Eliot's appropriately implicit garden metaphors early in the poem, with the latter allied in turn with the season of spring that symbolizes the fullness of the early English verse from which the belated poet has fallen. If the "shower of rain" (9) intimates the redemptive return to fertility or origins that the poem's end will supposedly signify, it also suggests the surprise of "summer" (8)—of fullness—that modernity lacks and, in Eliot's case at least, wishes to recall.

The increasingly regressive perspective by which the break into impersonation begins after the invocatory lines (8ff.) is itself symptomatic of Eliot's paradoxical atavism—going forward by going backward—that distinguishes the will to modernity in its aggravated rather than mollified or relieved form. The childhood fantasy is also classically quest-romantic, including noble birth for the children, with one child bearing the name of generative innocence itself ("Marie" [15–16]). The vertigo engendered by the vortex is, moreover, daunting in this hidden allegory of literary history: "he took me out on a sled, / And I was frightened . . ." (14–15). And, of course, eventually, "In the mountains"—the official site of Romantic revelation as we know it—"you feel free" (17). Hence the last line of the opening verse paragraph confirms what the childhood fantasy—and the secret reality of the poet—have only whispered: "I read, much of the night," and thereby "go south in the winter" (18). The northern cold of belatedness or estrangement engenders the customary desire for the Mediterranean warmth of origins. Despite such a frank late Romanticism, however, Eliot will also try to excise such a reality from the poem, neglecting, for example, to include the season of autumn—of Romantic landscape proper (Hartman 1972:1975)—in what otherwise seems to be a complete calendar of the seasons in the poem's opening paragraph, thus combining (or seeming to) the opening of Chaucer's General Prologue with Spenser's *Shepheardes Calender.* Like Shelley's mythmaking or Keats's beaker, the desire for the south to relieve the autumnal gloom of belatedness is a classical topos of Romantic desire, betokening, as we have seen, the lost freshness and clarity of vision imputed by Arnold to the Greeks. Here it is a virtually Platonic "sunlight" (10) that miraculously overrides the rain once "we stopped in the colonnade" (9).

But even this miniature wish-fulfillment of a Mediterranean imaginative holiday is put in question by the poem's larger strategy. In the poem's Fisher King mythic structure, it is rain that is desired and sunlight that is dreaded—the precise reverse of what Eliot's more traditional self-contextualization as a Romantic has required of his use of such categories within the exigencies of English poetry proper in the opening stanza. Surely the poem's overt tropologies of ruin, rout, and rubbish—of the waste that gives the poem both its title and the precedents that enable it to speak—is at variance with the mythical arrangement of the tropes of sunlight and rain in both the first stanza and, as we shall see, in the poem's mythic machinery at large. The inflection of the tropes unaccountably switches throughout the poem: light equals barrenness in the myth, darkness the promise of rain; darkness equals imaginative belatedness in Romantic tradition, light the recovery of original vision. Like the Oedipus complex, however, this otherwise unaccountably self-canceling articulation of simultaneous and incongruous significations—in myth and in the history of Romanticism—does have a reason. Eliot's mythic analogue is at odds, categorically, with the Romantic tropology through which it must be simultaneously articulated. It is perhaps just such cancellation of the Romantic arrangements he inherits that Eliot wishes the mythic to accomplish, and it is very likely why the "mythical method" is not itself a strictly poetic procedure. Rather than account for his use of myth in relation to language and literature, as Milton does in *Paradise Lost* or as Keats does in the odes or the *Hyperion* fragments, Eliot wishes instead to have myth predominate so as to silence the maddening reverberations of tradition as such.

It is no surprise, therefore, that the poem's overt polemic begins in the second verse paragraph with a question even more candid than those asked by Arnold in his greatest moments of doubt: "What are the roots that clutch?"(19). The contradiction is again exact as the poem answers its own question quite frankly: there are no such roots despite Eliot's wish for "organic wholes." And yet despite the admission of his belated status, Eliot will nonetheless maintain his seriousness as to the possibility of a fixed center outside of time by again bypassing, as he has in the criticism, the Paterian accommodation that his own images will offer here as well, but that the poem will reject in favor of its larger wishful desire. Eliot's self-noted borrowing from *Ezekiel* is true only of the phrase "Son of man" (20). The "stony rubbish" (20) with which it is juxtaposed is his own, the invocation as it is of the wasted landscape to come, an indication of a lack of fecundity rather than of a decadence or overripeness of tradition that such waste or "rubbish" signifies from the point of view of Pater and, as we shall see, of Joyce as well—the opportunity rather than the restriction to be found in belatedness as a poetic condition. Like Arnold, however, and unlike Pater, Eliot will not admit the possibility of the Paterian solution of recontextualization, but will instead continue his quest for absolutes despite their already cancelled possibility given the precondition of belated temporality by which all such ideals are produced. Indeed, "stony" and "rubbish" combine to produce a confusing, even self-contradictory, figure. If the landscape is dessicated enough to be all stone, its inability to grow anything is already plain. But to add the apparently clarifying term "rubbish" ends up contaminating the intent of "stony" rather than confirming it, since "rubbish" or waste suggests precisely that repressed fecundity—the waste that is also poetic influence—that Eliot, like Arnold before him, refuses to accommodate openly no matter his silent exploitation of it. It is, in short, a miniature intimation of the increasingly obvious clash throughout the poem between Eliot's mythic vocabulary of the barrenness of waste and his Romantic vocabulary of dank but fecund waste or influence that reverses the terms of the myth that tries to stifle it. Like the productive paradox of the protista or mycelia in Freud which grow as a result of—rather than despite—their own waste materials (Weber 1982), the Paterian possibility of handling waste as a scholarly opportunity rather than as a modernist restriction is, as we might expect, manifestly rejected. Eliot's desire to escape the system that enables him necessarily remains captive to a will to modernity whose mythmaking ambitions incrementally require the poem to engage in a contradictory or double movement designed to repress the contingencies of language and history to which the belated Eliot is defensively subject.

The admonitory "Son of man" (20) attempts to alert the reader to his own postlapsarian (but also pre-Christian) status, though in the bargain of the figure comes a revealing moment in Eliot's schedule of assuming poetic authority. The rest of the first verse of the second chapter of *Ezekiel* is instructive by its absence here, for it suggests in its own turn just what Eliot wishes to repress even as he uses it. The full passage (King James version) is as follows: "Son of man, stand upon thy feet," says God to the prophet, "and I will speak unto thee" (*Ezekiel* 2:1). Here the poet makes his reader or addressee Ezekiel, and, by implication, renders the text the very voice of God by virtue of the positionings required by the allusion. If the reader or "Son of man" knows no more than "a heap of broken images" (22), not only does the poem thereby claim to know such images whole, as does God in relation to fallen man; it must, by implication, also admit, however unwillingly, that, as poem, it knows its fragmentation to be no more than a device of empowerment designed in the final instance to place the poem's reader in a position inferior to the poem itself. In one sense, then, Eliot does use the symptom of his belatedness—the cracked or anthological stance of his overburdened imagination—as an opportunity for power rather than as a restriction boding failure; but, as we shall see, it is a strategy whose mythmaking ambitions have their goal, not finally in literature itself, but in a realm beyond it. That the poem is designed to gain power over the reader rather than over tradition is symptomatic of its Arnoldean pretensions. Already in possession of those continuities—poetic, theological, or both alike—that it claims at the outset to lack, the poem must therefore maintain that it is only the reader who lacks them (one recalls Blackmur's quip that "Mr. Eliot's desire for an illiterate audience should be considered" [1952:184]; Eliot did indeed remark in 1933, with only surface irony, that "I myself should like an audience which could neither read nor write" [152]). The burden of belatedness is thereby shifted away from the poem and vouchsafed a feature of its audience—and, by extension, of the modern world itself, maintaining its myth of the modern by disguising the sleight of hand that constitutes it. Designed to relieve Eliot of his relation to tradition, then, the poem will go on, habitually, to do so, not by surrendering its impossible quest for absolutes in favor of the Paterian "broadcast" it uses anyway without saying so; but by proceeding to excise, or at least to subjugate, the Romantic tropologies that enable it, thereby denying the degree of its implication in tradition in favor of its manifest project of mythic replication and recuperation.

The pattern is exact both locally and in the procedures of the poem at large. In the second verse paragraph, Eliot reverses the metaphors of light and darkness still again in order to recall and reassert the poem's primary structuring device of the Fisher King myth, now plainly in conflict with the Romantic vocabulary against which it is a defense. Hence the "sun" (22) and what is "dry" (24) once more become emblems of barrenness ("dry stone no sound of water" [24]) rather than of Platonic illumination. Eliot even magnifies the contradiction by suggesting a welcome "shadow under this red rock" (25) that is in direct contrast with the tonality of Platonic—and Romantic—revelation. In Romantic tradition, "shadow" is ignorance rather than the comfort Eliot claims it to signify—unless, of course, it really is ignorance that Eliot wishes to impute to his reader as the yield of his empirically unverifiable mythmaking. Indeed, Eliot's note here again directs us to a biblical allusion that already says as much, another example of the posture in which the poem must place its reader in order to produce its consummate myth of the modern. How else are we to make sense of this otherwise digressive excerpt from *Ecclesiastes* that suggests religious debasement to be the only road to redemption unless we take the "they" to signify Eliot's own readers? "Also when they shall be afraid of that which is high," says the sacred text, "and fears shall be in the way" (12:5). Again the poem covertly, marginally lets us in on its real aim, the attempt to simulate, like Arnold, the voice of absolute authority rather than of historical or properly poetic authority. "Desire" will "fail. . ." in life, as the poem will try to show, because Eliot's modernist desire for new authority never fails in its mythmaking ambitions. The poem's apparent mimesis is really the dialogical function of its effect on its reader, in whom Eliot thereby produces a crisis to be attributed to the world rather than to the poem's own inability to handle the vortex on and in its own terms.

The godlike "I," then, will show the son of man "something different" (27), although it is hardly Paterian "difference." It is neither the "shadow at morning striding behind you" (28)—the past—nor the "shadow at evening rising to meet you" (29)—the future. Short of the vulgar modernist conclusion that the "present"—that nonentity—is really the answer, it is something obviously hard to define: "fear in a handful of dust" (30). Whose "fear" is it, however, and how is it produced? The poem tries to make such "fear" the reader's representative modernist condition, when it is actually the poem's projection of its own "fear" that requires it to repress the burdens of tradition—of "dust," "waste," "rubbish"—that Eliot continues to reject in favor of his quest for Arnoldean universals. The subsequent quick cut to Wagner (31–34) is surely a defensive deflection of the cause of the fear by both admitting the poem's pervasive and enabling Romanticism while also safely distancing it across the plains of Europe—as it does again later on with an apparently digressive quotation from *Parsifal* (202). Indeed, when Eliot tries to pull away from the Romantic tropes that constitute his "fear," they tend to reappear rather directly. Hence one comes back "late, from the Hyacinth garden" (37), an expulsion from grace in which rain signifies, not redemption, as it does in the poem's mythic analogue, but Romantic failure ("my eyes failed" [39]). "Hyacinth" itself, moreover, is not only a gem and a flower, but also, according to the *Oxford English Dictionary,* a flower "native of the Levant"—a southerly spot par excellence, the seat of originary Mediterranean culture even geographically allied to the warmth it betokens metaphorically. "'Hyacinth girl'" (36) becomes in turn a double symbol of desire, the reduced Laura of a momentarily Jamesian Eliot—his Daisy Miller to Arnold's Marguerite. Intimations of the metaphorical strategies (or lack of them) of the *Four Quartets* also emerge as the second stanza draws to a close with a figure designed to draw attention less to its paradoxical qualities as a trope than to its religious connotations: "heart of light, the silence" (41). Like Milton's "darkness visible," "heart of light" is an oxymoron, thus calling attention to what is by now a familiar kind of rhetorical bind that Eliot's otherwise theological (but also suppressed Paterian) figure wishes to repress in it. As in the essays, here the problem—as the poem itself has already begun to show—is muffled beneath an appeal to an emergent absolute by which paradox functions not so much as a figure whose machinery grants it what meaning it may have, but as a kind of stoppage by means of which the paradox is not to be negotiated as a condition of language but to be sanctified as the pious sign of trying to say something altogether inexpressible.

The latter possibility, however, presumes a world outside of a language dubbed insufficient to what it wishes to express, buttressing the mythic intent of the poem while also suppressing its Romantic or traditional way of voicing such ideals. When the first section begins its crescendo with its tale of Tarot, Eliot's reader is again required to make those scholarly combinations that the poem claims one cannot make, demonstrating once more the extent to which the text's own readability is a function of just those systems it has pronounced dessicated, dysfunctional. To be sure, Eliot's logic is partially Joycean in that the readability of the poem is produced against a lack of overt connection that the reader's diligence alone must procure. As Northrop Frye nicely puts it, "the poet hands the continuity of his poem over to the reader" (1967:69). At the same time, however, Eliot, as we have noted, prefers to keep the implications of his reader's own scholarship as dark as his own equally decisive Romanticism. Thus the function of the footnote that glosses or frames our reading of the Tarot section, asserting as it does that the machinery of Tarot has been used "quite arbitrarily" for purposes of motif-association. The machinery of Tarot may well be chosen "arbitrarily," but that is hardly to say that Eliot does not deploy such machinery in a strict, if dissonant, fashion once he chooses to use it. "The drowned Phoenician Sailor" (47) is already implicated in other, far from arbitrary systems of symbolic usages ranging, quite incompatibly, from the death of imaginative inspiration he comes to signify overtly in part IV to the Christological figure of potential redemption that Eliot's New Testament allusions try to grant him as compensation for his symbolization of Romantic failure. "The Lady of the Rocks" (49) is in turn a harbinger of the debased proletarian love to come in parts II and III despite the image's status as the enduring sign of imaginative power in its real source in Pater's almost identical description of the Mona Lisa is his essay on Leonardo in *The Renaissance* (1873:125). Finally, "The Hanged Man" (55), like the drowned sailor, is a summary compromise-formation between imaginative death and religious salvation.

With the symbolic associations of the Tarot figures so supple, its potentially "alien" spillage requires Eliot to introduce the fabulous "Mrs. Equitone" (57). Mrs. Equitone is Mrs. Even-tone, Mrs. Harmony, Mrs. Equivalence-of-voices. Married as she is, her implicit fidelity to one mate only is an exact symbol for the poem's own desire to link all its mythic analogues in harmony rather than to contend with the myriad associations its language both detonates and wishes to cancel or inhibit. Eliot wants to be Henchard and Farfrae simultaneously—to allow language its spillage but also to enforce a set of absolute meanings upon it. Hence Eliot's project is not reflexive in its representationalism, since its two planes—the play of language and its product—are not parallel, as they will be in *Ulysses* or among Bloomsbury, but in conflict.

The images of the last verse paragraph of part I are also articulated in a manner inconsistent with the vision they produce. Until, ironically, the "dead sound" (68) at the "stroke of nine" (68), Eliot's language functions here so plainly that it really does seem for a moment as banal as the quotidian sleepwalkers it portrays on their way to work in the morning. That the "dead sound" occurs "on the final stroke of nine" (68), however, gives us the kind of association—in this case, another Christological one—that redeems these sleepwalkers by implicitly linking them to a fellowship with Jesus: a mode of connection that the barren modernity that Eliot claims to share with the sights he describes is, by definition, not supposed to possess. After all, even the Christological portent of the number nine is called into play within a field of historical context that the poem characteristically—and duplicitously—claims modern life to have lost at the level of *histoire*, but that the poem itself already possesses at the level of *récit*.

The closing montages of part I are a sequential, if unwitting, unpacking of the Romanticism of both English and American tradition at large that wounds Eliot enough to force him to build the poem's mythic, if not truly poetic, defense against its reality. First, the Americanization of Homeric quest produced by yoking "'Stetson'" and "'Mylae'" (69, 70) appears to be in the service of mythic replication. It also suggests, however, that the connection between the Greeks and the cowboys is not really the result of archetypal homology, but of the genuine history of mythology by which Greek quest-romance is eventually incorporated into a Romantic tradition in English that also produces the mythology of the American West through the mediation of the American Romantic Emerson as it once did the mythology of the Renaissance explorers. Next (71–75) we witness the suddenly overt conversion of the wishful paradisiacal garden allied with the earliness of childhood in part I into a blast-beruffled graveyard of a garden. In a manner akin to Marius at the mausoleum, corpses are planted in the grave admission that the dead cannot in fact be buried, as part I has promised but failed to do. And, last, the citation from Baudelaire (76) finally names Eliot's Romantic alliances while simultaneously distancing them by locating their locus (as with Wagner) safely cross the Channel, in neither England nor America.

The double pattern of mythic replication despite historical difference continues in part II as Cleopatra begins the section as a model for the various lovers who follow (Cleanth Brooks inadvertently notes a source for Pater's description of the Mona Lisa in Shakespeare's description of Cleopatra [1939:147]). Presumably, then, the structure of (even secular) love is repeated over the ages despite differences in the modes and manners of human history. And yet, at the same time, the sequence of archetypes that begins with Cleopatra is a downward trajectory as well as a set of identities, a clearly hierarchical social movement that disrupts what is otherwise voiced as a series of homologues: from royalty (87–110) to the aristocracy and upper middle class (111–27) to the nouveau riche (127–30), and, eventually, to the proletariat in the poem's memorable pub scene (139ff.). Again the one intention cuts across or against the other as the assertion of mythic reduplication is put in question by the simultaneous separation of its equivalences at the level of social rank.

Similarly, too—though here Eliot is overt about it—Philomel's loss of her tongue (99) clashes with the simultaneous maintenance of the nightingale's song (100–01). The contradictory vision is reflexively framed by the Keatsian figure "As though a window gave upon the sylvan scene" (98), a virtual repetition of the last three lines of the seventh stanza of the nightingale ode (though glossed by Eliot in the Notes as deriving from Milton) that teases out its Spenserian undertones (Keats's "faery and forlorn" becomes the "sylvan scene" that evades Keats but not Eliot himself). It is as though the text unconsciously prepares us for the subsequent use of Spenser as the emblem for a lost Renaissance fullness in part III of the poem. Hence the acknowledgment that the dead—influence—are the very waste that disturbs ("I think we are in rats' alley/Where the dead men lost their bones" [115–16]), a figure equivalent to the Hardyesque "wind under the door" (118) that follows it and the "staring forms" (105) of "withered stumps of time" (104) that precede it. And though Eliot characteristically denies that the "wind" (118, 119) of influence is up to "Nothing" (120), it has blown through the door of his own Paterian House Beautiful with all the dialogical force that the poem always requires but also always claims is unavailable. And as soon as the conversation about what one remembers begins (121–24), the famous "Shakespeherian Rag" (128) sequence is interposed in order to blunt the question by depicting the lazy habits of the rich despoiled. Eliot intervenes in this way not, of course, for political reasons, but because such languor is too like Paterian aestheticism—too like the image of Cleopatra on her burnished, Keatsian throne, as though she were Moneta—to be acceptable in a poem looking elsewhere than its literary precursors for a primacy their paternity has rendered lost forever.

In part III, then, the middle of the poem, the Spenserian refrain becomes the signature of the poem's belatedness. It is probably the central instance of the real, poetic grail from which the poem is so distant, and also the ironic means by which it tries to assert the unity, originality, and generation for which it supposedly stands by speaking in the language of a prothalamion that praises the harmony—the equitone—represented by marriage. More than even the status of Milton in the criticism, Spenser serves Eliot here as indication that "the nymphs are departed" (175, 179), with Spenser's line both the reflexive and referential token of Eliot's modernist desire. Again, too, a Romantic landscape of dank and stormy gloom ("the wet bank," "the wind" [174]) is juxtaposed quite overtly with the poem's mythic landscape ("the brown land" [175]). The latter still seeks to secure the desire for new authority canceled by the pastness of Spenser's fullness and whose loss engenders, as in Arnold, the necessity of extraliterary values in order to regain plenitude or transcendence in a realm beyond a literary tradition whose burdens apparently forbid its futurity any success. That it is the windy vortex that makes the poem frosty is undeniable: "at my back in a cold blast I hear / the rattle of the bones" (185–86), "on," of course, "a winter evening" (190) or, a little later on, "At the violet hour" (215, 220). The two systems—myth and tradition, Arnold and Pater—are at odds more and more overtly as the poem proceeds, with Eliot's rhetoric continually putting in question the ideals it proposes. While the absence of the nymphs equals the presence of Thames rubbish, it is also such a logical operation that requires us in turn to identify the causative link between loss and influence that Eliot, like the classicizing Arnold before him, seeks habitually to repress. The mythic equivalences are canceled by the dynamic that asserts them.

Again and again this double operation occurs as the poem continues·to switch registers in midstream, the differences among its vaunted personae hardly as decisive as the differences in the double epistemology that organizes all of the poem's voices into two antagonistic systems to which any single voice already belongs no matter its apparent dramatic role. Thus the persona "fishing in the dull canal / On a winter evening" (189–90) domesticates Romantic landscape "round behind the gashouse" (190), although in the process it also burlesques the vestigial figure of the Fisher King as well as adding to it the look of a Twainian character with toes dripping from a Thames momentarily turned Mississippi. In the latter connotation, the figure begins to split its own possibility of isomorphic recuperation by radiating, not homologues, but "alien associations." In the former, Romantic and mythic systems come dangerously close to mocking one another in a standoff, leading Eliot to try to clarify his terms once again.

As though to swerve from such dangers, the poem eases away from "the low damp ground" (193) of tradition by devolving from the Paterian "bones" in the Parisian aesthete's "garret" (194), through an allusion to Marvell (196), to the rhythms of popular song (199–201). Sealing the verse paragraph with the lines from *Parsifal* (202), however, forces the poem back to the problems of Romantic imagination in the next fragment. The "Jug jug . . ." (204) of the nightingale is now "rudely forc'd" (205) compared to its "full-throated ease" even in Keats. And yet the irony is once again plain, undercutting the lament as a precise function of the terms by which it is voiced. If the modernist's problem is his lack of connection, the fact that the phrase that expresses it is borrowed from *Lycidas* ("with forc'd fingers rude" [4]) suggests such connection to be instead the ground by which its nonexistence is articulated. Moreover, despite Milton's implicit status as the last example of wholeness before dissociation sets in, Milton already represents himself in the allusion as "rude," as though to usurp Eliot's own modernist lament before the dissociation that supposedly causes it even happens. And while "Mr. Eugenides, the Smyrna merchant" (209) may be a sign (like Blaustein) for Eliot's opinion of the superannuated races of the Levant, the name also combines *Eumenides* with Euripides, both instances of the epic past whose dignities the poet wishes to recuperate. Hence too—and in a recollection of the duplicate lovers of part II—Tiresias here links the lovers of Greece and the Renaissance with those of the present through mythic repetition. Once again, too, however, a hierarchical social register is, as in part II, simultaneously invoked as well, canceling the identities at the moment they are asserted. The typist and the young man carbuncular (222ff.) are on the one hand made mythically even with Elizabeth and Leicester (279) as the passage itself begins reflexively to climax, but are also clearly inferior to them from the point of view of social hierarchy. Again, too, if it is this dirty Thames (266ff.) that requires that earlier, clean one (279ff.), and these dirty lovers that require those idyllic ones, then the connection thereby produced erases its own possibility by virtue of the historical and social differences that allow the equivalence. While mythic replication may identify the typist with Elizabeth "'Supine on the floor of a narrow canoe'" (295) on the Thames, raising her knees "'By Richmond'" (294), the "'Trams and dusty trees'" (292) restrict the personification to the debased present alone. Eliot seems almost ready to put his strategy into question even when it can work. Still fixed in his desire to repress the systems of connection that the poem paradoxically requires in order to lack, Eliot will now begin to move us to the ground—or lack of it—of his own real, and quite nonliterary, desire. Like Arnold's, Eliot's impetus is to locate value outside the system of literature that binds him. More radically than Arnold, however, Eliot's ideal is, even in 1922, already rather frankly religious, and, by definition, also extraliterary, especially in its expectation that language can freeze itself in ways it really cannot. In an exact example, the apparently biblical figure of "burning" (308, 311) assigned to Augustinian revelation at the close of part III can easily be confused with Pater's most famous figure for success in life, "to burn with a hard, gemlike flame." No matter such "alien"—though really all-too-familiar—"associations" in its language, the poem begins to grow frank about its alinguistic strategy for maintaining the will to modernity or myth of the modern that literature proper disallows. The direct and shocking appeal by the Augustinian persona at the close of part III (307ff.) to plain Christian godhead is the poem's less-than-covert preparation for the religious and apoetic resolution toward which it will now try to move.

As though to dramatize the double operation at work throughout the poem, part IV almost acts it out. Is this short segment a movement of eternal return or of belated failure? Is Phlebas dead and gone or is he metamorphosed through the ages by the harmony of archetypal spheres? Dead, Phlebas is a failed Arnoldean visionary who can forget "the cry of gulls" (313), the latter the nadir of the nightingale's decline in stature following its earlier transformation by Hardy into a thrush (though not, by contrast, for the American Hart Crane, for whom the gull is the secular equivalent of Milton's dove in *The Bridge*). Dead, Phlebas is also relieved of "the deep sea swell" (313) or dangerous afflatus of the oracular poet who wagers himself for the sake of revelation. "Profit and loss" (314) are therefore unnecessary to calculate, since, in this Romantic context, it signifies, not the dirty business of daily life, but the compensatory strategies a belated poet must invent in order to turn waste to advantage—the kinds of strategies that Eliot himself abjures.

Or is Phlebas, as the mythic reading stipulates, an example of eternal return, of mythic replication, of static and harmonious archetypes unified throughout—before and beyond—history? Phlebas's otherwise simple Christian rising and falling (316) is also a passing through "the stages" of all life (317), suggesting him to be a model for a transmigration of souls that gives to all voyagers, "Gentile or Jew" (319), an equivalence as questers. But, of course, the figuration of such voyagers or sailors as pilots (320) not only prefigures the poem's resolving image, but also implicates all such imagery in the Christian system by which the pilot represents the fixed center of faith that the poem has only moments earlier still claimed to be lacking. Again, however, Romantic and mythic systems clash before the solution is found. It is only within "the whirlpool" (318)—the ineluctable medium of all poetic speech, whether Arnold's and Pound's "vortex," Pater's "alien associations," Woolf's "sunken meanings," or even Eliot's own "tradition"—that literary language can signify at all. Though still acting out the contamination of its systematic regularities by constantly invoking the connections it claims no longer exist so as to repair them, the poem has by now, however, found a seam of escape from its Romantic predicament by beginning to restrict the broadcast of its signifying potential only to the fixed, mythic systems beyond language with which it wants to replace its temporal, literary ones. Whether

Phlebas is a failed Arnoldean quester or an archetype is left undecided, since the poem will move away from such problems entirely as it enters its fifth and concluding section.

Now Eliot simply announces rather than earns his conclusions. The landscape crossed by the recapitulating reader/persona ("After . . . " [322–27]) is, of course, the landscape of the poem itself, a landscape of poetic or imaginative rather than worldly ruin. The opening images are a catalogue of the styles of poetic presumption the text has deployed: an aestheticism gone pop, whether in its imitation of Cleopatra, in its portrait of the nouveaux riches, or in an anticipation of fascism ("torchlight red on sweaty faces" [322]); the paradise lost of late Romantic desire ("the frosty silence in the gardens" [323]); or the religious domain beyond language to which the poem wishes to flee ("the agony in stony places" [324]). The poem can now even readily admit the Paterian scholarship (and in its selfsame figuration) that informs it: "Prison and palace and reverberation" (326). The line in fact forms a sequence from a notion of language as restriction ("prison"), to Tennysonian fetish ("palace"), and, finally, to broadcast or "reverberation"—the temporality of tradition that Eliot himself has theorized in 1919 but has increasingly repressed, especially as his central poem begins to draw to a close. (Eliot also appears to have substituted "Prisons" for "Gardens" in the manuscript [1971:71].) It is, however, only by means of such "reverberation" that the poem, as we well know, reads at all. The admission detonates the first inkling of the redemptive promise of "thunder of spring over distant mountains" (327) that will bring rain to replenish the barren landscape provided by the poem's mythic machinery as opposed to its Romantic. Of course, the coming of rain—success in the Fisher King schema—is simultaneously a sign for the contrasting protraction of dampened Romantic inspiration—failure, that is, in the poem's rival rather than complementary field of reference. The "hermit-thrush" who "sings" (357) here does so only momentarily and fantastically because he is to be located in a Romantic legacy from Coleridge and Keats to Hardy to which *The Waste Land* itself will no longer appeal, and from whose agonistic intertextuality Eliot as poet will simply depart as a writer.

"There is," however, still "no water" (359), even late in the poem. There is only a combination Tiresias/Christ/Marius figure available for ghostly companionship (360ff.), whether for good or bad it is hard to tell (is the "hood . . ." [364] a reference to the presumably Muscovite threat of "hooded hordes" to come [369], or is it the beneficent sign of a monkish cowl?). Such ambivalence suggests the poem's undecidability as to whether it proceeds from Pater on the one hand or from Arnold on the other. Addressing the project of

Romantic quest-romance as he seeks a route out of his double predicament, Eliot produces perhaps the poem's most famous passage as a function of the Romantic tradition he has tried, and will now go on, to disavow. The "city" (372)—the New Jerusalem in its Spenserian antecedent, the "house" or "mansion" of sensibility, as Pater and Keats put it, even the fortress of the self in some of Freud's figurations—is under siege from "those hooded hordes" (369) that are not so much an expression of Eliot's political or racial fears as they are a nightmare version of the ghosts of influence as represented, say, in Hardy's "Wessex Heights." Thus the "towers" are "falling" (374) because Eliot wants them to fall. They are not metonymies for the actual cities denoted, but the "towers" of Romantic or visionary power in a traditional landscape that Eliot will now ruin instead of allowing it to ruin him. Although Arnold's outright withdrawal from literature is the wider precedent for Eliot's only implicit exit from it, Browning's well-known refusal to enter the Romantic agon is Eliot's specific tropological precedent here in the poem's closing section. By ruining even the transubstantiating possibilities of searching for a tower already ruined anyway in "Childe Roland" (Bloom 1969), Browning, Eliot's chief precursor in monological technique, has already prepared the scenario to which Eliot comes, habitually, late, and in which he will invert and evacuate the tropology of "towers" outright by destroying them. And though they are "falling" because of a lack of visionary will, Eliot suggests their demise to be a function instead of a fallenness from the point of view of the Christian ground that now becomes the poem's larger court of appeal, and, eventually, the route of its safe passage out of the burdens of tradition altogether (for a more convivial reading of the passage, see Gregory Jay 1983:189ff.).

Eliot must nonetheless cross, like any poet who writes in English, an explicitly Romantic landscape of ruin in conflict with the tropology of both his classicism and his Christianity in order to allow for the emergence of his ideal, incongruous and unearned as it may be. The interpolated tale of the woman and her hair (378ff.) that alone separates us from the apocalypse of closure or resolution is in fact a miniature history of Romanticism itself, linking Coleridge's harp with the Gothic ("those strings / And bats" [379–80]) through the reverberant figure of a Grimm Rapunzel, and in an appropriately dim "violet light" (380). Thus we can suddenly see *The Waste Land* for what it is, an inversion of the late Romantic poem of ruin and ruins. Its visionary "towers" (383) "tolling reminiscent bells" (384) are, like the sleeping "bats" inside them (380), decidedly "upside down in air" (383), graphically overturned because the modernist Eliot has simply had enough of the authority of the past (the "reminiscent bells" also "kept the hours" [384], telling the only time there is to tell in the closed system of literary usage), of "voices singing out of empty cisterns and exhausted wells" (385). Romantic speech is an echo rather than an original and holds out no hope of real redemption or freedom from the system that kindles its desire for liberation from it.

This is not enough for Eliot, who forges the landscape of towers only to draw back from it. Now the reason is fully clear from figurations whose own genealogies reflexively account for the fear they produce as referential images. Influence (or waste) is not only figured here as "bats" (380)—as gloomy, nighttime creatures that feed off the blood of the living, much as the leeches do in Wordsworth's "Resolution and Independence." The figuration—"reminiscent," too, of Hardy's ghosts—also finds an exact, and decidedly decadent, source in Pater's memorable remark that the Mona Lisa's enduring influence makes her "older than the rocks among which she sits," because "like the vampire, she has been dead many times, and learned the secrets of the grave" (1873:125). Hence the figure's precedence to Eliot's in articulating influence as a perpetual "deposit" (1873:125) of the dead in the living is dynamically emblematic of the action it signifies. We have earlier seen Pater's Gioconda—"the Lady of the Rocks" (49)—reduced to "The lady of situations" (50), as though to remove from her figure the sinister atmosphere of the Paterian "disease" of "Romanticism," as Eliot puts it in *The Use of Poetry* (1933:128). Eliot's stance here is reinforced by the Mona Lisa's other appellation earlier in the poem as "Belladonna" (49), the name of a poisonous eastern plant also known as Nightshade (Ronald Bush finds her embedded in "Ash-Wednesday" as well [1984:141]). Yeats must have had a good laugh when he began his Oxford anthology (1936) by printing Pater's famous lines about the Mona Lisa in blank verse (1936:1) while leaving all parts of *The Waste Land* absent from his selections of Eliot's own work. The passage from Pater, says Yeats, "dominated a generation" (viii). Eliot himself, writes Yeats, produces "his effects by a rejection of all rhythms and metaphors used by the more popular romantics rather than by the discovery of his own"—this is precisely the problem. The result: Yeats "thinks of him as satirist rather than poet" (xxi–xxii). The poet of *The Tower* (1928) who could link the work of Hardy and Wilde (1936:vii–viii) obviously stands far away from the poet of the "Falling towers" of *The Waste Land*.

Much, then, as Keats's nightingale sends the poet back to his "sole self," so, too, does the toll of "reminiscent bells" here force Eliot back into the real place of literary ruin he still inhabits so close to the poem's close:

> In this decayed hole among the mountains
> In the faint moonlight, the grass is singing

> Over the tumbled graves, about the chapel
> There is the empty chapel, only the wind's home.
> It has no windows, and the door swings. . . .   [386–90]

The "chapel" is "empty" from Eliot's point of view because it is "only the wind's home." And yet, from a strictly Romantic perspective, this is precisely why the chapel, or site of revelation, is actually full—because it is windy with influence, anticipating the gaunt but gusty landscape of "Time Passes" in *To the Lighthouse,* doubling (though, as we shall see, with the reverse intention) Joyce's handling of the vortex in *Ulysses,* and recalling the haunted fields of Hardy's Wessex. By now, however, it is plain that the poem's Romantic vocabulary is fully at war with its decidedly different notion of value in the metaphysical rather than in language or tradition itself. Though Romanticism enables Eliot, it is the very plain or landscape of Romanticism that he puts "behind" him as the poem comes to a close (425)—not so much as a measure of his originality as a poet as of his quasi-Arnoldean surrender to the conundrum of belatedness that defeats him. "Dry bones," says an Eliot who forgets the necropolitan Marius at the mausoleum, "can harm no one" (391).

Poised, then, at the height of its imaginative crisis, the poem must now decisively repress its fecund Romantic landscape and insist that it is barren because of its waste rather than constantly fertilized by it. Hence the poem's final turn as it attempts a dialectical resolution on the model of Christian redemption (Frye 1963:65). In the midst of dessication, suddenly there is the "flash of lightning" (394) and the startling delivery of "rain" (395). Why the sudden upturn with no apparent reason? Deus ex machina, to be sure—but of what sort? The only explanation we can find is in the lines that separate "Dry bones . . ." from the "flash" itself, especially the first of the two: "Only a cock stood on the rooftree" (392). Here the poem resorts to the vulgarity that Eliot's earlier footnote on "*turdus*" has implicitly outlawed in its ostentatious protocol of linguistic omission: the use of crude and/or American inflections, especially for the purposes of the anarchic Joycean pun. And yet here "cock" is clearly meant to represent, in its denotative meaning of rooster, the phallus and its regenerative powers. Despite the "maternal lamentation" (368) earlier, Eliot's notion of generation is rather one-sided, putting all confidence in the figure of the male whose hegemony the figure of Tiresias has, in another of the poem's contradictions, supposedly neutralized by means of his blind polysexuality. Even the "leaves" that still await the rain, however, are correspondingly "limp" (396), while the "jungle" is "crouched, humped in silence" (399) as the chain of sexual metaphors is elaborated. (Notice, too, that the thunder speaks only "Da," never "Ma," although both articulations occur simultaneously in the origins of individual speech; see Fineman 1980:57ff.) How odd, then, that a poem supposedly guided by the posture of Impersonality is girded at its close by the most specific vocabulary of the personal we have, that of sexual intercourse, and, moreover, with dominance given over to the male member in still another unconscious valorization of precisely those psychobiographical categories that both Eliot's verse and criticism appear to forbid.

Hence the Objectivist paradox returns to provide us with still another register of structural contradiction in the poem at large. Like the problematic use of sexuality to symbolize imaginative regeneration, the use of subjectivist tactics, particularly the poem's influential use of point of view, is, by Eliot's own criterion, designed to achieve an Impersonality at odds with the subjective categories that produce it. Objectivity and Impersonality are also figurally at odds with the supposedly synonymous figure of the work of art as an "organic whole." How can the Impersonal produce the "organic" any more than the subjective can produce the Objective? The contradictions grow more and more overt as the pressure within the poem mounts, implicitly canceling the project it wishes to articulate in the act of trying to sustain it. Such impasses are, however, familiar to us by now, and, as in Arnold, remain unnegotiated by an otherwise sharper Eliot who must therefore have something else in mind.

At its close, then, the poem resorts to homily rather than restrict itself any longer to the exclusive realm of poetry as such. Its intensified montages are themselves symptomatic of the poem's increasingly paraliterary status as it now reaches out for the kind of faith language alone simply cannot provide. Eliot even admits his swerve from Romantic literature to theology when he answers Datta's question, "What have we given?" (402), with the defensively convoluted remark (assigned to whatever persona one might like to choose) that "the awful daring of a moment's surrender . . . By this, and this only, we have existed" (404, 406). "This," says an Eliot who foresees the life-in-death of properly Romantic or necropolitan achievement, is "not to be found in our obituaries/Or in memories" (406–08). With Romanticism behind and religion ahead, Eliot can then announce, despite the ironic echo of Casaubon in the remark, "I have heard the key" (412). The ironies linger, however, beyond the echo of Casaubon's false "key to all mythologies" that may reasonably be said to characterize the poem's own strategy of mythic recuperation or archetypalism. Theological though its intention may finally be, Eliot's "key" also unlocks another door. It tropologically responds to Pater's figure of solipsistic self in the conclusion to *The Renaissance*—"the narrow chamber of the individual mind" (1873:235)—by claiming to unlock it, too ("each in his prison" [414]; "each confirms a prison" [415]), releasing Pater's "solitary prisoner," like Eliot himself, from his Romantic "dream of a world" (1873:235). Of course, as with "burning" earlier, Eliot thereby also contaminates the atemporal realm of pure escape his "key" is meant to symbolize by virtue of such intertextual referentiality that confirms his indebtedness to tradition at the very moment he wishes to cut away from it.

With Eliot's language now vibrating well beyond its intent, however, some control must be reasserted. Thus "beating obedient/To controlling hands" (422–23) is the poem's summary emblem for the kind of reader it needs to organize "reverberation" rather than to relish it. But, in a mere inversion of the quite witting failure to see the sunrise at the close of *The Prelude*, *The Waste Land* is clear that, despite the promise of rain, the "plain" behind the poem's speaker is, at the end, still "arid" (425), even in the mythic replication schema. The point has not been to fertilize the mythic landscape anyway so much as to escape the Romantic one that coexists uncomfortably with it throughout the poem. Indeed, the poem's hope for a mythically redemptive rain is another sign that it has failed to relieve the dark gloom that signifies Romanticism. London Bridge is, after all, "falling down" (427). Rather than a literary triumph or failure, what we witness is the petrification of a modernist myth that is finally less interested in negotiating its anxiously enabling modes of influence than in finding an authority to be had by moving away from the determinations of language and literature altogether. Despite—because of— his confessed late Romanticism, Eliot has already reorganized his library as a critic by banning Milton and his heirs from tradition, dealing wishfully with a problem that the poem now maintains is extralinguistic rather than the result of the poetic belatedness it tries to repress as its real motive force. Though the poem strains, like Arnold's verse, to begrudge all mediation, it can only do so as a function of the tradition it has rearranged despite the unsatisfactoriness of such a procedure. The very moment of "Damyata" or control that shows us that, at last, "The boat responded" (419) is itself mired in the tradition whose repetitions Eliot wishes to avoid. At poem's end, Eliot is once again the Miltonic Fisher-poet of *Lycidas*, salvaging watery corpses in what is perhaps really an elegy rather than an epic. Eliot's implication in the system of English elegy even robs him of the godlike authority he has taken on earlier, since the Miltonic allusion also replaces the Eliotic speaker with Milton himself as the poem's pilot, another instance of why Eliot builds his defensive myths in the first place.

Hence literary ironies dog the poem at its metaphysical conclusion. Eliot's final note, translating the poem's Sanskrit "shantih," is still another instance of the kind of perpetual wake or recall of literary murmur that surfaces when one tries most to escape it. "The Peace which passeth understanding," as Eliot translates "shantih," following traditional biblical usage in his predictable Orientalism, is, alas, precisely the term Wordsworth uses in *The Prelude* (XIV:126–27) to describe a project not dissimilar to Eliot's, although one easily confused with it: the attempt to find the identical rhetorical ideal, "that peace / Which passeth understanding," one that for Wordsworth, however, is only in a tentative and metaphorical relation to "Holy Writ" proper (*Prelude* XIV:125). And not (already contra Eliot) because Wordsworth's poem lacks the authority of Scripture, but because Scripture may well lack the authority of Romantic imagination.

The single certain claim this strategically unsuccessful quest can make at its close is that, as the speaker puts it, "These fragments I have shored against my ruins" (431). Ironically, however, the "fragments" and the "ruins" are the same thing—the burdens of tradition that ruin imagination to the point of its fragmentation, and of which the tropology of fragmentation is but a projection. The poem's self-proclaimed shards are not fragments anyway, but parts of the larger, continuous signifying chains of which they are metonymies. Eliot's fragments in short are really only excerpts. And excerpts are not fragments, suggesting instead the continuity of the tradition from which they are taken. To maintain that the systems of culture need repair by dint of exercising the reader in their easily available complexities is, by definition, to put such a claim into question by virtue of the means of its articulation. The attempted repair is itself a failed imaginative fiction. Nothing is broken to start with, and that is Eliot's problem—not a world in ruins, but an imagination weakened by too much influence. The continuity of tradition often suggested to be the true affirmation of Eliot's apparently crisis-ridden verse is in fact what most assails it, and which it wishes to disrupt since it cannot conquer it. Much as Arnold's claim that Wordsworth and Byron have "no style" ironically removes the objects to which his remarks are directed, Eliot's constant claim that culture is troubled is made available to us only by means of what turns out to be a quite untroubled culture, at least on the evidence of the relative aplomb with which the poem's dialogical machinery may be variously handled. Eliot's influential ethos of such apparent difficulty in the writing and reading of modern literature does not correspond to its accompanying assertion that the modernist poet must force his meaning because meaning is harder to come by in the present than in the past (Eliot 1921:289). Such polemical difficulty actually makes the reality of the connectedness suppos-

edly lost all the more real the moment one begins reading the poem in the
ways it requires.

The Waste Land, then, can appeal to a set of feelings and beliefs in its
reader only insofar as it has succeeded in putting them there. With the wit of
the irony it consciously lacks, the poem thus becomes but another symptom of
a frustrated will to modernity in its raw, non-self-accounting form. Though
Eliot's repression of his literary problems is an acknowledgment of their exigencies, the poem itself, like the essays, is nonetheless insufficiently reflexive to
account for the predicament that both generates and consumes it.

Art and Ideology in the *Four Quartets*

By the time of the full publication of the *Four Quartets* in 1944, Eliot had, of
course, long been overtly religious, his conversion to the Church of England
coming just five years after the publication of *The Waste Land*. His poetics
become in the process no longer even the functionally dialogical poetics that
inform "Tradition and the Individual Talent" and that *The Waste Land* both
uses and represses. Now Eliot's poetics rest instead on an appeal, no longer to
the tradition that a younger Eliot deemed the single field of both literary
meaning and poetic authority despite the attendant frustrations, but to the
authority of a frankly divine agency whose truths the writer simply transcribes
as though a prophet new inspired. Northrop Frye both links and distinguishes
Eliot and Arnold from just such a point of view: "In Matthew Arnold's conception of culture, religion is a cultural product, a part of which culture is the
whole; hence the human value of a religion lies mainly in its worldliness. In
Eliot religion forms a third level above human society" (1963:12). Denis
Donoghue, too, insists that "for such a poet language is the only possible
home" (1974:197) and that, at least in *The Waste Land*, Eliot does "not call
another world in judgment upon the words" (193). The case is far different in
the *Four Quartets*, a case that "marks the transition" in the exemplary Leavis's
switch, according to Donoghue, from "a criticism of Eliot mainly appreciative
and a criticism mainly diagnostic" (1981:75). Leavis, concludes Donoghue,
came to feel that Eliot failed "to understand, as Blake understood, that a poet
gains his strength from the language," not from an appeal to "eternal reality"
(77, 76). Since Eliot's enduring will to modernity cannot be satisfied by an
agon with Romantic tradition, he will not only remove himself from the

landscape of the "tower" in *The Waste Land,* but go on to turn away from the exigencies of language altogether in the *Four Quartets.*

Notorious as it is, Eliot's later criticism (one need not repeat the unwholesome self-definitions in *For Lancelot Andrewes* [1928]) is even franker than Arnold's in its addiction to the transcendent. So defensive had Eliot become about his earlier lucidity that his 1964 preface to a reprint of *The Use of Poetry* (1933) carries with it "the faint hope that one of these lectures may be taken instead of *Tradition and the Individual Talent* by some anthologist of the future" (1933/1964:9). After his vicissitudes about Arnold, especially the link drawn with Pater in 1930, Eliot returns again to the more forthright estimate of his continuity with Arnold displayed in the Introduction to *The Sacred Wood:* "he discovered a new formula," says Eliot; "poetry is not religion, but it is," in the well-known words, "a capital substitute for religion" (1933:26). Only one slight step separates them, and Eliot will quickly close the gap. "For Arnold the best poetry supersedes both religion and philosophy" (1933:113). For Eliot himself, however, "nothing in this world or the next is a substitute for anything else" (this from a poet who uses metaphor), "and if you find that you must do without something, such as religious faith or philosophic belief, then you must just do without it" (1933:113). Not wishing to "do without something," Eliot has become plainly devout and less plainly poetic, even to the point of underwriting a belief in "an index of prohibited books," an idea "perfectly sound in principle" (136*n*).

After Strange Gods (1934) makes the position of the later Eliot noxiously clear. Two key terms in his criticism are in fact redefined there so as to distance his early work, even *The Waste Land,* as much as possible from faith and the corresponding relaxation in poetic principle it allows, perhaps entails. First, "tradition" is reassessed; no longer the "tradition" of language and literature to which the writer comes late as in "Tradition and the Individual Talent," it is now "all those habitual actions, habits and customs . . . which represent," in a strangely Lawrentian and/or protofascist trope, "blood kinship" (18). The advantage to be had from the redefinition is clear: less responsibility toward language, more toward belief in unquestioned ground. Second in the reassessment is the substitution of the term "orthodoxy" for the old term "classicism" (22). "As we [now] use the term *tradition* to include a good deal more than [even] 'traditional religious beliefs,' so I am here giving the term *orthodoxy* a similar inclusiveness" (22). The ground is now set. The religious poet of "Ash-Wednesday" and after even tells us at the start of that transitional poem, "I do not hope to turn"—to trope—"again." No longer a poet of language, Eliot now refuses to address what the 1930 poem is at least willing to call "our exile," preferring instead to "cry" "unto Thee" alone.

It is no wonder, then, that the homiletic tendencies of the latter part of *The Waste Land* become manifest in the *Four Quartets*; nor is it surprising that the later Eliot, now relieved of the anxiety of belatedness by stepping outside the tradition he once considered determinate, is at last free enough from his earlier agonistic "fear" to act out in summary form the fluctuating arguments his career has provided. The rhetorical dangers of the past no longer trouble Eliot, since, having now removed himself from the field of tradition, he no longer feels bound by the rules of what he calls the "pathology of rhetoric" in *The Sacred Wood* (1920:30). Helen Gardner is entirely unapologetic when she endorses the poem's thoroughgoing "doxology" (1950:15); even subsequent critics are far too generous in noting a free play of language in a poem designed to stifle the play of language altogether (Gregory Jay 1983; see, by contrast, William V. Spanos's antithetical reading of the *Quartets*, 1978).

The poem's four-part structure is in itself misleading, since parts I to III only summarize the habitual contradictions in Eliot's language in an oscillating repetition of them, with part IV serving as an epilogue or coda describing the ideal place beyond culture that the poem will have supposedly reached—peace with the dead, especially the literary dead, since Eliot's repressed Romanticism, despite the denial of the tower in *The Waste Land*, appears to be endemically wounding, the enduring reason for escape from its scholarly rigors. Eliot begins with the assertion of a realm beyond time and history that cannot, of course, logically be said to exist, nor can it be properly articulated by any manner of poetic figuration. The "end"—the "one end"—of "time" is, as the will to modernity wishes it to be, "always present." Eliot's posture is now a contradiction rather than a fruitful paradox. How can "one end," or even another—by definition points of closure that presume a past that is now absent—be also "always present"? The figure cannot be reduced to an oxymoron that suggests the rhetorical interdependence of the notions of closure and eternity, since its components are identified rather than opposed. This "end" is, of course, still assailed as an ideal by the Romantic ironies that have already required Eliot to retire from the landscape of the tower in *The Waste Land*. But so alienated from tradition has Eliot thereby become that its rules, like the rules of language at large, have become too strenuous to manage, even "rudely."

No matter, though, since language in the later Eliot is what it is in Arnold the essayist—the transparent instrumentality by which universal truths outside it may make their way to men. If there is an "end," there is, as Eliot starts to layer his hymn early on, also a beginning, a "garden," though one already full of "echoes"—Eliot's cautious admission that, strictly speaking, all such primacies are contaminated because they are actually installed after the fact. Indeed, Eliot is evidently free enough of his old anxieties to describe their aetiology in the belatedness that he can now overcome by faith, having failed to do so within language. Still, his enabling vocabulary remains Romantic in a reflexive example of why he abandons the cost of using it. Though he claims, for example, not to "follow / The deception of the thrush"—the "reminiscent bells" of tradition—he nonetheless proceeds immediately to pluck a metaphor again from the opening lines of Keats's first *Hyperion* ("the dead leaves"; Keats's "the dead leaf"), doubling the way he invokes Chaucer to ruin the opening of *The Waste Land* in order, paradoxically, to enable it. There is also an equivalent inversion of the initiating allusion that is similar to the standing of Romantic tradition on its head in the late stages of the earlier poem. In Keats, it is the Titans who grow extinct, not the leaves. Through his misreading, Eliot thereby kills off time in order to maintain power, the reverse of what Keats knows he cannot do. This is precisely the antithetical assertion that Eliot cannot live with in *The Waste Land*, bound as he is to traditional requirements until he releases himself from the strictures of the tower by poem's end. Indeed, it is a recapitulation of those strictures that we suddenly see early in the *Four Quartets* in a compact version of *The Waste Land's* largely Romantic landscape—"the empty alley," "the drained pool." Eliot even mixes the metaphors of barrenness and gloom that form separate tropological systems in *The Waste Land*, but that are now (despite the scholarly sloppiness the mixture entails epistemologically) apparently designed to signify synonymously rather than antithetically a lack of religious faith that the frustrations of Romantic tradition can only abet. Though we are still mired in the tropological rubble or "clot" of influence, remarks the poet, it no longer seems to matter.

Hence the sudden intrusion of the familiar ideal, the first appearance of the legendary "still point of the turning world" that the poem will not so much earn as take for granted from the start. This is the core myth of the poem—the absolute arrest of the (really Paterian) interval, the freezing of the temporal vortex whose mediations have, in *The Waste Land*, thwarted the absolute that Eliot seeks. Nor does Eliot seem to mind the wake of Pater's (and Yeats's) language as it litters the poem even in its figuration of the divine ideal as "white light" or "the dance."

But lest we overestimate the degree to which Eliot has moved away from the memory of his Romantic enablement, we should continue to note the extent to which he readily admits its ineluctability even in the fullness of faith. Hence Eliot gives us the belated preconditions that make his ideals impossible straightaway, although they are presented in a manner that again reverses the situation to his advantage, now by simply asserting the ideal in order to cancel his distance from it through sheer will:

> Except for the point, the still point,
> There would be no dance. . . .

The figure is an implicit chiasmus that can thereby be turned about again and again, making difference rather than fixity its true epistemological yield. Like Pater's deconstruction of Arnold's ideal through the metaphor of music, Eliot allows that anything "still" is to be produced only by a relation to movement. There is neither one without the other. So begins a series of logical inversions that the poem grows increasingly fond of using, although too often with insufficient rigor, hence symptomatically rather than successfully. While Eliot wants something outside of time, he knows—like Milton—that things are in "place" only "in time." Thus a merely pedantic Eliot asks us not to call his ideal "fixity," even though it is. Only overcompensation can account for such a warning in the first place. It is in fact no warning at all, but a blunt negation of what the poem—and "Tradition and the Individual Talent"—wishes to be true despite all the admissions to the contrary. Not only do "the dance" and the "still point" exist only in relation to one another no matter the simultaneous claim for the "one end" that is "always present." The ideals in question are also figured through an unworkable melding of Arnold and Pater in the phrase "concentration/Without elimination"—an *ascesis* that cannot exercise its defining power of "rejection . . .," as Pater calls it in "Style" (1889:13). Such a process is, of course, a contradiction rather than a paradox. Paterian "concentration" requires precisely the scholarly rejection or "elimination" of certain aspects of waste or influence as the writer's means of asserting a modicum of identity in a vortex whose elements, in Arnold's case especially, are incompletely sifted, and so tend to drown the poet's possibility of separate identity.

And yet no sooner does Eliot lapse into such wish-fulfillment than he turns about, just as easily, to explain why such a "still point" is, after all, an impossible ideal: "Only in time," says an honest Eliot, "can the moment . . . Be remembered." That Pater still follows Eliot, especially when it comes to the scholarly exactitude of one's metaphors, is especially clear when we suddenly see the ideality begin to collapse once life is viewed as "only a flicker."

The "flicker," reminiscent as it is of what the gemlike flame does in the Conclusion to *The Renaissance*, thereby thrusts us back into the familiar waste land of "unwholesome lungs" pocked by "dessication," "evacuation," and "inoperancy." The figure "flicker" is, as it turns out, a sign for or instance of the anxiety-begetting influence that produces the landscape of waste in the first place. Indeed, "Words move, music moves/Only in time." Eliot admits, too, that "the end precedes the beginning," much as the "still point" precedes the "dance." Things "will not," as the poem readily reports, "stay in place." Thus the frank, though momentary, representation of the vortex ("Shrieking voices"), with "Desire itself" a "movement," too. "Love," however, is suppos- edly (and wittily) "unmoving," even though movement is both its "cause" and "end." Existence at large is a "shaft of sunlight," another allusion to Pater (1888:133) that reflexively suggests the extent to which Eliot now voices his ideals in open opposition to what prohibits their realization.

Despite the narrator's seeming distance, the second section of the poem grows troubled about the temporal inevitabilities of language and tradition to which the first has so serenely admitted, rendering them frustrations and annoyances now, and, in turn, rendering the poem itself a hidden dialectic meant to abreact the Romantic realities from which Eliot's faith has distanced him. "East Coker," that is, exposes an enduring anxiety that "Burnt Norton" has apparently misrepresented as allayed. In a landscape understandably like *The Waste Land's*, Eliot now pontificates about what problems really beset him, chief among them literary history or tradition in his original sense (stanza one), and the accompanying fact that its wake or "haze"—the Arnoldean word for "influence"—"Is absorbed, not refracted." This is, of course, just the modernist problem, the problem of "concentration/Without elimination." Reminding us again of his defensive myth of our supposed fall from the Spenserian festival of "daunsinge" and "commodious sacrament," Eliot wishes as a result to obliterate temporality altogether by identifying the "rhythm" of dance with the transcendent rhythms of the seasons and the stars.

But again the tropology of late Romantic landscape disturbs the procure- ment of Eliot's ideal by insisting on the reality of belatedness. It is now "late November," and in asking why November gloom seems linked "With the disturbance of spring" ("April is," after all, "the cruellest month"), Eliot finally tells us, however indirectly, that the arid waste land of his earlier poem is really the flipside of the Romantic or "November" belatedness that motivates it as a compensatory myth. The nature of the burden is now clear; it is, of course, the "vortex," "the intolerable wrestle/With words and meanings."

No wonder things are "dark dark dark." The myth of the waste land is really the poet's projection of his own imaginative difficulties onto the world: "there is no one to bury," says a momentarily Hardyesque Eliot. The undead of influence still haunt the living, vampirelike, even here. There is, therefore, only "a hollow rumble of wings"; the dove or Muse is not yet ready to redeem Eliot, since the power of poetic voice is admittedly crippled no matter his desire or ambition to be whole. "You say I am repeating," says an Eliot who is indeed repeating himself at what becomes the poem's real moment of crisis. To be a poet is to be in a dizzying state of "echoed ecstasy / Not lost, but requiring." How does Eliot manage to get out of this familiar trap when the demands of tradition are, as always, absolute in their disallowance of absolutes as such?

The montage maintains the mood of lamentation—"Our only health is the disease." Still neglectful, however, of the opportunity presented by such exemplary paradox, and so still treating it only as a restriction, Eliot remains in crisis as he continues to repress the Oedipal structure of poetic dependence and desire even when he falls into a figuration that expresses it: we "Die of the absolute parental care / That will not leave us, but prevents us everywhere." What is lacking is the sense of the independence with which loss or prevention normally, if ironically, responds in order to fill the lack it generates. Like Arnold's Empedocles, however, Eliot seems ready to capitulate entirely to the anxiety of belatedness, reading it only as prevention and not as possibility. And to exacerbate the problem, two doubly systematic images suddenly collide that foreshadow the poem's concluding line: "the flame" and the "roses." The "flame" and the "roses" are, of course, Pater's two most famous tropes, although they are also—as Pater himself well knew—figures for Christian trial and redemption whose resonance Eliot wishes here to be stronger than the Paterian echoes with which they are inextricably mingled. But while the poem's language identifies the antagonistic idealities of Christianity and aestheticism, Eliot's subsequent assertion moves swiftly to insure no such contamination in his universal symbolism: "The dripping blood" of Christ is "our only drink"—not the once authoritative ink of tradition. "The bloody flesh" is in turn "our only food." Eliot maintains the dominance of the Christian layer of meaning in his figure, then, by repressing the Paterian layer beneath it in another reflexive example of how his unstinting will to modernity derives from a refusal to accept the Paterian scholarship that is the only real solution to the difficulties at hand.

So unenthusiastic is Eliot about Paterian scholarship, however, that he can seriously make the familiar modernist claim—entirely defensive in its patent reversal of what is true, and reflexively confirmed in its antithetical relation to

Pater's "Style"—that writing is "a raid on the inarticulate/With shabby equipment always deteriorating." It is therefore pointless for Eliot to compete with "men whom one cannot hope/To emulate"—one's precursors. And if, as Eliot suddenly announces, "there is no competition," then he has simply withdrawn, as *The Waste Land* has already suggested, from the agon with tradition with which his career began. To be sure, "There is only the fight to recover what has been lost," but that is only the defense speaking, another way of denying the reality of tradition (nothing at all has been lost) by reasserting the desire for lost origins that literature proper forbids because it is its cause. Thus Eliot can only move more and more closely here to a Christian rather than poetical conclusion as he removes himself more willingly and wittingly than in the earlier poem from the system of literature itself, his text materially a part of it while its intent resides beyond it.

The poem must somehow find a way out of its crisis, however, once we reach its midpoint with "The Dry Salvages." This third section, though, is, as we have already suggested, actually its resolution, with the fourth little more than a reprise. Thus in part III the vortex that burdens the poet in part II gets apostrophized as another Eliotic river that, like the Thames, "tosses up our losses" as waste or rubbish—as the influence that weakens us by exposing our repetitiveness. Indeed, Eliot is now unusually direct. He not only goes on to recapitulate the seasonal sequence at the start of *The Waste Land*, but in the process includes just that decisive Romantic season absent in the earlier calendar: the autumn of belatedness that is now grudgingly admitted to be potentially bountiful as well as inhibitive in, for example, Keats's decadent imaginative harvest ("grapes on the autumn table"). With tradition so admitted, Eliot will now also dramatize his (wishful) exit from its burdens by actually extending rather than contracting the visionary figures by which he has already begun to step away from the tower in *The Waste Land*. In the *Four Quartets*, the tolling bells are no longer "reminiscent," but prophetic of something earlier than the golden age itself: "a time/Older than the time of chronometers," a time before or beyond culture, the very site of modernist desire, a place that is, however impossibly, "an end to the drifting wreckage" of the otherwise inescapable past.

Like the posing of the question of "roots" in *The Waste Land*, however, such overt wishfulness here must prompt a similar question: "Where is there an end"? Eliot the realist admits that there is "no end, but addition," only haze upon haze—the history of distortions that Arnold has tried to eradicate so as to possess the origin, and that Pater has instead shown to be productive of the thing it hides. So perilous is the poet's vortical situation that "there is no end of it" because of influence—"the voiceless wailing, / No end to the withering of withered flowers." Hence Rimbaud's "drifting boat" in the tides of intertextuality becomes a sign for the belated poet amid an Arnoldean flood. The image also suggests our constitutional inability to "think of a time that is oceanless" (sure ground without such tides, even if that is un-tidy), "Or of an ocean not littered with wastage." Eliot's rhetorical keenness has reawakened. Much as the ocean of influence is "littered with" a "wastage" that contaminates its purity in the second figure, so, too, does the first figure contaminate the primariness we might assign to either of its terms because of their reciprocal relation to one another. In both cases, the figures are in the service of a desire for the kind of primacy that their articulation prohibits. This is, however, as far as Eliot will go. Again the challenge of belatedness is discarded as though it were only a difficulty: we can only "restore . . . ," says an unsatisfied Eliot—implicitly formulating a structure of deferred action that is not good enough—"experience / In a different form. . . ."

Once the paradoxes begin to mount up as part III reaches its peak—"Time the destroyer is time the preserver," and so on—Eliot, however, may seem at last ready to negotiate the rhetorical impasse such apparently calculated figures imply. And yet, astonishingly enough, Eliot will again refuse to execute the salutary implications of such paradoxes by refusing to admit, as Pater or Freud do, their rhetorically constitutive rather than empirically inhibiting possibilities. Eliot even wonders momentarily whether the divine Krishna had in mind an unacceptable if inevitable deferred action ("The way up is the way down") in a theology finally too tentative for Eliot's iron will to modernity.

With retreat the only route left, Eliot can at best offer some equally familiar idealist countermoves: the assertion of "a voice" "not in any language " whose primitive, primal source represents (in a figuration ironic on the face of it) the original he seeks. Though he knows such an original is forbidden by the nature of the rhetoric he will strategically use to produce it, Eliot will nonetheless present it as the recovered center. After all, it is the "lawful traffic" of "ships" and "fish" that Eliot desires, probably more, as it turns out, than he desires strictly or officially literary authority. The meaning of "lawful" is now far from unclear. "Fish" tilts the figure toward a Christian symbolism that alone is "lawful" in Eliot's eyes, a symbolism that can link all his figures univocally and so point the way to the sacraments of a church of universal truth that even poetry is not worthy (not able) to express given its duplicitous rhetorical requirements and the ironic phantasms or vampires that serve as its burlesque originals.

The poem's core ideality is therefore suddenly announced rather than demonstrated: "to apprehend / The point of intersection of the timeless / With time. . . ." As the poet already knows, however, such an "intersection" is functional only rhetorically (and always absent empirically) because neither time nor timelessness can exist without the other. To speak of their intersection is to speak tautologically. Though now the poem appears to parade such generative paradoxes as "The Dry Salvages" begins to conclude ("music," for example, "heard so deeply / That it is not heard at all"), these figurations are not paradoxes at all, but catachreses—false paradoxes that result in semantic confusion rather than in the relief of poetic anxieties. This is again the language of homily rather than of literature. With one last gesture, to be sure, Eliot recalls the Romantic genealogy of his ideals, "driven" as they are "by daemonic, chthonic / Powers." Eliot still, however, wishes to promote as absolutely as he can the transcendental primacy he believes he has found despite his admission of its deferred means of production. What remains is the hope of the "prayer" the poem now recommends as the only way to secure the admittedly "impossible union" of early and late, first and fallen.

With the third and actually resolving portion of the poem having announced resolutions good enough for its extraliterary conscience, the fourth, "Little Gidding," recapitulates both Eliot's ideals and his better wisdom. On the one hand, then, we can find a rational assessment of the ironic belatedness within which Eliot remains implicated as a modern writer, even though he brackets it: "Midwinter spring is its own season," the unnatural season of the belated imagination's recombination of old and new alike. On the other hand, we also find the equally irrational assertion of faith despite the rhetorical difficulties it presents: time's real "covenant" is not, says an escapist Eliot, "in the scheme of generation" at all. Outside both history and biology, Eliot's ideal resides in a timeless absolute or primal state in which "It would be the same at the end of the journey" no matter the otherwise determining point of departure. Despite all in Eliot himself that makes such a claim untenable, his authority has by now become so plainly theological that even the pious ending of *The Waste Land* pales next to the subsequent imperative here: "You," says Eliot to his reader, "are here to kneel."

"The Dry Salvages" goes on to repeat the movement of both *The Waste Land* and the *Four Quartets* itself by revisiting the four elements of life— "air," "earth," "water," and "fire"—as Eliot dramatizes a transcendence over sense as theologian if not as poet. Indeed, Eliot now feels so free of his Romanticism that he can remember, without anxiety, "the sudden look of some dead master" that once constrained—and so impelled—his desires, even the whole tradition rolled into a single shade: "a familiar compound ghost."

Eliot briefly acknowledges, too, the lingering lesson of "Tradition and the Individual Talent"—that it is the later poet who makes the earlier one. But having removed himself from the landscape of the tower in favor of the plain of faith, Eliot is blithe about the agon of influence itself: "Knowing myself yet being someone other—/ And he a face still forming." Eliot will not, as a poet at least, finish forming such a face himself, rearranging the canon with his essays perhaps, but merely smashing it up some with his verse. He can now also admit the contradictions that have consistently structured his stance by their very inconsistency: "So I assumed," he says, "a double part."

We are due a formal peroration here, and we are about to get it as the poem ends by surrendering entirely to religious rather than aesthetic principles. "All shall be well," says Eliot, making his newly empowering Mosaic ventriloquism a refrain as the poem concludes. Now the "dove" can unfurl its curtailed power, no longer a gull but the Holy Spirit proper, even though it "breaks the air" by means of a distinctly Paterian "flame of incandescent terror" whose aesthetic figuration not only diverts its manifestly religious intent, but almost flamboyantly calls attention to its literary genealogy from Milton to Yeats and Hart Crane. While such Paterian "associations" reflexively exemplify Eliot's anxiety about a tradition—and a language—that cannot speak transparently or originally, Eliot knows that his Arnoldean exit from it can never be complete no matter the earnestness of his withdrawal. Indeed, he is remarkably candid about the regularity of his contradictory stances—though "every word is at home" when the ideal is achieved, every word is nonetheless also in "its place to support the others." Home—fixity, primacy—is the ironic, because belated, function of a relation rather than the showing forth of an essence. With his rhetoric again sharp, a surprisingly Paterian Eliot even admits that "We are born with the dead," and that they "return, and bring us with them."

Achieving his modernist myth of primacy as he undercuts its possibility in a pattern of fluctuation early and late, Eliot concludes by claiming he can see "the children in the apple-tree" (they presumably do not eat), complete with an assertion of the immediacy the recovery of such resonantly figured innocence also entails: "now, here, now always—/ A condition of complete simplicity." Though we "know the place for the first time" only because we "arrive where we started," such deferred action can, somehow, coexist with the absolutes it forbids. At poem's end, Eliot allows his Christianity to be overtly flecked by the rhetoric of Pater's suspect aestheticism by remarking at the text's very close: "the fire and the rose are one." Unlike Arnold, Eliot at least remains, in the final instance, balefully aware that his modernist desire, theological late, classicist early, is perpetual captive to any of the various means he may use to express it. Even Frye's decidedly Christian reading of the poem (1963:72ff.) is cautioned not only by his remark that Eliot's place within Romanticism cannot be overlooked (98), but also that "one cannot both accept tradition and decide what it is to be" (99). Blackmur, too, was troubled by "the problem of the moral and technical validity of Mr. Eliot's Christianity as it labors to seize the actual for representation in his poetry" (1952:165); indeed, "Mr. Eliot would prefer the advantage of a literal to that of an imaginative faith" (1952:172). Surely Paul Jay is too generous when he maintains that "Eliot's belief seems to control the representational problems he confronts in writing his poem" (1984:174).

Belatedness, of course, can also be transformed, in Pater's words, from a restriction into an opportunity, though we shall have to turn to Joyce and Bloomsbury to see how. What *The Waste Land* calls the "reminiscent bells" of tradition or belatedness place both Eliot and Arnold in the rather exact stance of the Freudian hysteric who, in the historical period that separates them, suffers, in Freud's selfsame word, from "reminiscences" as well (Freud and Breuer 1895). No treader of the loom, Eliot, like Arnold before him, is caught in the same modernist bind that Joyce will, by contrast, loosen with enormous wit and ease.

"Double Writing" in *Dubliners*

We can now begin to see how the difference that separates Arnold from Pater also separates Eliot from Joyce, and so produces two divergent lines of High Modernism in English at large, each with considerable and enduring influences of its own. As a proleptic example, compare the difference between the title *The Waste Land* and a key joke and pun-system in *Ulysses*, the term "throwaway" (1922:86). The latter is a polyvalent term for what Leopold Bloom takes to be the newspaper he is about to throw away, but which his friend Bantam Lyons overinterprets as a tip on the name of a horse running that day in the Ascot race. For Eliot, on the other hand, waste signifies what is barren and lost because it is really the sign of the dialogical reality of the precedents and protocols of English poetry that Eliot, as modernist, wishes, like Arnold, to repress—the reality of influence. But if waste or influence is wishfully invisible for Eliot, for Joyce it is, by contrast, not an Arnoldean restriction but a Paterian opportunity. For Joyce, the waste of influence is not to be flushed or repressed, but used, as Pater recommends in "Style." Neither stance is, by implication, as much a response to the world as it is to the conditions of influence under which each labors as a modernist. In kindred opposition, the punning title of Joyce's early volume of poems, *Chamber Music* (1907), anticipating Bloom's first appearance in *Ulysses*, simultaneously signifies the activities of, say, string quartets with those of the chamberpot. The pun's importance is less a function of the conventional Freudian reduction, for example, of identifying art with excrement than it is of the reflexive weight of its exemplification. For Joyce conflates at the level of the structure of language itself—the structure of structures that makes the pun possible—the products of classical or high art and the products of daily life. The waste of modern civilization and imagination alike (their difference will soon be elided in any case) is precisely its richness, much as, reflexively, the waste of influence is, for Joyce, fertilizing rather than distasteful. Moving us from Pater's mausoleum to what he will call "the green grave" in *Ulysses* (50), Joyce works through, rather than acts out or represses, the metaphor of organic decay that distinguishes rhetorically what is quite properly called the literature of the decadence, with Pater, of course, at its head in English. If Eliot's habitual strategy, or lack of it, is to short-circuit or repress the temporal means of his literary production in order to secure the static ideals they put in question, then Joyce's is precisely the reverse. Joyce's is a Paterian rather than an Arnoldean project, and succeeds in taking fiction to the limit.

It almost goes without saying that Joyce will begin where Pater leaves off (Harry Levin long ago insisted on the centrality of Pater in Joyce's work [1941:25, 56]; see also Hélène Cixous 1968); and that his argument with Eliot (an implicit one, to be sure) will surface most exactly when we examine Eliot's (mis)reading of *Ulysses* against what Joyce's text actually does to such reifying treatments of it. Joyce's most recognizable language, already nascent in *Dubliners* (1914), is a wild(e) Paterian scholarship that makes both overt and dynamic what Eliot wishes to repress in "The Function of Criticism," and, by implication, what generates the discourse of all supposedly fixed referents: that all criticism—all reading, all signification—is already interpretation anyway. If the title of the first section of *The Waste Land* represents the wishful will to modernity incarnate—"The Burial of the Dead"—the title of the last chapter of *Dubliners* is instead the will to modernity recognized as such—"The Dead" undead, the anxiety of modern enablement dramatized by *Dubliners* as a whole, and, by book's end, distanced and assessed in preparation for the strategies of the Joyce of the *Portrait* (1916), *Ulysses* (1922), and *Finnegans*

Wake (1939). No wonder, then, the customary lore about *Dubliners*—the paralysis of its world and the consequent desire for freshness or regeneration it prompts in its parade of defensive Romantic fantasies of exotic escape to balmy warmth, whether among seamen or in the American West ("An Encounter"); in tropical romance ("Eveline"); or in the pathetic romanticism of "Araby." It is, of course, the "twilight greyness" of northern Romanticism, as De Man puts it, that calls up the contrastingly "sunlit noonday landscape of Mediterranean poets," or poets of the origin (1984:132). With all three examples ones of ultimate frustration, such a catalogue becomes one of symptoms, suggesting the plain extent to which Joyce is no victim of his late Romanticism, but is in fact so explicit about the typology of lament and desire it entails that it is fair to say that the will to modernity is itself the subject of *Dubliners* rather than its motive force. Joyce has already superseded the anxiety that places him within tradition by virtue of being able, especially so early, to represent its terms rather than to capitulate to mere expressions of them.

The novel even renders its world in a way that represents living itself as a belated condition. Dublin is figured as a series of representations, much as Wessex is, and Joyce's representation of such representations as the condition of both life and the art that represents it renders both in turn devoid of the originality we might otherwise assign to them. Like the traditions of language and literature to which Joyce comes late as a modern writer, the traditions of Dublin life are systems of precedent that determine destiny from before birth. Hence the paradigmatic repetition of the words from "the Euclid" and "the Catechism" in the book's opening paragraph (1914:9), as though Joyce wishes to alert us to the kinds of representative codes that mark out his hero's range of emotional capability, from "fear" to desire (9). That such a world is functionally a text as well becomes obvious once Joyce tells us how his hero "puzzled" his "head to extract meaning" from his uncle's "unfinished sentences" (11), or that the stranger in the second story acts out his obsessions as though "magnetised by some words of his own speech" (26). "The language of Dublin *is* the subject," says Hugh Kenner; Joyce's "books are about words" (1956:12); as a result, Kenner goes on to describe *Dubliners* itself as a kind of "double writing" (7ff.). Joyce's realism in *Dubliners* is, in other words, also reflexive. Story is a version of narration because the world of Dublin as Joyce represents it is already a function of the representations of which it is constructed.

Nor is the implicitly enduring characterization of *Dubliners* as a novel either novel or undue. "All these stories," remarks Kenner elsewhere, "are the one story rotated" (1971:39; see also Kenner 1956:48). With a categorically if not nominally consistent hero or heroine organizing a developmental trajectory of stories that moves from childhood through all the stages of life—and in all its social and sexual variety—*Dubliners* is actually a kind of communal *Bildungsroman*. To say so is to appear to produce a mixed metaphor, since such a characterization seems to combine, illogically, the structure of the individual with the structure of society. To ask, however, how the structure of the self can be allied with its apparent antagonist in the structure of society is to presume what Joyce himself does not—that the two categories are distinct, when, in fact, they are mutually interdependent phenomenologically as well as rhetorically. Though Joyce's protagonists are without proper names early in his series of portraits, their combined attributes eventually come to be gathered up in the composite and summary figure with whom the book culminates, the wonderfully resonant figure of Gabriel in "The Dead." By building such a locus as the tales accrue in Gabriel's exemplary character, Joyce actively impugns the sharp fixity or givenness of individual personality assumed by an Eliot who has nonetheless also demonstrated that such a personal inside is already a function of that outside to which it is customarily opposed. For Joyce, by contrast, it is just this interdependent relation—the production of an inside by an outside that necessarily precedes it and makes it belated preconditionally—that is the thematic counterpart to his reflexive stance as Paterian scholar in relation to language and tradition as a whole. Maintaining an extreme version of such reflexive realism even as late as the *Wake*, the early Joyce makes Gabriel emblematic of the fluctuating status of personal and literary authority alike, and so provides us with a kind of grammar, both representationally and reflexively, for the curve of his career to come after "The Dead."

Hence the structure of Gabriel's epiphany is far more than an exacerbation of the boy's sudden discovery of his vanity much earlier in "Araby." Gabriel is already compromised in a number of ways, and, as a writer, already a reflexive as well as a realistic vehicle for the kinds of Irish anxieties about the hegemony of English language and culture against which Miss Ivors's pedantic Romanticism is (like Yeats's enthusiasm for the Gaelic revival) mounted as an almost comic defense. For Gabriel, of course, such anxieties may be equally real, but they are also abundantly—and inexorably—ironic. Like Joyce himself, the English-speaking Gabriel knows no other language and never did, even though such native English is not native to him at all. Built into the conditions of life and letters alike, in other words, is the objective fact for all subjective realities in Joyce's manifestly Irish world that the system of language into which one is born and through which one feels and writes is, by the same token, not one's own at all. Like American English or any such colonial discourse, Irish English is, as a formation, belated in relation to an original that is itself absent. Much as Euclid and the Catechism are, domesticated though they may be, imports from the principal sites of Mediterranean origin the modernist distance from which they ironically signify, the English that Joyce must deploy as a writer is also an imported tradition, even though it replaces no functional original (thus the logic of Fritz Senn's contention that any reading of Joyce is a translation [1984]).

Compact in the paradox of Irish English, then, is a highly pressurized version of our customary modernist paradox: that the belated conditions that enable one also make one anxious, inhibit one in the act of empowering one. In Joyce's case, what may be largely metaphorical for our other writers is quite real as well. And it is through Gabriel, the vessel into which all the characteristics of those who have preceded him in the book are poured (here, too, Gabriel's lateness in appearing at the end of the narrative triply reflects the already doubly belated conditions of his status as both a man and as a writer), that Joyce will arrange the coordinates of his work to come, securing his own literary independence (unlike his hero) by means of the curious logic he finds in his dependence. The techniques of Paterian scholarship will not only be used to convert what is otherwise a prohibition into a new way of playing an old instrument; Joyce will, in "The Dead," also use Pater himself in a dynamically reflexive—and paradigmatic—instance of just such a conversion of inhibition into expression, prevention into cure.

What is remarkable about what may be called the primal scene that is the catalyst for Gabriel's famous epiphany in the closing paragraphs of "The Dead" is, ironically, that it is really someone else's. Gabriel fully expects the early memory that has moved Gretta to tears to be one of himself in the freshness of her desire for him in their youthful love. And yet Gabriel's extrapolated imagination of his wife's early desire is in fact contaminated by—indeed, usurped by, preceded by—the presence of someone else who has priority over him, an unexpected precursor discovered in the place supposedly reserved for him alone as the author of Gretta's original love: "While he had been full of memories of their secret life together, full of tenderness and joy and desire, she had been comparing him in her mind with another" (219). Joyce's devastatingly unexpected point is that the scene represents, not so much Gabriel's vanity, but precisely the lack of an identity to be vain about in, quite graphically, the first place. Gabriel is ousted from his own self-securing primal scene, no longer the begetter of Gretta's desire but merely a repetition of it. Already the thematic and reflexive depositary for literary and cultural estrangement from the systems of language and culture that empower him, Gabriel thereby suggests that alienation is not a distance from a real plenitude to be overcome, but the acknowledged precondition of both subjectivity in life and authority in literature.

Joyce's use of biblical / Miltonic allusion upon which the two Christian names of Gabriel and his usurper, Michael, pivot also confirms such a reversal of customary priorities. It is Gabriel who tells Adam about the past and Michael who tells him about the future. At the close of "The Dead," however, Gabriel's power to narrate the past is not only removed, foreclosing whatever claim to originality he may be said to have; it is also replaced by the voice of futurity in Michael that is, by the schedule of precedent, supposed to precede it in both the Bible and in *Paradise Lost* (for a catalogue of such precedents, see Walzl 1966). To make Michael prior to Gabriel—to make the voice of the future prior to the voice of the past it supposedly follows—is, as we shall see, not just to reconfirm the ironies of Gabriel's primal scene, but also to intimate the larger strategies to which Joyce will turn by the time of *Ulysses*.

The scene's reflexive counterpart, moreover, is that Gabriel's epiphany is, in addition to all the other lacks that distinguish it, also a repetition from the point of view of literary history. An apparently new or original vision, Joyce's is, however, also already someone's from the past, from the dead, too—Pater's. Unlike Eliot, Joyce not only thematizes belatedness, but also doubles its action at the level of narration as Gabriel enters the fullness of his epiphany in the book's penultimate paragraph. Moving on a grand and visionary scale unusual in Joyce, and virtually unique in *Dubliners* except perhaps for the parodies of such emotion in the book's symptomatic exotica, the celebrated passage is, as it turns out, largely a palimpsest of that difficult passage in the Conclusion to *The Renaissance* in which Pater dissolves the category of self under the name of reducing experience to pure subjectivity. Joyce intercepts this rift or double option in Pater, turning, as Pater himself does, the rhetoric of the ego into the rhetoric of what Eliot calls the Objective or Impersonal. Here is Gabriel at his epiphany, followed by the matching passage in Pater:

> The tears gathered more thickly in his eyes and in the partial darkness he imagined he saw the form of a young man standing under a dripping tree. Other forms were near. His soul had approached that region where dwell the vast hosts of the dead. He was conscious of, but could not apprehend, their wayward and flickering existence. His own identity was fading out into a grey impalpable world: the solid world itself

> which these dead had one time reared and lived in was dissolving and dwindling. [1914:223]

> At first sight experience seems to bury us under a flood of external objects, pressing upon us with a sharp and importunate reality, calling us out of ourselves in a thousand forms of action. But when reflexion begins to play upon those objects they are dissipated under its influence; the cohesive force seems suspended like a trick of magic; each object is loosed into a group of impressions—colour, odour, texture—in the mind of the observer. And if we continue to dwell in thought on this world, not of objects in the solidity with which language invests them, but of impressions, unstable, flickering, inconsistent, which burn and are extinguished with our consciousness of them, it contracts still further: the whole scope of observation is dwarfed into the narrow chamber of the individual mind. [1873:234–35]

Joyce repeats, microscopically, the Paterian images of fire ("flickering" by both accounts), and, macroscopically, the shared communion with, as Pater puts it in the paragraph before, that which "extends beyond us," including the dead (1873:234). Moreover, Gabriel's "generous tears" (223) repeat Marius's in the hours before the latter's death, both in the precision of its diction as well as in its familiar Paterian cadences, with Marius the particular original for Gabriel's quiet bleeding of self here. Even "the form of a young man"—of Michael Furey—"standing under a dripping tree" teases us (as do the number of figures at table in the story's dinner sequence) into identifying him as the implicit image of Jesus that cools Marius as the fever of death approaches. So ironic is the play of symbols, however, that Furey as a Christ figure is also canceled or put in question by the impossibility of such redemption or resurrection that his different function in Gabriel's (now post-) primal scene suggests instead.

Of course, it is precisely the "alien associations" of language's "broadcast" that account for the play of meanings in both passages. Gabriel's personality fades into the dead who have already usurped his primacy in the primal scene that precedes the vision proper, thus elaborating the argument in each passage that puts in question the difference between subject and object by loosening both into the larger forcefields of signification out of which subject and object emerge reciprocally rather than essentially. "That clear, perpetual outline of face and limb is but an image of ours," says Pater earlier in the Conclusion (1873:234), and Gabriel's epiphany has the pursuant result of acting out Pater to the letter. But if for Pater the result of the passage from the Conclusion is the fortification of self despite the alterity that produces it, for Joyce the result is instead the dissolution of the category of personality as such. Rather than battle ghosts in orthodox Oedipal fashion, or, like Eliot, repress the reality of such ghosts, Joyce simply unravels Gabriel's personality altogether, thereby evacuating the site such influence could make anxious in the first place. Recapitulating the paradoxical structure of Romantic revelation at large, Gabriel's epiphany represents the subject as a vessel of the kind of visionary experience that overwhelms subjectivity itself, and so ceases, like Woolf's Septimus Smith, to be a subject as a result of it. Joyce, in other words, defuses the anxiety of precedent by taking it at its word. Hence influence, particularly when it is Pater's injunction not to be influenced, is, ironically, turned back upon itself so as to undo the kinds of categories that may be said to absorb or repeat it.

Joyce's strategy, however, does more than simply disrupt the terms by which influence may be received. If it is the loss of personality that the influence of Pater reflexively requires a defensive Joyce to enact at the level of *récit* even as he dramatizes it at the level of Gabriel's *histoire*, Joyce's calculations also allow him a route out of Pater altogether by means of going on to follow him even more strictly, first in the *Portrait* and then, decisively, in *Ulysses*. For Joyce, language is not a transparent instrument designed to signify alinguistic truths, whether Arnoldean or Eliotic, but a palace of reverberation the scholarly Paterian art of which comes to distinguish more exactly than any other precedent formulation his exceedingly particular and ironically original achievement in *Ulysses* and, more ostentatiously, in the overdrive allowed the same kinds of procedures in the *Wake*. In *Ulysses*, moreover, Joyce will again repeat the Conclusion to *The Renaissance* when Stephen's Hamlet lecture explains just what it is that gives latecomers an ironic advantage over their precursors. The advantage—as even "Tradition and the Individual Talent" suggests, but which Eliot goes on to repress—lies in that perpetual production of the past by futurity that Joyce's inversion of his mythic materials at the end of "The Dead" already intimates. An exact analogue to the structure of deferred action, Michael, ordinarily the narrator of what succeeds the origins narrated by Gabriel, changes places with him instead, preempting his traditional position of discursive priority. "The Dead" is therefore cautionary rather than expressive, less a description of Gabriel's fatuity than of a deferred action that serves as a pedagogical instance for the relief of the anxiety of belatedness that *Ulysses* will be. The future, the later, thus assumes a logical if surprising power over a past that otherwise precedes it and so makes it anxious.

The future is the sole site of the past's enduring presence, its prior reality always a function of a narrative belated to it phenomenologically but precedent to it discursively.

Such an apparent evasion of the Oedipal paradox that defines the structure of modernism is, as we shall see, actually the shrewdest negotiation of it among all our writers. With the *Portrait*, Joyce will prepare the ground for *Ulysses* by dramatizing, both representationally and rhetorically, the almost absolute degree to which we are, to recall Trilling's words, implicated in a culture from which we therefore wish to be freed. *A Portrait of the Artist as a Young Man* is an exercise in the irony of such pervasive discipleship. It takes as its initial concern the belated emergence of the supposedly new, and as its final concern a deconstruction of the Arnoldean ideals repeated by a Stephen who will change completely in the subsequent *Ulysses*.

A Portrait of the Artist as Critic

Dubliners is, ironically, a less-influenced text than the later *Portrait*. In fact, the *Portrait* is Joyce's most Paterian text, almost flamboyantly burdened by a precise precedent in Pater's imaginary portraits, and so rendering its genealogy both conscious and exact. As a text, then, it functions as the reflexive counterpart to Stephen's sense of the burdensome precedents provided by the signs around him that constitute what world he has. As the pedagogical allegory of the novel's opening will suggest to us in a moment, the narrative as a whole is designed to question belief in the myths of personal and aesthetic liberation for which it is largely, as a mistaken rule, praised. After all, the book is customarily received as Joyce's decisive step forward after *Stephen Hero* (1907/ 1944) to a new, close-up method of narration that supposedly distinguishes the modern Joyce from the Victorian Joyce of the omnisciently told and largely discarded (if ever fully written) earlier book. By beginning, unlike *Stephen Hero*, not during Stephen's college years, but with early childhood sequences that supposedly render the primary in its selfsame tongue, the modernist *Portrait* begins, or so it seems, at the beginning in order to render Stephen's consciousness from its very start. And yet the leap forward to the *Portrait* is actually a profound—and profoundly overt—step backward from the point of view of the kind of influence that Stephen and Joyce alike are supposedly bent upon overcoming. In its stance a lengthy rewriting of Pater's first imaginary portrait, "The Child in the House" (1895b), the *Portrait* is also a virtual dictionary of the tropology of Pater at large. It is even marked by repetitions of instances from Pater's other imaginary portraits, especially one from "Emerald Uthwart" (1895c), in which the scene of the inscribed schoolroom desk in Cork in the *Portrait*—the theater in which Stephen's father searches for the trace of his own initials (1916:89–90)—finds its own apparent source or origin. The representation is itself—in an active or self-dramatizing exemplification of what it represents—something already written, even doubly so, since, like Simon Dedalus, Emerald, too, signs his name belatedly in the first place, on an old and scarred desk of prior usage. Even the diary form with which the book concludes—and which is usually read as a breakdown of generic form in favor of direct personal witness seeking no form but the real—returns us, in a perfect deflation of the diary's apparent symbolism, to another of Pater's imaginary portraits, "A Prince of Court Painters" (1887), told in just such diary form by a female narrator.

Hence the *Portrait*'s status as a narrative duplicates the belatedness that assails Stephen as a character. Joyce's apparently manifest project of mounting probably the most famous of all modernist flights from influence in English is, like the formal bravado that it already owes to Pater rather than to its own solitary inspiration, is in fact a virtually Gastonian tract on why Stephen's exemplary will to modernity is all wishfulness and irresponsibility, especially if Stephen wishes to be a writer. So secure is Joyce in contrast to Eliot that he will, in other words, actually allow himself to regress to the reflexive dramatization of influence—to an imitation of Pater—in order to establish the absurdity of seeking to overcome it by means of any mythology of liberation whatsoever—sexual, religious, even aesthetic, the three stages through which Stephen will pass. So profound is the imitation that it not only drew notice from Levin in 1941 (49–50, 56); it also prompted Richard Kain in 1947 to render the negative judgment that the *Portrait* is "more limited in scope" than Joyce's other work because "often self consciously literary in the vein of Walter Pater" (142). Demonstrating the irony that constitutes modernism as a structure rather than symptomatically expressing the will to modernity built to resist the reality of belatedness, the novel, not surprisingly, casts Stephen himself in the Arnoldean light of the late Romantic drained of belief and wanting in inspiration. After all, it is just such Arnoldean modernism that lies behind Stephen's wish to become the free modern artist, "soaring," as he puts it (225), beyond the "nets" of culture (203), although, as Kenner long ago reminded us, "we are not to accept the mode of Stephen's 'freedom' as the 'message' of the book" (1956:132). Such a wish is, to recall Trilling again, one of culture's most generous and appealing myths. It is, thereby, already an ironic version of the ideal that structures the *Portrait* at large and that undercuts its Arnoldean assertions even at its outset. The Daedalus/Icarus myth is in effect an antimyth anyway—it is, like "Sohrab and Rustum," an illustration of the son's weakness (believing so much in his father's powers as a craftsman, Icarus flies too close to the sun's strength), and so of the father's own ultimate failure despite his earlier success in constructing the labyrinth. Already a *renversement*, it is the myth itself that requires Joyce to exchange the names of father and son in the *Portrait*, a reversal whose yield will be made apparent in *Ulysses*.

The opening sketch of the baby Stephen seems, on the face of it, to be the very center of modernist success in its procurement, both thematically and formally, of the kind of early or primary moment that the will to modernity relishes in stance and style alike. Seemingly a vision of the world directly from the child's point of view, and so the vehicle for a new method of narration that supersedes its original in *Stephen Hero*, we may tend to respond to it with too eager an assent, satisfying as it seems to do the overriding modernist wish to have been there first, in the beginning, without the sorrows of influence. And yet this is probably the most symptomatic misrecognition in which we could possibly engage. The first page of the novel is, as Kenner pointed out in 1956 (116), hardly the discourse of a child at all; nor is it the record of a consciousness, since Stephen is only just beginning to come into being in the belated and preconditionally alienated fashion that Joyce has already mapped out for all subjects in *Dubliners*. In fact, of course, the opening of the *Portrait* is the recitation of a nursery rhyme, a rhyme that the infant Stephen hears, but which is told to him in his father's voice. Rather than a portrait of the self-reliant child whom the narrative discovers, the novel's opening actually presents the paternal voice reciting a traditional discourse whose ritual performance produces and determines the child from the start, indicating to us the place we will find Stephen, as though he were already there. The function of an inscription that assures his subjectivity as an effect of its determinations, Stephen is, not unlike Gabriel, already destined to be an aggregation or composite of influences that establish him by means of the very terms he will fruitlessly try to use later on as a means of breaking away from them.

Thus the paradox rather than the possibility of liberation for the citizen and the artist alike is immediately set out, confirming what the novel's plot will also tell us under the similar cover of appearing to fulfill the kind of modernist wish for the apprehension of a lost primacy both simulated and satirized in its opening paragraph. Authority doesn't so much oppress the individual from without as it helps to formulate the world within from the very beginnings of life—a world whose conditions thereby simultaneously strengthen and weaken the subject, and that produce in turn the defensive will to modernity compact in any desire for autonomy. As we shall see when we examine Stephen's childhood assumption of language in the retroactive light of his undergraduate theorizations, language is not, as the collegiate Stephen will wish, a transparent medium for the expression of original feelings; nor does language allow for the aesthetic unity the defensive myths of religion and vulgar aestheticism will alike assign to the work of presumably autonomous art. Ironically, the individual can resist the precedents that provoke him—can be willfully modern—only by virtue of the languages that oppress him (Joyce's enduring recourse, however burlesque, to the vocabulary of the sacrament he rejects is probably its most overriding example). Similarly, the work of art can be presumed to have an equivalent kind of autonomy only as an ironic function of its relation to tradition, and so, like the structure of the individual, must thereby relinquish any claim to real originality it may seem to possess.

Hence Stephen's desire for primacy in the various keys or registers of sex, religion, and art is, on the one hand, a sequence that replicates in large the teleology of each of its components, and so renders the novel the dialectically constructed *Bildungsroman* it seems to be (see, for example, Van Ghent 1953:331)—the consummate expression of a will to modernity that expects the plenitude of both personal and aesthetic liberation at the end of its quest. Like the classical novel of development, it does, to be sure, have as its realized goal the production of a coherent subjectivity in Stephen, even though it is, unlike the nineteenth-century *Bildungsroman*, a subjectivity articulated against rather than as an extension of precedent, both social and literary (also another way of reducing the possibility of rebellion by equating its structure with that of conformity). But while sex, religion, and art may be articulated dialectically, with the conflict between religion and the senses synthesized in the religion of art that emerges in chapter 5, they may also be articulated, quite contrastingly, as mere variations one upon the other. No system grants originality or revelation any more surely than another—save, perhaps, for the final illusion of original revelation in art to which Stephen eventually succumbs in the last chapter, and for which Joyce will chastise him before going on to change his critical vision entirely in *Ulysses*. Along with the dialectical romance by which Stephen's apparent progression through the influences of sex, religion, and art result in his new vocation as hieratic aesthete, the *Portrait* also gives us a set of metaphors designed instead to equate these otherwise distinct realms or components of life rather than to maintain them as separate. Thus Stephen's early sexual passion with the whore at the close of the second chapter is figured through metaphors of language that triplicates "brain," "lips," and "speech" (101) as all versions of a code of sexuality whose epistemology as a trope suggests the language of the flesh and the language of texts to be structurally coincident rather than qualitatively opposed (for anatomies of the novel's metasemiotics, see Maud Ellmann 1981, 1982). And when we find the suddenly religious Stephen mapping out the days of the week according to their various religious significations at the start of chapter 4, the irony of the earlier figural equivalence of sexuality and textuality is reinforced by their like adequation in turn to the structure of a spirituality similarly figured as a system or code. Stephen works, simply enough, within different systems of order, different systems of signs. Distinct as they may be doctrinally, they nonetheless perform almost identical social functions as organizing structures despite their manifest differences.

It is, nonetheless, the religion of art that is Stephen's compromise-formation or resolution in chapter 5, and it is here that Joyce allows him his first real lecture, one in which Stephen theorizes the Arnoldean ideals that the novel's dialectic appears to have won for him. Preparation as it is for the correction of his aesthetics that Stephen will make in *Ulysses*, both on Sandymount shore and in his Hamlet lecture, his lecture in the *Portrait* is, by contrast, a promulgation of all that he will later learn to surrender, and that is already enormously problematic even now. Indeed, the terms by which Stephen articulates his ideals in the *Portrait* put them into question, and, just as clearly, also repeat once again the debate between Arnold and Pater that Joyce will solve with *Ulysses*.

The young Stephen has three principal criteria for the production and judgment of art, terms borrowed from Aquinas, but effective here as those recognizably Arnoldean categories subject, as Joyce, if not Stephen, well knows, to the undeniable pressure of Pater's analytic assault upon them. (1) The category of wholeness or autonomy, the quality a work of art must have to separate it from the rest of the world; the artist must, as Stephen puts it, set up a "bounding line" (212) between the art-object and the world. (2) The category of harmony, that every piece of the work have a component place in its unitary and perfect functioning. (3) The category of radiance, which Stephen rather weakly takes to be the art-object's *"quidditas"* or *"whatness"* (213)—its supposed essence or quiddity. All three categories are, however, made questionable by virtue of the arguments Stephen uses to adduce them, recapitulating with surprising exactitude the difference between Arnold and Pater, and so locating Joyce as Pater's disciple next to the Arnoldean or

Eliotic Stephen, who, by *Ulysses*, will have also moved into Pater's camp instead. How can works of art be truly "modern"—whole, autonomous, and essential—given the temporal conditions of their emergence? Hence Stephen's lecture in chapter 5 is about the problematic way in which *integritas*, *consonantia*, and *quidditas* get produced as ideals. Joyce in short recapitulates here (implicitly, to be sure) Pater's deconstruction of his manifest—and manifestly Arnoldean—musical ideal in the rifts or unspoken logical breaks in Stephen's argument.

First, "*integritas*" or "wholeness":

> —In order to see that basket, said Stephen, your mind first
> of all separates the basket from the rest of the visible uni-
> verse which is not the basket. The first phase of appre-
> hension is a bounding line drawn about the object to be
> apprehended. . . . The esthetic image is first luminously ap-
> prehended as selfbounded and selfcontained upon the im-
> measurable background of space or time which is not it.
> You apprehend it as one thing. You see it as one whole.
> You apprehend its wholeness. That is *integritas*. [212]

Surely, however, Stephen's conclusion is put in question by the language that asserts it. How can his basket be "one thing" when it is clearly a function, not of its own self-reliant essence, but of its difference from "the rest of the visible universe which is not the basket"? Thus the "bounding line" that is drawn is— like Freud's self-productive boundary between ego and world or like Heidegger's *Spiegelspiel*—the result of no more, and no less, than the difference between them that creates both in turn, signature of the birth of the "one" only by means of its relation to that "which is not it." The notion, moreover, that this impossibly "one" or single thing is also "one whole" is also discredited by the terms of its production, since the notion of integrity or wholeness, like the notion of the "one" for which it is (ironically) also a sign, is, properly speaking, equally impossible to maintain when autonomy or separation is a clear function of its difference from all that it is not.

The terms of Stephen's argument, if not Stephen himself, plainly admit such problems as we proceed to the second of the ideals, "*consonantia*," or harmony:

> — . . . you apprehend it as balanced part against part within
> its limits; you feel the rhythm of its structure. In other words

> the synthesis of immediate perception is followed by the
> analysis of apprehension. . . . That is *consonantia*. [212]

Not only does the difference by which such singleness or wholeness is articulated put such ideality in doubt ("balanced part against part"); such a structure is also necessarily temporal when we consider that the thing's presence is a function of an apprehension of its "rhythm." For, like harmony—or, indeed, tonality or atonality—rhythm exists, by definition, only in its temporal unfolding. Moreover, "the synthesis of immediate perception" is a patent impossibility, since a synthesis of the immediate requires us to admit, by its repression, a history prior to or earlier than the immediate that can come into being only as a function of such pastness.

Finally, *"quidditas"* or *"whatness,"* the work of art's concreteness or quiddity, a reifying interpretation of the quite different notion of "radiance" with which Stephen tries to make it synonymous:

> You see that it is that thing which it is and no other thing.
> The radiance of which he [Aquinas] speaks is the scholastic
> *quidditas*, the *whatness* of a thing. This supreme quality is
> felt by the artist when the esthetic image is first conceived in
> his imagination. [213]

Here the Arnoldean ideal is summarily questioned by Stephen's language ("that thing which it is and no other thing," another example of how we recognize one thing by noting its difference from others). If Stephen's desire here is to confirm not just the thing's singleness and its harmony, but also its whatness—its empirical reality—it is such quiddity in particular that his relational terms forbid as an epistemological possibility. For the production of phenomena by temporal and relational means also means that discourse does not discover an essence outside itself, but rather produces its objects in a chiasmatic or interdependent structure of relation that grants each of its terms its apparently single or original place thanks to its differences from the others.

Looking back, then, we can now see with what prescient exactitude the memorable scenes and images early in the novel already represent the ways in which Stephen himself is likewise produced in quite distinct relation to the world rather than as an autonomous being sometimes in contact with it, sometimes in disapproval or exile. In only the book's fourth paragraph, we get the first outline of a model for the way signification or sensation situates the young Stephen, and that schematizes the difference by which the autonomy of both the work of art and the modern artist's Eliotic pose is rendered impossible. "When you wet the bed first it is warm," thinks Stephen, "then it gets cold" (7). As in Pater's "Child in the House," the first distinctions the child remarks are distinctions in and of themselves, almost for their own sake. Indeed, the next two paragraphs accelerate and intensify the centrality of differentiation as the real dynamic of the child's inscription into the world. "His mother had a nicer smell than his father" (7)—again the comparative. The paradigm is elaborated in the memorable emblem of Dante's "two brushes" (7): "The brush with the maroon velvet back was for Michael Davitt and the brush with the green velvet back was for Parnell" (7). Not only does the child now recognize difference as such, in this case the difference between maroon and green; he is also able to understand how such differences are in turn coded to symbolize other things which they are not, again as a function of an emergent hierarchy of differences that intimate the constitution of the world at large and one's place within it.

Hence Stephen's early schooling reflexively elaborates the structure of difference at increasingly higher levels. We are privy, for example, to Stephen's memory of someone saying he'd like to give Cantwell a "belt" (9)—a punch— this just after Stephen has been meditating upon "that . . . belt round his pocket" (9). Stephen rather quickly draws the necessary conclusion that the same word can mean two things at once. Much as the colors of Dante's brushes are the same in Fleming's geography book even though they signify a wholly distinct opposition (15–16), so a term like "belt" can signify altogether differently in another context, too: "And belt was also to give a fellow a belt" (9). Much as the two different meanings of "belt" must be simultaneously preserved and cancelled in order to understand the term in either of the contrasting contexts in which it may be used, so the two meanings to which the difference between green and maroon lead in Dante and Fleming, respectively, require Stephen simultaneously to preserve and cancel both meanings in order to understand either one. So, too, with the equally exemplary word "suck" only a few pages later on. "Suck," says an already punning Joyce, "was a queer word" (11). It means, thinks a puzzled young Stephen, both a flunky and the sound heard, for example, "in the lavatory of the Wicklow Hotel" as "the dirty water went down through the hole in the basin" (11).

Joyce thereby also rejects the onomatopoeic fallacy of iconic signification— that a sign is naturally motivated by what it signifies, such as the sound of the water in the basin that seems to be reflected in the word "suck" that represents it. Stephen's bewilderment here is that, despite the apparent possibility of such motivated signification, each meaning of a word is only one in a number of meanings that a signifier can simultaneously detonate. Hence Joyce's Paterian notion of the relational buoyancy of language rather than the fixed or transparent signification of alinguistic states or objects that Arnold and Eliot, by contrast, hold language to be. Appropriately enough, too, this lesson in the surfeit of language takes place in a memory of the lavatory, in what is the same tropological site for the elimination of just such multiplicities of meaning that Arnold and Eliot alike wish to evacuate as mere waste. Indeed, the lavatory memory elaborates Joyce's notion of language even further if we continue to follow the chain of Stephen's associations. For in the lavatory, "there were two cocks that you turned and water came out: cold and hot. He felt cold and then a little hot: and he could see the names printed on the cocks. That was a very queer thing" (11). Here Stephen again learns that the same signifier ("cock") can mean two different things at once ("hot" and "cold"), just as Joyce himself knows it can mean something else, too, especially when the word "queer" in turn thickens the context in a way that Stephen himself barely notices.

As chapter 5 makes clear later on, then, Joyce already lays out the differential and temporal conditions of language at the start of the novel, describing overtly—rather than repressing—the ways in which its mechanism requires the simultaneous cancellation and preservation of meaning as the price of its use. One is reminded of Farfrae's machine, which, like Arnold's and Eliot's wish that language remain merely transparent, represents, by contrast, the desire to keep the various and incongruent signifying registers of "belt" or "cock," for example, harmonious or univocal by means of a repression of language's inherent polyvalence. Joyce himself, of course, will go on in *Ulysses* to practice what he seems only to preach here: encouraging *sèmes*—seeds or signs—to spill about and contaminate the proper meaning a given context assigns to them—luxuriating, in short, in that Paterian "brainwave" of "quite alien associations" to which the scholarly Joyce will at last turn in *Ulysses* itself (see "Style " 1889:18).

In addition to its requirement of the simultaneous preservation and cancellation of meaning at the level of language itself, the recognition of "difference" also entails the attendant cautions of the paradox of liberation that follows from it, and that joins Joyce's theory and practice of language with his theory and practice of the individual's—and the individual talent's—relation to tradition. Recall, for example, the chastising ditty with which Dante threatens Stephen at the start of the novel when he expresses the desire to marry the Protestant Eileen Vance. It is not only a graphic instance of difference in action, juxtaposing as it does the alternatives that position the positive values of tradition as a function of their negation; it is also, more particularly, a difference structured according to the trope of chiasmus, which foregrounds the paradox of liberation not only in its rhetorical structure, but also in the psychological double bind it shows to be the precondition rather than the price of subjectivity:

Pull out his eyes,
Apologise,
Apologise,
Pull out his eyes.

Apologise,
Pull out his eyes,
Pull out his eyes,
Apologise. [8]

Each stanza is, of course, the inverse of the other, a structure that figurally reduplicates the ditty's manifest message by identifying submission to the world ("Apologise") with what happens when one tries to resist it ("Pull out his eyes"). Much as the boundaries of manners and custom appear as a result of the attempt to transgress them (Stephen is also the addressee of this second nursery rhyme that shows him the horizon of his world only when he unwittingly tries to violate it), so his place in it is formed in a way that leaves no room for anything but either conformity or the symbolic threat of castration. Nor is it an either/or question, since submission and rebellion alike are the reciprocal rather than the antagonistic poles by which individuality is ironically conduced. With the structure of subjectivity (like that of the work of art) a function of such reciprocity between conformity and resistance, what is affirmed is the law of the world rather than the subject's choice in either accepting or rejecting it.

In both its frankness as a Paterian portrait and in its wit in producing the kinds of primacies and resolutions that it also puts into question, the *Portrait*, then, presents us with a recurrent structure of belated production in all registers of life and letters. Belatedness is, however, also now regarded as an opportunity rather than a restriction. If belatedness will become the overriding strategy of *Ulysses*, the hidden recursive movement of the *Portrait* summarizes it beforehand. For the development of the artist that Stephen famously recommends (214–15)—the movement from lyric to epic to dramatic—is quite plainly reversed by the movement of the novel itself. The text, after all, proceeds from dramatic to epic to lyric, beginning in the third person (the dramatic or impersonal mode appropriate to it) and concluding with the first person of Stephen's diary (the admitted sign of lyric, provoking in still another way the contradiction signified by Stephen's assumption of independence at the novel's close). Indeed, a pervasive structure begins to emerge in Joyce at large in which enabling terms are set up to produce arguments or new terms that put their origination into question. Such a structure rhetorically manages, as a result, to cancel the priorities that allow it to speak. Joyce thereby explodes the will to modernity by programmatically dissolving rather than repressing its paradoxical Oedipal terms of empowerment. It is precisely the disadvantage of belatedness that Joyce uses to gain an advantage over the past by eventually becoming its recursive or belated father. *Ulysses*, of course, is the consummate expression of Joyce's success, a monumental act of Paterian scholarship both in its atonal orchestration of language moment to moment, and in the ironic arguments that organize it as a whole.

Ulysses: On Translating Homer

The tower that Browning eschews and that Eliot tries subsequently to level is, of course, the very site upon which *Ulysses* begins. The Martello tower may be decayed, although it is just such originary contamination—ruination at the beginning—that alerts us immediately to Joyce's frank and explicit implication in the tropology of Romantic tradition from which Eliot, by contrast, tries to flee. Already broken at the start, such a blasted place of origin for the narrative is reflexively entailed anyway by the belatedness of the Romantic tradition that enables it, and that almost requires so candid a novel to introduce itself with so precise a genealogical metaphor from the point of view of literary history proper. From the point of view of myth, the precedent analogue here is the parapet of Christ's temptation, with Mulligan, salty purveyor of a black mass, cast in the role of Satan, teasing Stephen to renounce his earnest belief in aesthetic transcendence with which the *Portrait* has apparently closed. Unlike Eliot, however, Joyce will let the two systems—literature and myth, history and Christianity—collide in all their incongruity. Like Pater, Joyce will make no claim to endow myth with the ability to reach beyond or behind tradition. He will work only within tradition—and by an extension of it—rather than resist its authority. Even Joyce's tone is different from Eliot's. The aesthetic Stephen and the medical Mulligan both call the ruined tower home rather than exile, a sign not of anxiety but of luxuriant decadence. What accounts for the difference? Why does Joyce delight in the waste that Eliot wishes to repress?

It is to Stephen's progress from the Arnoldeanism of his desire to create anew in the *Portrait* to the Paterianism of his recognition that all creation is in fact criticism in *Ulysses* that we should turn first.

On the beach, amid the garbage or waste on Sandymount shore in "Proteus," the Stephen with whom Joyce presents us is no longer an undergraduate snob but a bohemian aesthete who, in the chapter just before, identifies a noise in the street with the meaning of the word "God" (1922:34). No wonder Stephen becomes engrossed in epistemology as he kicks his way through the pollution in the third chapter, crackling through a waste land that is a compost heap rather than an unregenerate barrenness ("a sprouting of new growth through decay," as Forster remarked of the Decadent imagination [1949:91]). Stephen has become an outright picker among the ruins, a man on the dump in Stevens's words (prefiguring, too, Bloom's first appearance), sifting through heaps of images, like Marius, though seeking less to restore epiphany in a world of garbage than to come to terms with the world as garbage, as the accumulation of the waste or influence that informs tradition rather than inhibits its continuity. As the childbirth conceit of the "Oxen of the Sun" chapter suggests, the earliest English already works under conditions of labor rather than in the wishful freedom Eliot may assign to it instead.

If there is an especially appropriate Joycean gloss for the problematic of modernism at large, it lies compact in Stephen's Miltonic remark in the first chapter, "Dead breaths I living breathe" (50)—the sense that one's life or one's art is the echo or repetition of another's. And yet Stephen's quintessentially modernist lament for proper originality in the light of such frankly remarked precedent is followed immediately by a movement away from what for Eliot is an inhibition, but what for Joyce is the opening that grants the modern a single, and ironic, privilege over a past that otherwise owns it beforehand:

> Dead breaths I living breathe, tread dead dust, devour a
> urinous offal from all dead. Hauled stark over the gunwale
> he breathes upward the stench of his green grave, his leprous
> nosehole snoring to the sun. [50]

The movement from "dead" to "sun" (or "son") is managed through a strategy that recuperates the nonoriginality and noncreativeness of belatedness by turning it instead into a stance of salutary critical recontextualization. The sordid ruination of living among waste products (at first sight merely "urinous") is, by means of the pun, turned from bad to good. "Urinous offal" ("You're in us, awful") may on the one hand be the modernist lament proper ("tread dead dust"), but what is "awful" is also awe-ful. There is no denying not simply that the past endures in the present, but also that such a condition means that the present—"us"—now houses the "you," or tradition, that the will to modernity maintains houses it. If it is, however, always the other way around, as Joyce suggests here, then it is the very belatedness of the modern that gives it a narrative power over the discourses it otherwise claims to wound it. In a Homeric gloss that anticipates Stephen's cunning reading of the Oedipal paradox in his *Hamlet* lecture later on, Joyce hints at the answer implicit in the question. "Hauled stark over the gunwale" intimates the sedimented figure of Odysseus looming up behind the dog's corpse—the supposedly original quester in the book's mythic analogue—a corpse not only unburied, but, by virtue of its slow putrefaction, made to rest ("snoring") in the light of the enduring "sun," the perpetual future or "son" that will always have the power of dealing with the father's remains in any way he sees fit(s). Hence an oxymoron that signifies an adjudication of the modernist impasse rather than a repression of it: the "green grave," the old and the new simultaneously. The dead are always fresh in death, or, really, ghostly, vampirelike. The image is, however, celebratory rather than mournful, elegiac only in the structural precondition that the novel as a whole will go on to invert.

The older Stephen has, in short, made the change from Arnold to Pater: the haze, the waste, the garbage, *is* the history it seems only to obstruct, the vestiges, the "offal" by which we (re)construct its presence from the tokens of its absence. *Ulysses* is tersely clear about it: "Dirty cleans" (68), thinks Bloom later on. Rather than wish to repress the haze or waste—the first Arnold's term, the second Eliot's—Joyce will in fact make it the subject—and the medium—of his mature art. The awe-ful "offal" becomes its own relief. By means of the admission that language is an inherited condition whose mere usage defines us all as latecomers, Joyce opens the art of the Archive for which he is duly famous, an art that unleashes the reverberations of language through a radical Paterian scholarship. Such scholarship makes the book a machine (quite the opposite of Farfrae's "agricultural piano" despite its ability to turn bad into good) that can produce incessantly fresh meanings based on the theoretically infinite number of possible connections to be found among the "quite alien associations" of the semantic inventories it detonates by means of the pun in particular. Such connections are infinite even under the terms of an epistemic horizon that may itself be finite, but within which a text such as *Ulysses* may defy all odds by appealing to the metaphysically random permutations of language itself so as to overwhelm its horizon of historical closure by constantly rearranging its terms (hence, too, the endless readings of Joyce that line our shelves more than he does).

Before we turn fully, then, to Stephen's cogent explanation of how the Oedipal structure of modernism is to be managed—and the roles that Bloom and Molly play in it—let us summarize the extent to which the text of *Ulysses* already takes into account all that Eliot tries to repress in the problematic of modernism at large. The dominant subjectivizing mode of Joyce's representationalism has, of course, as its consummate reflexive counterpart the implication of the reader in the same structure of experience that the narrative only pretends to re-present in its characters, but that is actually identical with it. The reader must, as the price of admission, deduce the larger context from which any given signifier of subjective experience is a metonymy; must search for the text's proximity to any of the numerous systems, grammars, competences, that can impart to it (and/or its reader, with little distinction now left between text and audience anyway) even the customarily given first or denotative meaning in narrative. Hence Joyce's extreme subjectivism of representation makes the reader keenly aware of what is otherwise merely automatic in the experience of subjectivity and narrativity alike: the understanding of how any utterance, moment by moment, can occur (can be heard as well as said) only as a function of knowing the grammar or context that produces it, usually by means of some curiously constructed mixture by which public signs combine to produce private meanings. If the Joyce of the *Portrait* shows us the paradox and ultimate impossibility of liberation in any form, citizenly or artistic, in *Ulysses* he goes on to force his reader to realize for himself—directly, as it were—the extent to which we, like Stephen, are also already made up of predetermined influences or traditions that precede our birth, and whose funding Joyce asks us to make conscious and to use overtly in order to make sense of the text before us. It is, of course, a generous sign of presumed connection rather than of its Eliotic opposite. My earlier suggestion that Stephen realizes in *Ulysses* that there is no epistemological difference between creation and criticism now finds its rationale, though the contrast with the Eliot of "The Function of Criticism" so produced is remarkable. There, of course, Eliot suggests that "interpretation" ought to be removed from reading, already a duplicitous remark, since *The Waste Land* not only requires but actually highlights (albeit by negation) precisely the kinds of interpretation of which reading (and writing) is composed. Eliot represses no less than the plainly interpretative mode by which reader and writer alike function as theorized so clearly in "Tradition and the Individual Talent" and subsequently forgotten. If Joyce's reader must, however, be, by contrast, an interpreter par excellence, summoning up the frames that give various meanings to the signifiers in the text as a constant and necessary habit of reading it, Joyce himself must, by implication, be an interpreter, too, not a godlike creator (indeed, he is likely "paring his fingernails," in the famous phrase [1916:215], because they are quite dirty). In another reflexive exemplification of the novel's equivalent—and equally overt—thematic deconstruction of origins, in other words, the text itself is, to the extent we can secure it moment to moment, already secondary by definition, either from the reader's or the writer's point of view. Each mirrors the other in the second tier of the novel's reflexively foregrounded strategy of double articulation that adequates the location of lexical frames by the reader with the text's arrangement of such references to them by its putative author, the latter another primary or causative category retroactively installed by customary interpretation to give the text the ground it not only lacks but deliberately eschews both thematically and reflexively (the "more accurate" text of the novel published in 1984 is, by definition, but another misprision of it). As Kenner remarked in 1971, Joyce "is said to have let typists' errors stand when they were good ones" (273). Besides, the novel is, according to Fritz Senn, "consistently autocorrective" in any case (1984:69).

Such attempts to normalize *Ulysses* in the name of honoring an originality it abjures both in principle and in practice have probably no more representative source than Eliot's short review (1923b), one that has exerted as much influence on the study of Joyce as it has on the study of *The Waste Land*. Eliot's reading of Joyce is, of course, predictable, falling as it does into the reifications by which he tries to maintain order in his own poem, and against which Joyce's text is a foil rather than the match Eliot implicitly claims it to be. It is Eliot whom we may thank for promoting a reading of *Ulysses* based on taking, without apparent irony, its wryly announced correspondences to *The Odyssey* as a way not simply of beginning to contextualize the novel, but as a way of decoding it that is, quite contrary to the real behavior of the text, designed to repress the play of readerly temporality that sustains its ability to signify at all. So defensive was Eliot about Richard Aldington's claim that the novel is "an invitation to chaos" (1923b:269)—the cacophony of Joyce's scholarship taken, as it is, to the limit—that he responded in *The Dial* with an argument that actually sharpens our sense of the differences rather than the similarities between the two writers. Sufficient concentration upon Joyce's Homeric equipment, according to Eliot, can hush the Paterian associationism of *Ulysses* that Eliot himself must polemically abnegate in response to Joyce's assumption that no extrasemiotic realm of universal truth, fact, or order is available to us because of our entire implication in the nets of culture. With such motivations, Eliot's brief review bristles with anxiety when, even before its decisive peroration, a momentarily lucid Eliot acknowledges that the "parallel use of the *Odyssey*"—"using the myth" and thereby "manipulating a continuous parallel between contemporaneity and antiquity"—"has never before been necessary" (270). The historical dubiety of the claim aside, it is just such overt scaffolding that is "necessary" to Joyce's effort to estimate the modernist problematic without succumbing to the will to modernity (270). For Eliot, however, it is not mere scaffolding, or, to put it more fairly than Aldington himself, merely the most obvious of the novel's numerous devices by which to make sense of it; the "parallel use" of the myth is, says Eliot, "a way of controlling, of ordering, of giving a shape and significance to the immense panorama of futility and anarchy which is contemporary history" (270). We know by now that the "immense panorama of futility and anarchy" to which Eliot refers is proper to imagination rather than to history as such, and it is Joyce's ability to crack the problem rather than to compound it that requires Eliot to pull Joyce into his own camp. By the end of the piece, Eliot's desire to repress the central—and saving—temporal dynamic of the novel in favor of the stasis of myth is overt: "Instead of narrative method," writes an Eliot relieved of the burdens of time and history, "we may now use the mythical method" (271)—the method that the narrative necessities of his own contemporaneous poem have, consciously or not, already put in question. The temporal procedures of reading that rule *Ulysses*—and, covertly, *The Waste Land*—are what Eliot and his critical influence wish to repress in a preference for the kind of mythic replication at which even *The Waste Land* eventually fails.

The stance of *Ulysses* is, however, the exact reverse of that of *The Waste Land*, although the modus operandi is the same for the reader of both. If Eliot represses the temporal flux of the various meanings that flow through his poem in order to recontain them in a series of archetypal harmonizations that the nature of their articulation actually forbids, Joyce by contrast allows the free play of language to put in question the seemingly equivalent—and equally famous—strategy of mythic or archetypal replication by which his Homeric analogue seems to give a fixed order to what is otherwise a porous and pleasurable chaos. In fact, tracking down a source in Joyce may well end up in discoveries that overtly mock the validity of such searches for meaning in any fixed sense (a humorous E. L. Epstein, for example, finds that "the legitimate grandfather of Odysseus, Autolycus, was a most distinguished thief and deceiver" [1982:78]).

Of course, Eliot's remarks on what is the presumably Homeric anchor of a Joyce more disciplined than assumed beforehand (the notion of discipline without fixities is, of course, inadmissible from Eliot's point of view) recall as well, with all the irony its reflexivity entails, Arnold's overvaluation of Homer as the sign of the origin or primacy that both he and the later Eliot seek in their undaunted will to modernity. No matter the now-familiar self-canceling articulations (Homer as a symbol for the origin deoriginates it by virtue of such symbolization), Eliot's use of Homer to organize Joyce is quite plainly akin to Arnold's own sense of Homer as the real and enduring "object" behind the "haze" of history's distortions. And yet from Pater's—and Joyce's—point of view, such idealizations are also equally impossible, all this despite Joyce's teasings as to the Homeric parallels in his work (Gilbert 1930). Recovering an origin that can be said to exist in the first place only as a belated function of our distance from it is just what Pater's definition of the indefatigable will to "modernity" in *Gaston* has already uncovered, and just what *Ulysses* puts into practice with abnormal vengeance. Much as Pater has shown that the kind of ideal represented by Arnold's Homer is canceled by the terms that express it, so the dynamic of *Ulysses* puts in question its own finally quite ironic gesture toward the kind of mythic replication erected by Eliot as the novel's ultimate organizing device. Any reading of *Ulysses* is, to use Kenner's phrase, one of "so many trial alignments" (1978:60) or, to use Senn's terms, reading *Ulysses* is a "polytropic endeavor" based upon any variety of "serial approaches" (1984:208). The novel's dynamic is an enormously witty instance of just why and how *Ulysses* is no capitulation to the will to modernity but, along with psychoanalysis, probably modernism's most impressive negotiation of the impasses that structure its problematic. The cost, of course, is massive—it is no less than the implosion of English upon itself, an act of literary terrorism that solves the problem of waste or belatedness by wasting the absolutes that it forbids as well as the tradition that forbids them, and, in the process, relegates the form of the novel itself, along with the will to modernity, to one of the book's objects of inquiry. Except for its own progeny, its *Wake*, the novel's devastating influence upon the subsequent practice of fiction—in England by negation, in America by adulation—is the emblem of its deliberately nefarious ambition, comparable only to Milton's influence on the eighteenth century and beyond, and, as time will likely confirm, more purely disastrous. The novel suggests just what it cannot do by calling upon the Arnoldean figuration of Homer as origin—as, yes, "home"—that Joyce's own epistemology will vilify. Even Richard Ellmann must admit that the "parallel" is "in fact discontinuous" (1977:17).

The novel's title should tell us as much anyway, insisting so compactly on the deferred temporality by which we install ideals or origins retroactively that it goes almost unnoticed. The title is itself a signature for the Paterian recoil or reality of belatedness by which it responds to the will to modernity that it may seem only to reduplicate. By virtue of a Latin rather than properly Greek title, the novel gives us a graphic clue for its programmatic failure to complete Eliot's "parallel" even on its face. If *Ulysses*, as Eliot claims, is a mythic replication of *The Odyssey*, why, then, is the book not called *Odysseus?* The Latin translation that obscures the eternal return the Homeric correspondence supposedly signifies is the mark of Joyce's Paterian insistence that the recovery of such primacy is simply impossible. To be sure, the Homeric conceit appears to enact Joyce's will to modernity by expressing the desire to retrieve origins in the novel's pose as a modern-day *Odyssey*, as an exercise in mythic replication (Kenner calls such replicas "homeomorphs" [1971:33]) that will sanctify the quotidian by virtue of its hidden conformity to eternal archetypes. But the professedly belated Joyce gets graphically waylaid or bogged down on his way back to the warmth of Greece, his project breaking down somewhere in the vicinity of Rome—not as a sign of its failure but as a sign for the process that makes such a quest impossible to fulfill. Such an apparent breakdown is in fact an unavoidable factor in any idealist regression toward the certitude of an origin. Joyce inscribes the process in the book's title as well as in its readerly dynamic and, as we shall soon see, in its thematic as well. Even the reverberations that might seem in turn to favor Rome over Greece lead only to further questions about priority rather than to any kind of priority as such—is the Roman locution of the title a reminder that the vocabulary of Catholicism, for example, is more decisive for Joyce than that of Homer? is it a notation for the belated antiquity of Rome proper in its own anxious relation to the golden age of Greece? or is it both, whether in conflict or congruence a function of how it is interpreted?

Ulysses, in short, burlesques its own attempt to recuperate origins by appearing to fashion mythic Eliotic homologues (biblical, as we shall soon see, as well as classical), but whose own terms make the possibility of such a project palpably absurd, ignoring as any such will to modernity does the mechanism of deferred action by which both life and literature constitute origins only after the fact. Even S. L. Goldberg's claim that the Homeric analogue lends "historical universality" to the novel is cautioned by his reminder that "the structure of *Ulysses* is completely its own" (1961:150, 145). For Joyce, unlike Eliot, the text of the world and the world of the text are alike abundant precisely because of their Keatsian ripeness or belated, autumnal decadence— an "art of surfeit" (201), as Stephen enigmatically calls Whitman's. To say so and, even more, to dramatize it by making the book's readerly dynamic of deferred action dependent on such (over)connectedness is to fashion a modernist text suspiciously like Eliot's—as is customarily believed—but that is its exact reverse in both stance and epistemology. Not only does Joyce presume no dissociation of sensibility; he also presumes neither wishful origins nor, as we shall see a bit later on, wishful resolutions, all such cautions the result of the admission and exploitation of deferred action rather than of its repression. As a text, *Ulysses* doesn't just betoken Stephen's lesson in the *Portrait* that there can be no immediacy, no priority, no origin(al) in a world to which we all come late. It actively, decisively implicates the reader in the acting out of such a precondition in the labor required to make a book out of it at all. For we like to forget in our pretension that the problem of the text's readability is always its overriding point. Like the tower with which it begins, *Ulysses* is, from the start, always (about) the (re)constructions that make it available as a text in the first place (hence Budgen 1934 and Blamires 1966). The novel's world—the real it presumably renders—is always already a belated or deferred function of its narration rather than of a direct, unmediated mimesis which the novel necessarily outlaws as a category by which to describe any poetics. Narratologically, the original—the story it tells—is itself made (up), belatedly, by means of the reader's work with the fragments that produce its wholeness only after the fact. Like Freud, Joyce presumes secondary revision or deferred action to be the structure of reading as a process, the original a retroactive function of its later report (hence John Paul Riquelme's reading of Joyce's entire career backward [1983]).

Ulysses is, in short, the circumstance it describes. By implicating the reader in a process of having to recuperate—in fact, to produce in the first instance— the novel's *histoire* or "original" from its *récit* as an overt and laborious activity, it makes the act of reading itself reflexive of the novel's thematic as it will appear in Stephen's theory of paternity, and, as we shall also see, in Stephen's position next to the Blooms. Once Joyce puts the question of the desire for a return to origins in the rather strictly Oedipal terms that organize what plot the book has, we can see the exactitude with which *récit* and *histoire* are adequated. Joyce's disarming of the Oedipal structure with which he is already familiar enough to use as an ideological item rather than as a meaning ("the new Viennese school" [205] is mentioned in the same chapter that contains Stephen's lecture on *Hamlet*) is channeled through Stephen's relation to Bloom and Molly. But even the terms by which Joyce has Stephen find a way out of the dilemma posed by his displaced and secularized Oedipal Trinity are themselves reflexive of an equivalent Oedipal relation on Joyce's own part to Pater, and one that in turn puts in question the interpretative certitude by which Pater, like Homer, can make the text cohere. Joyce is so fine a student of both Pater's notion of dissolving personality and his requirement that the artist be a scholar that he breaks his own Paterian umbilicus in *Ulysses* by using influence as a tool rather than feeling it as a weight, heeding Pater's own strategies—indeed, Pater's own language—in order, paradigmatically, to overcome them in the triply reflexive tour de force of Stephen's lecture on *Hamlet*, a mirror of the Oedipal tensions that structure *Ulysses* at every moment (hence, too, Shakespeare's face in the mirror stage of "Nighttown" [567]). Stephen's lecture is no less than the *summa* of his exemplary progression from the Arnoldeanism of the fifth chapter of the *Portrait* to the unexpected Paterian mouthpiecing in the Library chapter of *Ulysses*, an act of ventriloquism that lays out the novel's structural policy even more unabashedly than Birkin does for Lawrence in *Women in Love*—probably because few of us suspect Stephen to be taken seriously any longer by an older Joyce who has by now supposedly displaced his sympathies onto the new invention of Bloom.

Stephen's analysis of the Oedipus complex in his lecture is, of course, both symptomatic of its reality (for Stephen looks to undo it), and a sign of the means of its dislocation that contains the logic of *Ulysses*'s own ironic originality as well. Though still bound superficially to his earlier ideals ("Art has to reveal . . . formless spiritual essences," says Stephen at the chapter's start [185]), it is again the rhetorical structure of Stephen's reasoning that carries the full weight of Joyce's own argument, and one that he will now allow Stephen himself to win outright as well. If the ghost of Hamlet's father is, as Stephen argues, really Shakespeare himself, it is due to Shakespeare's strategic response to his own Oedipus complex, a defensive inversion based on what Freud calls identification with the aggressor, and an inversion that also explains why the play's otherwise autobiographical hero bears a name not unlike that of Shakespeare's own son, Hamnet. For Shakespeare projects in Hamlet, not himself, but his own futurity, a futurity that he, like Joyce, knows to be the ironic, because belated, site of the past that supposedly precedes it. In the biographical fiction that Stephen produces as evidence, Shakespeare knows that his own identity is a function of what succeeds it because it is only the future that narrates or pre-serves (or threatens) it, whether in the belated *méconnaissance* that defines subjectivity from its own point of view (belated in relation to itself by definition—"I . . . am I by memory because under everchanging forms," thinks Stephen [189]) or, in the overdrive into which Joyce here shifts, in the belated *méconnaissance* of historiography (Strachey's subject) that makes futurity the discursive father of the past that precedes it chronologically.

It is, quite simply, the Oedipal analogue to the structure of the book's readerly dynamic: the original is a function of what succeeds it, since *histoire* can be situated only by means of its belated (re)construction through *récit*. Hardly a "doctrine" of "aesthetic trinity" (Kellogg 1974:169), Stephen's notion of *Hamlet*, in other words, is one in which the figure of paternity—of power, authority, influence, tradition—resides, strictly speaking, not with the father, but with the son (no wonder the Trinitarian Eliot's dislike of the Satanic Hamlet). Knowing Freud's argument as he did (Joyce had a 1911 German copy of Ernest Jones's book on *Hamlet* in his library [Quillian 1983; R. Ellmann 1977:54]), the stance is prescient indeed. Though the son biologically succeeds the father, in so doing he also precedes him rhetorically by virtue of having the single privilege belatedness bestows: the power to narrate the past, and so to possess it by virtue of the distance that otherwise prevents its possession. "Loss," says Stephen of Shakespeare, "is his gain" (197). Shakespeare's is an anxiety, not of influence, but of anticipation—the result of his knowledge that futurity will, as it does Joyce as well, forever father him. "The corpse of John Shakespeare does not walk the night. From hour to hour it rots and rots. He rests, disarmed of fatherhood, having devised that mystical estate upon his son" (207). "Paternity may be," in the famous phrase, "a legal fiction" (207).

Thus the unexpected leverage that relieves Stephen's will to modernity: "the now, the here" is not an immediacy that can be possessed; "the now, the here" is, properly speaking, the perpetuity of the medium of temporality alone "through which all future plunges to the past" (186). Tradition now enables without the accompanying anxiety, the latter rendered a feature of the unknown future's reception of it (hence the intentional violence of Joyce's influence, the problem of After Joyce). Restoring power to the structure of weakness represented by, say, "Sohrab and Rustum," Stephen says of the son: "His growth is his father's decline, his youth his father's envy" (208). Thus even Stephen's customary image for the stifling burdens of tradition ("Coffined thoughts around me, in mummycases" [193]) is overturned by the new articulation, which animates a past that is otherwise immovable when its components are viewed as the necessarily static kind imputed to them by the funereal figure of embalming. Like Marius, Joyce proposes instead to make the most of deferred action—to move the bones around in the mausoleum, not even respecting the supposed integrity of the body that is mummified in its apparent wholeness (nor does the pun that here identifies Oedipus with the mother or "mummy" produce problems, since the mother, too, is, as we shall see with Molly, also part of the complex of influence).

It is in fact just such Paterian suspicion of the notion of the wholeness of the body that gets embalmed that makes such strategic inversion possible for Joyce as well as for his critical fiction about Shakespeare. Joyce's argument is, of course, grounded upon what he learns from Pater's Conclusion, though, as we have already seen, it is a lesson about the disassemblage of the terms by which its own influence can be measured. Stephen in fact sets the stage for his argument by nearly repeating (a second time in Joyce, following the close of "The Dead") both the stance and the tropology of its origin or authority in the precedent Conclusion, even bringing Pater's fondness for scientific metaphors up to date, as Woolf does in "Modern Fiction" (1919):

> —As we, or mother Dana, weave and unweave our bodies,
> Stephen said, from day to day, their molecules shuttled to
> and fro, so does the artist weave and unweave his image.
> And as the mole on my right breast is where it was when I
> was born, though all my body has been woven of new stuff
> time after time, so through the ghost of the unquiet father
> the image of the unliving son looks forth. . . . That which I
> was is that which I am and that which in possibility I may
> come to be. So in the future, the sister of the past, I may
> see myself as I sit here now but by reflection from that
> which then I shall be. [194]

Among the passage's self-announced multiple or radiant significations, we can isolate a vision of the belated recognition that defines subjectivity itself ("I may see myself as I sit here now but by reflection from that which then I shall be"), and, in turn, a vision of the nonautonomy of the body and the work of art alike, the fibers of each "woven of new stuff time after time." The "new," then, is simply a shuttling or shuffling of the inherited "molecules" or, in Pater's word, "particles" (1889:20), of life and letters that "weave and unweave" an object-world that, again in Pater's words, is "but an image of ours" (1873:234). Such weaving and unweaving as the belated modality of life and letters alike is, thereby, the epistemological precondition behind Stephen's theory, and that, as suggested before, also reflexively enacts its assertions by weaving its vocabulary as a function of unweaving Pater's otherwise authorizing one. Of course, Pater's injunction already requires its own cancellation anyway as the price of the action it recommends. Like Shakespeare, Joyce becomes his own father as a function of, rather than despite, the belatedness that otherwise makes him a disciple.

Hence too the equivalent advantage to be had in the accompanying implication that the artist, like the son, is a critic or interpreter rather than a creator in his own right. Like Stephen's earlier claim as he meditates on his mother's death that he is, like art itself, "made not begotten" (38), his demonstration that Shakespeare is himself his own father is made possible in the first place by the evacuation of the notion of autonomous creation in all its registers, from the biological to the aesthetic. Much as Stephen's own body is woven and rewoven out of that which, in Pater's words, "extends beyond us" (1873:234), so every work of art is woven and rewoven out of the materials or "molecules" of tradition that the nonscholar treats only as a problem. If the notion of an original text is foiled by the book's readerly dynamic, then the notion of the original writer is, like the original subject, a fantasy, too. Again repeating a Paterian strategy—this time using the results of a biographical inquiry to overturn the categories by which biography or portraiture proceeds—Stephen thereby again reflexively does what he says by dispersing the category under consideration. As Stephen's joke about the question of Shakespeare's authorship suggests ("Rutlandbaconsouthamptonshakespeare or another poet of the same name" [208]), even a living Shakespeare is always already "a ghost, a shadow now" (197). There is, to use Virginia Woolf's words that conclude a rather similar argument in "A Sketch of the Past," "no Shakespeare" (1939:72) at all. Hence all artists become what Stephen himself has become: a critic or even a kind of committee (the latter the metaphor for artistic production that Orwell, like Arnold and Eliot before him, will go on to reject in 1984 [1949]), constantly in dialogue with the texts of the past, a circuit or agency of influence rather than an integral, creative essence. And it is again the wounding that is for Joyce the balm: the supposed demotion of the creative figure to a critical one is what gives the candidly dialogical writer a new and peculiar kind of power. Though founded on necessity and mounted initially as a defense, it becomes an extraordinary mode of authority in its own right, since it allows every artist the power of the critic to make the past over again in his own image.

Once we turn to Bloom, we instantly revisit the problem of originality as well, though in a less orthodox fashion than we do with Stephen or with the book's abstract structure. Bloom, of course, famously relishes the production of a waste that fertilizes his urban garden rather than renders it a waste land (his chamber is full of music), planning to sow it with the "peas" (68) upon which he and Stephen will pee later on. Such "urinous" fertilization is not only no longer "offal" in either sense of its sound, but is the very activity that grants the book its single genuinely commemorative moment: Rudy's imaginary resurrection in the "green grave" of a necropolitan garden in which Stephen substitutes for him in a structure precisely the reverse of that of Michael Furey's substitution for

Gabriel in "The Dead." Bloom also relishes the "inner organs" (55) of other beasts, a suggestion less readily of his primitivism than of a universe of interchangeable parts that makes him not only the long-acknowledged and happy representative of the age of the machine, but also not necessarily—as is customarily assumed—the opposite of the Romantic Stephen. Despite the superficial differences in the rhythms and materialities assigned to each character in turn, both believe the world to be a vortex or "whirlpool" (196) rather than a seat of hidden absolutes. While Stephen and Bloom do represent a difference between an orthodox and a popular Romanticism, it is a difference of degree or type rather than of kind. Much as Stephen has put in question the category of the proper from a theoretical point of view, Bloom does so dramatically when Molly asks him early in "Calypso" what "metempsychosis" means (64). "The transmigration of souls," he replies (64). Molly, however, cannot accept Bloom's answer, bound as an earth mother must supposedly be to belief in origins. Her hilarious response: "Who's he when he's at home?" (64). But as we have seen, there is neither proper identity nor absolute home within the conditions of the whirlpool—the overdeterminations of tradition both literary and popular—only borrowings and ragtag riches that we patch together into the simulacra of selves and works of art. Bloom's world is simply a homespun version of Stephen's more abstract one; his equivalent notion of the advantage the latecomer has in reordering the past is to be found in the notion of parallax to which the scientific Bloom is attracted: "Parallax. I never exactly understood. . . . parallel, parallax" (154). "Parallax" is, unlike "parallel," the change in the position of an object that results from a change in the situation from which it is viewed—the astronomer's version of Stephen's reimagination of the past as a moveable feast rather than as an immovable mausoleum. (Moreover, Bloom's claim "never" to have "exactly understood" it is a reflexive instance of its meaning, one not unlike that of misrecognition that allows the subjectivity that is its apparent rival or opposite.) If an object's position changes as a function of its perception, it is not only a function of its reading, but also an instance of the same principle by which the novel itself must oscillate between mythic "parallel" on the one hand and the more particular shifts of linguistic and literary "parallax" or genuine dialogism on the other. When Bloom mutters, immediately subsequent to "parallax," "Met him pike hoses she called it till I told her about the transmigration" (154), he has, consciously or not, identified the two procedures, each versions of Stephen's notion of intersubjectivity in life and art alike. Parallax, in other words, is the Paterian mechanism by which a belated gaze is different from an earlier one, and therefore capable of seeing the components of tradition in an always new, if always retrospective, way. It is, on the one hand, the mechanism by which the belated writer, as Eliot describes it in "Tradition and the Individual Talent," continually shuffles the particles of tradition from the point of view of his advantageous futurity, history itself changing both his position and that of the tradition upon whose gaze it props itself. On the other hand, however, what such advantageous belatedness or parallax cannot produce is the "ideal of order" Eliot claims for it. By virtue of the relations that constitute the objects it seems merely to behold, parallax can only arrive at a Stevensian "idea of order" that is never absolute because, in Stephen's phrase, order itself is "everchanging." The difference between the impossible "ideal of order" and the functionally effective procedure of parallax or belatedness is the same as the difference between the parallel—the Arnoldean mode of reading *Ulysses* that Eliot recommends—and parallax proper, Joyce's Paterian mode of relief from belatedness through the latecomer's singular power of recontextualization.

If Stephen is the academic Romantic and Bloom the (punning) pop Romantic, their difference is really one of style and degree rather than of stance or kind. Belatedness or diaspora is, of course, the precondition of Bloom's being as a Jew, forever distant from the origin of the origin and with no promise of redemption even with what faith he may possess. Diaspora thereby graphically allegorizes and magnifies the structural preconditions of the novel as a whole—and of Stephen's theories in particular—at the most basic level of Bloom's representation. Redoubling the structure still again, Bloom's father is, moreover, dead, while his proper name is itself a translation of a prior German "original." Diaspora is also an exacerbated version of the structure of Gabriel's paradigmatic relation to English itself in "The Dead." Diaspora or belatedness by definition produces a defensive will to modernity, a thirst for origins that makes Bloom a member of a communal Romanticism by the ironic virtue of his preconditional estrangement ("we are all foreigners," says Senn of *Ulysses*, "lost in a labyrinth" [1984:49]). Bloom himself breezily indulges his will to modernity, knowing its status to be merely wishful thinking anyway, and also, as we shall soon see, because he has a compensation in mind that will largely assuage the irritations of exile that otherwise make the will to escape so inescapable. The novel's recurrent metaphor for Bloom's quest for origins lies in what is at first another "throwaway"—his thoughts during the day about Palestine, oranges, Zionism; about the warmth, in short, of that Mediterranean cradle that represents lost earliness for the northern European, Hebrew and Hellene alike, whether in officially literary forms or in the popular mythologies they disseminate. Much as the novel's title suggests it to get caught in Rome on its way back to Greece, so Bloom's equally representative Levantine desires have long beforehand found a compromise-formation in the sweet topography that has furnished him the wife to whom he is still faithful: Gibraltar, simultaneously facing the cold Atlantic and the warm Mediterranean, much as the Molly who was born there now simultaneously shares the cold of Bloom's bed and the warmth of Boylan's body.

Bloom's pop Romanticism and its self-containment or self-bridling under the conditions of reality are summarized in his vision of a radiant suburban villa in what will serve as an earthly surrogate for what Joyce calls in "Night-town" "the New Bloomusalem" (484). Filiated to the same quest-traditions of the culture from which he is also estranged, Bloom's "ultimate ambition" (712) is, as we find out in "Ithaca," a realistic one by contrast to its ideological origin. It is simply to have a house in the suburbs. Note, however, the terms of its representation: "Not to inherit by right of primogeniture, gavelkind or borough English, or possess in perpetuity an extensive demesne," "but to purchase by private treaty in fee simple a thatched bungalowshaped 2 storey dwelling-house of"—can there be any doubt about it?—"southerly aspect" (712). Though local, Bloom imagines its location as the balmy "Flowerville" (714), just as there is to be a year-round "summerhouse" with "tropical palms" (713). The main house is also to have a "vulcanite automatic telephone" and a "handtuffed Axminster carpet" (713)—the technology superadded rather than opposed to a pop Romanticism whose genealogy Joyce both charts and deploys.

Bloom's wishes and the means of their representation are, therefore, hardly throwaways, representing as they do the book's ability—and intent—to switch from the hieratic to the secular, from abstract metaphors to mundane ones, even as it maintains them as the same in stance. In the process, Joyce reciprocally sanctifies the everyday while sullying the absolute in the oscillating inflections that convert Mass to mass and back again in the simultaneous contexts invoked by the play of his language. Complete with dictionary and encyclopedia (713), the villa's Romantic genealogy is both officially literary as well as popular or ideological. Indeed, Bloom's mass-culture Romanticism is a precise sign for the mass inscription of the tropology of Romanticism—of the will to modernity—that has always been literature's companion since the age of exploration, and that, after Joyce, the world has uncannily acted out in Bloom's image. An ironic possibility to emerge from one of the most scholarly texts in the language, such unexpected and unlikely predictive power is another example of Joyce's newly won anticipation of the future rather than fear of the past.

Bloom's insistence on "purchase" rather than inheritance also carries with it the logic that sustains *Ulysses* throughout. By the rhetorical negation of the hegemony of the rule of "inheritance" and the "right of primogeniture" behind it, Bloom will accept the mantle of real property only under the same conditions by which he has already been inscribed as a subject: the conditions of diaspora, belatedness, metempsychosis. Property, in short, has been implicitly redefined as a function of the waste that—as Arnold's exacting appeals to the term's etymology have shown—turns out to produce rather than inhibit it. Much as the text itself is a belated function of its exchange of signs with its reader, or subjectivity the belated function of its exchange with the signs of the world, so even real estate—"property" in its plainest sense, though carrying its stack of connotations with it—is demystified as a function of temporality and exchange, too, rather than as the natural sign it may appear to be. Indeed, the novel's implications require us to realize that, just as there is no original to which Joyce's (re)constructions are necessarily faithful (all this despite the novel's cartographical exactitudes), neither is there an origin to which any kind of copy corresponds; rather, the book suggests that everything is a copy of originals that do not exist, an incipient typology of mass rather than Mass production by which the novel takes into account the nature of its effects as well as the effects in the real that it reflexively (re)presents (hence, too, Stevens's "Canon Aspirin"—the classic as copy). For Joyce, the world itself is a copy or representation without an original—a set of discourses that realize rather than reflect us.

From a literary historical point of view, moreover, Bloom's rejection of primogeniture and inheritance is not simply a reflexive outcropping of anxiety of influence either. Such rejection also means that Joyce excises from the tradition of the nineteenth-century *Bildungsroman* of which *Ulysses* is both a part and the finish the residue of the form that produces it genealogically. Now it must be cleansed from it if the novel itself is to become the fully bourgeois extravaganza for which it is usually celebrated (Patrick Parrinder quite aptly calls Bloom and Molly "the bourgeois utopians" [1984]). Like Hardy—but still under the guise of quest—Joyce eliminates a precise component in the romance sediment in English narrative familiar to us as early as Shakespeare: the hidden aristocratic lineage that gives the wandering child that is lost and then found the proper name and prior financial property and correlative psychological wholeness that Joyce's epistemology forbids. As with Hardy, here there is no aristocratic secret—no hidden original, no d'Urberville lineage, no reborn Rudy—that the novel can recuperate despite its numerous but unstable mythic parallels. Like Stephen, Bloom presents us with an endless cycle of gain and loss in the whirlpool of life, one that joins the imagination's compensatory agon with tradition as represented by Stephen and his vocabulary with the world of social reality represented by Bloom as well as by the novel itself as a form.

And yet despite the text's insistence on the copy without an original—on no proper homes or origins—it seems to conclude, in a willfully dialectical fashion, with the celebration of natural primacy in the figure of Molly. Molly is the Mary/Mother/Penelope who mediates between Bloom the Father and Stephen the Son, not only psychologically and mythologically, but also dialectically (Richard Ellmann's "triadic organization" [1972:2, 167]), resolving the supposed tension between Stephen's art and Bloom's science in their like appeal to the nature Molly customarily represents. The apparent spontaneity of Molly's interior monologue (accompanied by the parallel flow of her menstrual blood) is the overriding sign of her legendary symbolization of the fecund and the vital—of precisely the kinds of originary terms the novel at large forbids, much as it also forbids the kind of mythic and dialectical resolution Molly's traditional role in the structure of the text historically enjoys. Even the category of interior monologue by which (with Joyce's own belated assent) "Penelope" is customarily glossed already presumes a genuine dichotomy between an inside and an outside that may be a real distinction for, say, Eliot, but that Joyce's novelistic practice and policy alike forbid (Dorritt Cohn's attempt to maintain the category notwithstanding [1978:229]; see, by contrast, Riquelme 1983:131ff.). As the *Portrait* has already shown—and as Stephen and Bloom have each rearticulated it in *Ulysses*—subjectivity is a function of the object-world to which it is positively rather than mournfully opposed. The interior is by now a familiar product of the exterior that sustains rather than restrains it in the overt semiotics of *Ulysses* at large and in the new theories of Stephen in particular. Impossible to construe as genuinely interior, Molly's soliloquy is not monologue either. The play of any subjective discourse is a variegated function of the overdetermined forcefields of influence that contribute to it. "Penelope" is instead a polylogue, the swathed tissues of prior discourses that find their locus in Molly, and among the "offal" of which Molly in turn tries to narrate memories in order to lend coherence to her own subjectivity. The polylogues of Stephen and Bloom have already required the reader to contextualize laboriously the public frames of reference from which the privacy of subjectivity is itself paradoxically constituted, an effort designed to reproduce consciously the means of its production in the reader himself. Molly's polylogue is more demanding because it makes it harder still for the reader to locate the sources or origins of her utterances, since, unlike the men's common predisposition to fashion themselves largely by means of overtly public languages such as literature or science, Molly's more personally centered discourse tends to blur the fact that even her own most private thoughts are the result of equally social or exterior frames of reference despite their particularity to her own experience, especially in her memories of love.

Such problems, however, are but more ironic signs of Joyce's success in exploding the forms he completes. *Ulysses* locates itself in the kind of readerly subjectivity that it cannot properly be said to represent from any point of view at all, contaminating as it does what is proper to inside or outside, past or future. The novel thereby ruptures the category of subjectivity upon which it is founded and appears to take for granted in its reader. But the reader, like the novel's characters, can no longer be conceived of as a pure subject either, since what readerly competence is already proper to the reader personally and what must be hunted down from the outside before joining the reader's inside is always a unique and undecidable occasion, the function as it always is of the peculiarities of each of its readers in turn. Like the characters' implication in systems that precede their birth—and like Joyce's like implication in the tradition that precedes him—the reader's implication in the text doesn't presume his self-sufficient subjectivity so much as his availability as a circuit for its reception. Indeed, like Eliot, but with grace, humor, and generosity, Joyce doesn't so much appeal to a reader already in place, but instead produces a new one as a function of the demands his text makes upon whatever agency can be constructed to receive it. If the *Portrait* reverses the successive modes through which an artist must pass in order to show that it stages a regression under the guise of a progression, *Ulysses* in turn reverses the earlier book's reversal by actually following the sequence from lyric to epic to dramatic—from the subjective to the impersonal—though characteristically producing in turn another irony still: the achievement of a mode of representing subjectivity in polylogues that depersonalize it as the price of its representation.

Hence, too, the enormity of Joyce's strategic duplicity in resolving the tripartite myth of Homer/Christianity/Oedipus in the dialectical movement that seems to assert the third term of nature or primacy with the figure of Molly. Any such resolution is put directly into question by the "everchanging" temporality, readerly or writerly, that presumes to secure it. We overrate Molly's heroism in our desire to see *Ulysses* complete itself as the recuperative romance it only appears to be. Even to use the grammatically inescapable masculine locution is already to suggest what is especially problematic in asserting Molly to be privileged in any dialectical triangle—the assumption of a femininity essentially different from its masculine counterpart. Aside from such an epistemological difficulty is the plain fact that Molly is likely more masculine in the power she brandishes and in the images of her desire than either Stephen or Bloom, less an earth mother than a phallic mother, a bearer of the Law far sterner than the father, whose own limp authority in Bloom's case actually pales by comparison (see also Unkeless 1982 and Hayman 1970). Rather than the missing third term of the dialectic that will make the book the at least symbolic romance it seems to be, Molly is but one more element in a giant machine that overrides all the categories upon which it depends as a paradoxical function of them.

Even Empson's suggestion that *Ulysses* fails to deliver its truly ultimate implication (1982:217ff.) looks to be insufficiently ironic to Joyce's uncannily proleptic ability to predict and account for the novel's own futurity or reception. If the Oedipus complex is the sign or formula for the anxiety of influence that both empowers and prohibits, and that Joyce himself has so plainly overcome, why, wonders Empson, does he merely tease us with a classical— that is to say, symbolic—Oedipal resolution when the biological injunction has been lifted, thus allowing Stephen to sleep with Molly? Why, in short, does Joyce not follow out Molly's fancy for Stephen in the few glimpses she gets of him by bringing Stephen to her bed rather than Bloom? If the book has both theorized and practiced the new authority of the son or latecomer, why is he not rewarded with actual possession of the primacy or paradise he has apparently regained?

Radical as Empson's suggestion is, it is, however, also quite conventional when compared to the novel's own principles (in Empson's deadpan words, "the Bloom offer was never actually made" anyway [1982:253]). Possession of the mother by the son is itself no more than a weak or literal Oedipal version of the wishful will to modernity that *Ulysses* habitually thwarts—the successful recuperation or repossession of (one's own) origins. This is not at all what *Ulysses* does, though our various ways of wishing for it, Empson's included, suggest in turn why the novel must constantly, even programmatically, forbid it. Its success lies not in the practice of the kind of Arnoldean or Eliotic myth of eternal return of which Empson's symbolic incest is itself an unintended example. It lies instead in Joyce's relentless refusal to submit to the will to modernity not only by demonstrating the impossibility of its project, but also by revealing its undesirability. It is not power over the past that Joyce wants any longer, in the image of either the father or the mother, or even in the image of the son that comes between them. So powerful is the art of *Ulysses* and its wake that Joyce no longer shares the known desires of the past, but the unknown desires of the futurity that will father him. The book is infinite in its possibilities because it is directed at the horizon always before it.

THREE

The Bloomsbury Novel and the Production of the Real

One man opposing a society
If properly misunderstood becomes a myth.

> —Stevens, "Lytton Strachey, Also,
>   Enters into Heaven"

Let them take a wider, a less personal view
of modern literature, and look indeed upon
the writers as if they were engaged upon
some vast building, which being built by
common effort, the separate workmen may well
remain anonymous.

> —Woolf, "How It Strikes A Contemporary"

"Psychic Economy"

How, then, does literature continue to proceed under conditions fraught with the impossible desire for Arnoldean immediacy or Eliotic fixity on the one hand and the burdensome reality of precedent on the other? Short of sacralizing art, as Eliot does far more aggressively than the Pater he represses, or destroying its futurity, as Joyce does, is there no middle ground? No resolution or compromise, however frail, neurotic, or subject to the rush of time as it may be? How, in short, does High British Modernism mediate between Eliot's defensive and finally irresponsible project and Joyce's garrulous intertextuality in which representation itself runs riot in a ceaseless recoil or reflexivity that eventually unhinges it?

It is no less than the canonical texts of Bloomsbury that provide the middle, saving ground, forming as they do a uniformly balanced kind of discourse that negotiates the will to modernity by both staging its wishful fulfillment of a return to origins, and, simultaneously, putting the reality of such ideals into question by exposing the belated means of their literary production. A genuinely collective and evolutionary sensibility from Forster to Woolf to Strachey—an achievement that ought to bear the name the Bloomsbury novel—it incrementally summarizes and solves the problematic of modernism at large in a way so typically understated that its genuinely common project has too long gone unnoticed despite the customary but problematic link to G. E. Moore (see Poole 1978), or even recent—and far more problematic—attempts to continue to construc it through Roger Fry's and Clive Bell's theories of painting (Dowling 1985).

Bloomsbury's solution is based upon the compromise-formation of a programmatic reflexive realism in which both illusionism and its demystification—Arnold and Pater, Eliot and Joyce, the symptomatic will to modernity and the larger structure of modernism that accounts for it—invisibly coincide in a deliberate form of prose that silently identifies the story it tells with the way it tells it. Plot and narration, *histoire* and *récit*, are versions of one another, although, unlike Hardy's reflexive realism or even Joyce's, Bloomsbury's is schematic rather than subjectivist in the stance of its representationalism, impersonally taxonomic and demographic rather than intent, as are Hardy and Joyce alike, on implicating the reader in the kind of labor that structures the experience of its characters (after Naremore 1973, J. H. Miller 1970, and DiBattista 1980, it is in any case axiomatic that the Woolfian narrator in particular is anonymous and omniscient). Like Hardy and Joyce, however, Bloomsbury takes as an informing structural principle the notion that the world it represents is itself a tissue of representations in the first place, already secondary in its supposed immediacy because it is a fluctuating ensemble of signs or traditions to which everyone comes late as a dubious birthright. And if Bloomsbury fiction represents a world of belatedness from the start, then it has also already succeeded at the level of policy in producing an unavoidably reflexive scene of writing in which the world it portrays is, in its very realism, equivalent to the belated situation of narration—of the modernist writer's burdened project—in relation to literary tradition.

Although more modest than Joyce despite its focus on the *langues* or competences that produce the personal metonymies or *paroles* that the narrative of the exemplary *Ulysses* gives us in the experiential randomness that asks us to reconstruct the codes from which they come, Bloomsbury's strategy is also more specific and schematic. It lies in the development of a prose that catalogues and interrogates the guiding and unconscious ideological systems embedded in common speech through the resources of a literary language equally belated in relation to its own history. This Bloomsbury accomplishes technically by joining a language of Joycean "scholarship" with a language of traditional representation, thereby identifying by means of its reflexive realism the structures of the world it represents with the structures that represent it. Like Joyce, but at the level of master codes rather than of experiential particularities, Bloomsbury writes a language of reverberation about the linguistic reverberations that constitute the real, especially the idioms of ordinary life, while simultaneously maintaining the coherence of its representationalism so as to thematize and account for the terms, dynamic, and history of the conceptual items or categories out of which its illusions are constructed: the components of the myth of the modern at large in Forster's *Howards End* (1910); the structure of subjectivity in Woolf's *Mrs. Dalloway* (1925) and of deferred action in *To the Lighthouse* (1927); and the history of the emergence of both the components and the structural dynamic of the myth of the modern in the sequence of Lytton Strachey's three major works, *Eminent Victorians* (1918), *Queen Victoria* (1921), and *Elizabeth and Essex* (1928).

Serenely taxonomic rather than hellbent on either ultimate chaos like Joyce's or ultimate fixity like Eliot's, Bloomsbury orchestrates the puns and "sunken meanings" it finds in its focus on ordinary speech in astonishingly uniform ways writer to writer, even, as we shall note briefly, among its paraliterary writers such as Moore, Keynes, and James Strachey. Organized with a clear thematic intent that punctures the notion that Bloomsbury is hermetic or irresponsibly formalist, the common strategy lies largely with puns that characteristically identify the vocabulary of the private with the vocabulary of the public. From Forster to Strachey, private worlds are a product or function of the public languages to which they are customarily opposed. Bloomsbury's thematic use of "alien associations" plainly links what James Strachey's translation of Freud (1953–74) calls "psychic economy" with the sphere of real economy as the result of a habitual and strategic identification of the vocabulary or figurations of private life with those of the public. Even the fact that we can propose such a solution to an aesthetic crisis exemplified by the wake of Joyce's achievement by citing a collectivity or group sensibility rather than another single or personal one is emblematic of the conclusions regarding the unstable status of the ego in Freud or of the problematic status of autonomy and property as categories from Arnold to Joyce. In the surprisingly common brand of prose practiced by virtually all Bloomsbury's members, such transubjectivity also finds its reflexive counterpart in the collective sensibility that produces it.

Hence the witting and consistent design of the Bloomsbury text—the deployment of unexpected lexical crossings that quietly but systematically put in question an otherwise familiar modernist thematic that usually deceives us into reducing Bloomsbury, too, to but another mythography of the will to modernity rather than as a solution to it or an account of its structure. The customary establishment of a myth of the modern at the level of story is habitually put in question by the migration or spillage of the language that describes it, making the will to modernity the same kind of object of inquiry it is for Hardy or for Pater or Joyce rather than a meaning in its own right: the ideology of modernity itself in *Howards End*; the allegorical loss of Mrs. Ramsay in *To the Lighthouse*; the substitution of modern fact for Victorian hypocrisy in *Eminent Victorians* and after. Moreover, the strategy of semic spillage that directs the punning identity of private and public simultaneous with their apparent thematic separation—a combination of Farfrae's machine and the broadcast it means to repress—is also the reflexive counterpart of what it represents. The linguistic slippage that allows for puns is based on the overdeterminations that allow language's associations to take place at all—on the necessity of what Pater calls the "residue" of past and collateral usage and the "quite alien associations" to which such contaminations may lead. And if the associations are in the service of a thematic that means to identify the operations of language with those of the world and the identification in turn of the vocabularies of the private and the public, it is because the economy of language and the language of economy are already structurally similar in Bloomsbury's reflexive realism. Indeed, if it is the residue or "surplusage" of prior usage that allows value or signification, especially puns, to happen in language, then it is also such residue or surplus that, in the apparently distinct sphere of economics, allows value to emerge in the world itself. The structure of signification—the exchange value of signs based on "surplusage" and the polysemy it engenders—is homologous with the structure of the surplus value that produces the value of material goods in a startling adequation of the production of texts and the production of the real to which texts supposedly only refer. Both, however, are functions of equivalent social processes that Bloomsbury will map.

Hence, too, the surprising but equivalent participation in such a collective design by at least three of Bloomsbury's key paraliterary productions: Moore's *Principia Ethica* (1903) and its (unconscious) identification of spiritual "goods" with material ones as an effect of the linguistic slippage that causes the systematic puns in Moore's otherwise straightforward moralizing about the value of "personal relations"; Keynes's treatises on money and their like figural adequation (following Marx as well) of exchange value in the marketplace with the exchange value by which all systems of human signification function, especially the system of language by which the adequation is itself made available to us; and James Strachey's *Standard Edition* of Freud, in which the linguistic identification of private or psychic economy with real economy leads to a socialization of the notion of the unconscious that produces in its own turn (and in a prophecy of Althusser's Lacan [1964]) the reciprocal relation between the private and the public that are otherwise taken to be separate categories in the reception of psychoanalysis and modern literature alike.

Our Bloomsbury itinerary will be both microscopic and paradigmatic. Readings of *Howards End, To the Lighthouse,* and all three of Strachey's neglected major texts will be close; the incremental comprehensiveness in our coverage as we move from Forster to Woolf to Strachey will in turn be consistent with the differing degrees of refreshment required to reassess all three writers, especially the now-unfamiliar and decanonized Strachey, for whom a look at all three works is likely more necessary than a summary review of the careers of the securely canonized Forster and Woolf, for whom the central texts upon which we shall focus remain exemplary.

Howards End summarizes all that we have seen before. A manifest myth of the modern that appears to repress or recontain the migration of its *sèmes* or tropes, its linguistic coincidences instead reveal that the privacies and primacies the novel supposedly champions are in fact functions of the public and belated world to which they are customarily opposed. Thematizing belatedness, Forster makes his characters the unfortunate victims of the inherited discourses that deny them authenticity at the moment of its expression, jettisoning the story's distinction between private and public by means of the narration's calculated language.

Paterian scholars as they are, Woolf and Strachey go on to exploit Forster's rather more hidden ironies explicitly. If Woolf's *Mrs. Dalloway* is, as we shall see, an instance of the self's paradoxical status as a vessel of the externalities to which it is by definition opposed, *To the Lighthouse* goes a step further by cataloguing and interrogating in almost summary form the three central myths of the modern that our strong writers have abnegated, but myths to which our weak ones have succumbed: belatedness or anxiety of influence in its exact Oedipal form in Woolf's use of James (Strachey) Ramsay; the usually unexamined centrality of the will to modernity in the failure of the empiricist presuppositions of Mr. Ramsay's analytic philosophy; and the vulgar-modernist aesthetic assumptions of Lily Briscoe, with whom, despite traditional opinion, the novel itself hardly identifies in the distance it wishes to draw between its own epistemology and Lily's contrastingly quaint and unacceptable one. In *To the Lighthouse*, moreover, Woolf also actually—actively—dramatizes the dynamic of belatedness or deferred action in the structure of the text's reading, thereby doubling its legendary thematic of loss, but also articulating it in a way that preconditionally requires the alienation or belatedness that it seems only to lament in the death of Mrs. Ramsay.

With Strachey, we will see a sequence of three texts that summarizes the movement from Forster to Woolf within Bloomsbury, and that goes on to historicize the emergence of the will to modernity at large: the reflexive representation of the world itself as a set of texts in *Eminent Victorians* that runs counter to its legendary pretence to distinguish between myth and analysis; the ironic production of the private by the public in *Queen Victoria*; and the historical emergence of both distinctions in the reflexive Renaissance of *Elizabeth and Essex*. Strachey, moreover, takes the apparently mimetic or empirical procedures of realism and historiography alike and transforms them, not just into the Eriksonian psychodramas that Freud admired (see Meisel and Kendrick 1985: Appendix II), but also into an interrogation of all such customary procedures and categories that topples the epistemology of positivist historiography in particular by revealing its purported raw or original materials to be no more than texts themselves. The supposedly extradiscursive originals to which Strachey's texts are directed are in fact no more than an effect or function of his revisionist inquiry into the representations out of which they are made rather than found out. For Strachey, life and letters are remarkably similar in both style and action, rendering all history historiography, much as the Homeric origin is, for Joyce and Pater at least, a function, not of its preexistent reality, but of our constitutive inability to grasp it. Strachey's concern is not simply with the history of our categories, but with their influence or effectiveness—their truth and its history—as a precise function of the power of those representational activities in the real most like those that represent them: the activities of reading, writing, and interpretation upon which Strachey habitually focuses at the level of story itself. Like Joyce (though, to be sure, far more literally), Strachey takes belatedness as an exact opportunity for power rather than as a rein on its possibilities. Hence the guise of the historian is enormously appropriate. Belatedness *is* power, since, from the historian's rhetorically unexamined (thus protected) point of view, coming late and knowing it is the announced precondition of the trade, allowing Strachey himself not just the freedom but the duty to exploit the resources of the otherwise burdensome past as an astonishingly direct way of gaining power over it—the opportunity that allows the latecomer the power of fathering his precursors. Thus the real is produced by means of a technology of power not only depicted in Strachey's texts as he elaborates in turn the methods of the Victorians and the Elizabethans, but also a technology of production and power also explicitly practiced by Strachey's narratives themselves, and, by implication, all narrative.

Howards End: Private Worlds and Public Languages

The senior Forster's *Howards End* recapitulates the myth of the modern at the level of story while simultaneously putting it into question at the level of narration. The manifest thematic that leads Forster, quite ironically, to ask that we "Only connect" in the book's epigraph turns out to be evacuated by the conspicuous connections systematically demonstrated by the behavior of its language, especially those between the supposedly sundered realms of the private and the public. Like *The Mayor of Casterbridge, Howards End* has a calculating myth of the modern that is the wittingly defensive function of a belatedness that its rhetoric takes into account.

Like *The Waste Land,* however, the novel as a whole appears to be the romance announced at its conclusion, replacing at its terminus the loss of Leonard Bast with the gain of a pastoral child—a lost one now found—who serves as the ideal of a primal harmony that is as wishful as the elf's own ritual invention. Howards End itself, of course, is a garden or paradise regained, with the child's resurrective emergence a symptom of the novel's ironically willful romance rather than a guarantee of the epistemological surety it appears to represent instead. Unlike Hardy's Elizabeth-Jane or Joyce's Rudy/ Stephen, Forster's child is still partly privileged in his twin social genealogy, half-rich, half-poor, as though the novel wishes to leave a clear trace of its ambivalence about the impossibility of the ideal of landed or grounded identity that Joyce and Hardy alike plainly eschew. As in Eliot, moreover, the pastoral conclusion emphasizes the ease with which the structure of romance at large contains the redemptive romance of Christianity. But while the two are identifiable ideals for Eliot himself, for Forster they are positioned as structures of irony rather than as assertions of truth. As the book's secular Eden, after all, the property of Howards End is a symbol of that realm beyond culture to which literature may appeal when it is in the kind of crisis required to produce such desire. The book's goals are apparently those "endless levels beyond the grave" (1910:332) that signify an eternal truth represented by the summary figure of "the sacred centre of the field" (335) at the narrative's close. With the "wych-elm" (3) serving as a protective "boundary between the garden and meadow" (3), Forster obviously perhaps too obviously grounds a mythical primacy in the figure of the enigmatic Mrs. Wilcox. "'Already in the garden'" (4) in the early morning early in the novel itself, Mrs. Wilcox is located in a fanciful landscape of redemptive origins consonant with her primal beatitude whose light overrides the kind of imaginative despair betokened by Coleridgean twilight or Gastonian dimness. "From the garden," says Forster at the novel's close, "came laughter" (342). The ground or property of Howards End is, in short, consecrated as a center, a home, an origin that the will to modernity uniformly produces as a defense against the belatedness that assails it.

So suspiciously programmatic are Forster's spiritual homologues, however, that not only is Christianity but one token of the generic type of romance. So, too, is the structure of native, pagan religiosity that identifies in sequence the will to modernity in its Renaissance, Romantic, and properly High Modernist forms. Howards End has "goblins" (33–34) as well as a garden, the intimations of Shakespearean romance suggesting in turn the Romantic strategy, as in Blake's early sonnets, of invoking indigenous deities in order to regain original inspiration. By so identifying "folklore" (267) and the "Holy of Holies" as alike "transfigured" (85) in their primacy or simulation of godhead, the novel allows Christian and pagan romance to coalesce. Not surprisingly, then, a "halo" (68) surrounds Mrs. Wilcox's hands as she lies ill. Like the romance ideals with which she is thematically coincident, she represents, at least in Mr. Wilcox's mind at her funeral, "unvarying virtue" (89), almost absolute "innocence" (89)—in short, a static and eternal ideal of virtue and spirituality, although one that remains in the ground of Howards End even after she dies, since it subsequently transmutes or transfigures itself into Margaret. The origin represented by ground or property—the "end" or telos that Howards End is—is, in the pagan sense, the function of a *genius loci* for which Mrs. Wilcox is but a transient habitation and a name, as Margaret will be too. Mrs. Wilcox's divinity is, of course, a product of the ground of Howards End, not the other way around, its spirit allowing Margaret to become its vessel in her turn, and also situating the novel's overly obvious symbol for lost primacy not in a personality but in actual—not metaphorically philosophical—ground, real estate, property. In fact, once "under the earth" (90), Mrs. Wilcox becomes a double emblem for her representation of the soil, roots, ground to which the novel aspires in its synonymous romantic, Christian, Romantic, and modernist terms.

If the term "genius" means spirit or indwelling of origin, the equivalent aesthetic ideality of originality it also represents is, of course, the formal underbelly of what Howards End and Mrs. Wilcox signify from the point of view of literature proper. A wonderfully reflexive instance of the modernist desire she represents from the point of view of literary belatedness, Mrs. Wilcox predictably "worshipped the past" (22) and has "that wisdom to which we give the clumsy name of aristocracy" (22)—the same name to which Forster's elfin child remains partially attached as well. Like the garden she inhabits both dead and alive, Mrs. Wilcox is the paradise lost of the soil at large and the belated imagination in particular, the latter the former's projective condition of representability. Thus Forster's litany of ideals grows more explicitly literary as the novel proceeds—from "aura" (153) and "supernatural life" (171) to the "nymphs" (197) and "new sanctities" (222) of a "Fairyland" (223) that, says Forster openly, even "Prospero" (230) could have commanded. If Mrs. Wilcox begins the novel as an emblem of modernist literary desire, the Shakespearean conclusion is its balancing reflexive counterpart in the text's almost overcoded disposition of motifs that are ideological objects of scrutiny rather than expressive messages. Preparing us for the novel's climax and functioning also as the prototype for Mrs. McNab in *To the Lighthouse* is the aptly named Mrs. Avery (aery, sprightly), who looks after Howards End after the original

Mrs. Wilcox's death and resurrects it for the transmigration of Howards End's genius into the new habitation of Margaret. True to her name, Mrs. A(v)ery is to be found "airing," of all things, the "books" (264), as though the text means to remind us that its ideals are calculated exercises in dealing with a literary problem rather than Forster's personal lament as to the fate of civilization. Forster even admits the real nature of his motivating anxiety:

> Why has not England a great mythology? Our folklore has never advanced beyond daintiness, and the greater melodies about our country-side have all issued through the pipes of Greece. Deep and true as the native imagination can be, it seems to have failed here. . . . England still waits for the supreme moment of her literature—for the great poet who shall voice her, or, better still, for the thousand little poets whose voices shall pass into our common talk. [267]

Though it is an inversion of this latter possibility from which the idiomatic art of reflexive realism will be made ("common talk" passes into literature rather than the other way around), Forster's implicit identification of "the great poet" with the role of mythologist is of special concern. While a "great poet" may well be a mythologist—a self-evident identity for the pioneers, especially of epic—for the latecomer, by contrast, strong art can no longer be persuasion or belief alone; it is, rather, an interrogation of the categories by which one dreams, not a rank presentation of dreams alone. Forster's novel is, to be sure, just such a metacritical art, taking as its raw materials, not some avowed chaos in or of the real, but the ideological grammar that produces the real—structuring mythologies like Hardy's "ache of modernism" or Pater's "modernity." *Howards End* even looks rather like *The Mayor of Casterbridge* in the efficiency and clarity with which it seeks to catalogue and question the chief ideological assumptions that govern modernist speech and desire in both novelistic discourse and general cultural competence.

Whether religious, romantic, or Romantic, then, *Howards End* is a catalogue of the will to modernity rather than an example of it. It is a meditation on modernism at large, finding among its other players the same structure of assumption to be found in Mrs. Wilcox despite the many differences that otherwise appear to divide them. The world the novel depicts is, in fact, one constituted by the ideology of a will to modernity that the novel itself will attempt to account for by describing the structure that produces it. The buzzing name "Schlegel" is probably the clearest instance of the novel's focus on the structure of the ideology of modernity, particularly its Romantic genealogy. Whether it is a question of "truth" (195), "earth" (199), the "fertility of the soil" or the "intensely green" (200) season of "Easter" (198), all such modernist notions of regenerative primacy—of the "earth and its emotions" (214), in a decidedly deliberate pathetic fallacy—are nonetheless shared notions or representations to which Schlegels, Basts, and Wilcoxes all alike subscribe, even if they differ in their particular interpretations of what living "deeply" (214) may mean. The soil of the colonies is as basic to Paul Wilcox's imperialism as the soil of England is to his mother's romanticism.

Like the "life of the body" trammeled by the unnecessary "appliances" (218) of the moneyed classes, it is the category of the original or the eternal that remains central to almost all the characters' recurrent and shared ideality of regeneration in a world of forms to which they come late. Even Bast has a partially direct connection with the earth in his ancestry; his forebears are, as he puts it, "'agricultural labourers'" (237) whose roots are in that "unspoilt country" (88) that represents what is left of the natural in the urban sprawl that threatens it. Pop Romantic modernist that he is, Bast wants simply to get "'back to the Earth'" (117), despite the phrase's equal foreshadowing of his subsequent death. Indeed, much as the soil upon which London sits precedes it, so Forster's staged myth of the modern, prescient as it is of Eliot's "dissociation of sensibility" eleven years later, also requires "an elder race" of "rural" folk (268) to whom "we look back with disquietude" (268) because of their more direct relation to the soil than ours. Forster even goes so far as to try to equate, like Wordsworth, the images of the garden and of childhood, both versions of primary innocence that Forster wittingly identifies as the kinds of assumptions that predetermine our ways of thinking and living. It is, in short, "the peace of the country" (315) that makes up the book's set of consistent ideals, all of them based on a notion of truth epistemologically intact beyond history, circumstance, and, apparently, beyond language as well. Margaret gives us the ideal in a compelling summary form: "Her conclusion was," says Forster of her mind's development as a little girl, "that any human being lies nearer to the unseen than any organization, and from this she never varied" (30).

So astute—so scholarly in Pater's sense—is the apparently breezy Forster in his interrogation of the forms the myth of the modern takes as an ideological formation that *Howards End* is almost an encyclopedia of the kinds of permutations its oppositions can produce. The opposition between the aesthetic Schlegels and the worldly Wilcoxes is, of course, only one example among many in the novel's scrupulous catalogue of the dualities that structure the myth of the modern, and one isomorphic with the equally recurrent opposition between nature and culture. Even in Bast's imagination of the composing process, for example, the poet Jeffries must work by having a prior state of feeling that he only subsequently turns into the secondariness or belatedness of writing: "the spirit," as Bast thinks, "that led Jeffries to write" (120). Here, and again symptomatically, the imagination of imagination is figured as identical with the structure of its religious and romance ideals: the certitude of a prior state of nature upon which or against which civilization uneasily sits, and the desire for which the novel readily identifies as a will to modernity defensively understandable but empirically problematic. One's job in life is to get to the " 'real thing' " behind the " 'husks' " (145), to the "root" of the "earth" (150); to penetrate the "husks" that "enclose . . . emotion" (311). In short, to keep, impossible as the mixture of metaphor already predicts, " 'memory green' " (152) in the hope that such a realm beyond culture really exists.

Much as Bast assesses writing as a function of an opposition between the primacy of feeling and the secondariness of language, so the opposition between the Schlegels and the Wilcoxes is likewise one between depth and superficiality, art and business. To the Schlegels early in the novel, the Wilcoxes are a "fraud," with only "emptiness" behind them (26)—affectation as opposed to authenticity or sincerity (10), the "lips" to the "heart" (37), the "eyes" to the "smile" (48). So, too, to see the world "half sensibly and half poetically" (12) not only tells us that Margaret is a balanced and judicious woman, but also that the informing oppositions that allow us to make such a judgment are in turn those between, for example, pose and reality, " 'romance' " and " 'prose' " (174), "prose" and "passion" (186); hence, too, the notion of a "rainbow bridge" between them (186), one of a number of Forster's phrases to be repeated by Woolf. And along with oppositions such as reason and passion, sense and sensibility, male and female, come other logical permutations, especially the key opposition between outer and inner worlds (174–75), the vaunted separation of "public" and private, the without and the "within" (28), "the outer life" (103) and the inner, one's "head" and "the universe" (50). The opposition between private and public is likewise aligned with the opposition between "surface" and depth (220, 240), much as the narrator distinguishes between "true imagination and false" (121), and, just as paradigmatically, between "Romance" and "work" (138). Epistemologically akin to the split between public and private, the split between civilization and soil also leads to the oppositions between "imprisonment and escape" (86), "trade" and "spirit" (84), body and soul or spirit (102, 115, 186), "cold culture" and real "art" (310); even the "orderly sequence . . . fabricated by historians" as opposed to the "chaotic nature of our daily life" (106). Nor should we fail to note the familiar opposition of "dirty" and "pure" (167) and Forster's accompanying lament about "muddles" (e.g., 308). Thus the differences between Schlegels and Wilcoxes—between spirit and trade, intimacy and "'telegrams'"(103)—also inform the notion that the "stench of motor cars" (15) and "metallic fumes" (53) "cut off the sun" (56) and desecrate the "soil" (47). Even at Howards End, a garage replaces the old pony paddock (71), reminiscent of the various urban technologies that replace the rural ones in Hardy's Wessex. Within such a world, the Schlegels "breathe . . . less of the air" and see "less of the sky" (107). "Nature," in short, "withdrew" (107–08). Indeed, Forster goes so far as to admit his quaintness in maintaining such oppositions, since "the Earth as an artistic cult," as he puts it, "has had its day" (108).

The myth of past freshness is so general in the political unconscious of the contemporary world that the novel depicts (and of which it is itself a function) that even the visit to Simpson's with the Wilcoxes displays the novel's selfsame literary and religious ideals in quotidian form: "Though no more Old English than the works of Kipling, it had selected its reminiscences so adroitly that . . . criticism was lulled, and the guests whom it was nourishing for imperial purposes bore the outer semblance of Parson Adams or Tom Jones" (153). In such a world structured by Romantic or modernist desire in its popular mythology as well as in its literary history, "'Houses are alive'" (155), at least according to the central animating Romantic trope of personification that Ruskin recognized by condemning and trying to outlaw. So different is modern life from the wishful glories of the past that the "nomadic civilization" (261) of modern cities, says the narrator, will "receive no help from the earth" (261), the sacred soil that the urban scorns and seeks to destroy or neutralize.

The novel's most famous trope in the organizing mythology its oppositions produce is surely the "civilization of luggage" (150), the wasteland into which we moderns have fallen and whose coherence as a target of attack relies on still another series of organizing oppositions, chief among them the opposition between transit and rest, hurry and serenity, luggage and home, and, of course, city and country. As though the real had really changed on its own, modern ideas, too, are "portable" (61) rather than secure. People, likewise, are always "'moving'" (137) and speaking "the language of hurry" (109), both counterposed to the natural stability of home, rest, and leisure; of seeing things "steadily" and seeing them "whole" (161), as Forster says in his wittingly Arnoldean refrain (see also "empires of facts" [30]) that is perhaps chief among the officially literary motifs included in the novel's survey of (its) hegemonic ideological presuppositions. Forster even soliloquizes, with hidden irony, upon the metacritical rather than mimetic status of his project through

Margaret's maintenance of the familiar myth of the modern that has structured her youth as it does the ideology of modernism at large: "London was but a foretaste of this nomadic civilization which is altering human nature so profoundly, and throws upon personal relations a stress greater than they have ever borne before. Under cosmopolitanism, if it comes, we shall receive no help from the earth" (261). With such oppositions so securely in place and so capable of organizing the world the book represents—a world divided between earth and civilization, steadiness and "flux" (261), private and public—the novel is almost merciless in the thoroughness of its inventories. Forster's catalogue of modernist ideology may therefore be said to formulate a grammar that will account for the symptomatic manifestations of the will to modernity in all its forms. By so isolating the means of production of its wishful primacies, Forster can thereby simulate the reality they engender in his (meta)realism while, at the same time, go on to disassemble it in the simultaneously reflexive arrangements of his prose by which the oppositions upon which the myth of the modern is based are, with equal systematicity, also identified by the language that expresses them.

If we begin to inspect the novel's language in any detail at all, then, we find that Forster's vaunted (and only apparent) thematic intent—his myth of the modern—is simultaneously undermined as programmatically as it is set up by a rhetorical contamination or slippage of the oppositions that put it in place. Central among the novel's dualities is the classic modernist antagonism between self and society, private and public, and one that leads Forster to recommend the Moorish ideal of "'personal relations'" (174) as a means of building that "rainbow bridge" (186) between self and community that turns out to be unnecessary because the two are already conjoined. Even Terry Eagleton remains captive to the belief in a straightforward "Forsterian affirmation of the 'personal'" (1981:138), as though there is no real irony in Forster's art. "Personal relations" is, however, an oxymoron, since, as Pater and Joyce—and even Eliot—have shown, self and world are mutually constitutive in the semiotic play of culture that produces subjects and objects alike in a series of gestures that privileges neither side of what is a productive rhetorical opposition rather than one expressive of a condition in the world. A thorough focus on Forster's vocabulary will show just how the oppositions that organize his manifest myth of the modern also turn into one another so as to wreak semantic havoc with the categories the novel's manifest thematic has erected.

If Bloomsbury is indeed programmatic in its use of the unseen poetic arrangements of ordinary language, the real object of a text such as *Howards*

End is to join linguistically those colloquial terms that are customarily articulated as oppositions. Thus the novel's oppositions turn out to link, paradigmatically, human and fiduciary relations—private and public, spiritual and material, "personal" and "relations"—in a common set of signifiers, throwing the relationship between denotation and connotation into chaos as one of the numerous side-effects that render privacy a function of its dependence on the publicity to which it is normally counterposed. Most pervasive as well as most focused are the similarities rather than differences between psychic and real economy and their mutual interdependence in the tropology that identifies the vocabulary of business or the Wilcoxes with the vocabulary of private emotion or the Schlegels. Private virtue itself, for example, is thereby always grafted, linguistically at least, to the same terms by which we calculate the world of material value to which it is customarily opposed ("worth . . . ," 165, 259, 262, 292), making it no wonder that an idiom such as " 'tender hearts' " (169) suddenly reveals an economic aspect to the figure that cautions the degree of epistemological integrity we like to assign to our private worlds. Thus a surprising parade of tropological identifications: one can be " 'worthy' " (66) or " 'unworthy' " (244) as a person; "tender" (245) emotionally; repose "trust" (37) in another person (shades, too, of *The Confidence Man*); or take an "interest" (103) in someone else. Even more exactly, Helen's stocks, like her emotions, are characteristically "reinvested" (256), while the contrastingly stable Mrs. Munt possesses stock in her more appropriate style of "safe investments" in "Home Rails" (14). One can, moreover, "cancel . . ." one's "mistrust" (37) in a person by means of the same idiom by which one cancels a check. Thus, too, a " 'girl with no interests' " (57) is, like the otherwise comfortable Helen, tropologically at least, nevertheless akin to a girl with no money at all—Jacky, for example, with whom Helen in fact changes places when she becomes Bast's lover. Likewise, " 'the will to be interested' " (57) directly implicates the vocabulary of the personal in that of the public. " 'The very soul of the world is economic' " (61), admits Mr. Wilcox, not only for the materialist reasons that escape him even in the first instance, but also because of the semiotic spillage that thwarts his like investment in the absolute difference between what is one's own and what is another's.

The vocabularies of the marketplace and stock exchange, in short, programmatically collide with the vocabulary of personal relations. Even throwaway colloquialisms denoting (connoting?) one's private mood such as "on Helen's account" (70) or to give an "account" (85, 106) of something coincide figurally with the public language of commerce and exchange. Such common or idiomatic usage almost endlessly infects the difference between private and public throughout the novel, whether we "'make a great deal of it'" (75), "evoke our interests" (79) or "withdraw" them (79). Thus an emotional "check . . ." (96, 109) has fiduciary connotations, much, amazingly enough, as does Mrs. Wilcox's extraordinary "tenderness" (89) and what is "tender . . ." (182, 193, 318, 325) in others throughout the novel. The property of Howards End has "tenderness" chief among its manifest atmospheric qualities (206), legal tender as it is of the value of the property as real estate. Indeed, one goes on "trusting" one's "husband" (93) or shows "mistrust . . ." (79) for someone in implicitly economic figures meant to describe the private alone, even when it comes to one's "life interest" (99). Though life is, says Forster, "unmanageable" (107), his descriptions of it are, by contrast, scrupulously managed by a language that joins the "alien associations" of the public discourses of management, finance, and exchange with those we (also) use to describe what is most private to us.

Hence the sudden resonance of apparently innocent idioms such as "'on no account'" (112, 248), "on her account" (162), "on his account" (320); the wish to "'tender . . . apologies'" (116); the economic murmur of phrases describing personal relations such as "'managed him'" (144), "trading on" (147), "deposited" (149), "cost" (158), even the matter-of-fact "owing to" (157). People try in short "to balance their lives" (150) through the management of psychic investments etymologically laced with economic ones such as those that make up Henry's bank balance. Thus Margaret's annoying recollection of "the stock criticism about Helen" (277) raises still another series of economic murmurs in an otherwise purely personal idiomatic signification. Even to be "rent into two people" (315–16) by psychological shock carries the quite alien associations that intimate the settled or unsettled state of one's psyche as a form of tenancy. Late in the novel, Helen's "'interests'" (305) slip between fiduciary and psychological meanings almost overtly, the family "'goods'" (306), like Moore's, both blessed and tainted by the oscillation of philosophical and material meanings in the same signifier. And once Forster describes the condemned Leonard as one who does not "count for much" (311), his fate is sealed tropologically and representationally in the same figure.

Hardly random events in the novel, *Howards End*'s linkage of the public and private in an exemplary set of shared or common expressions not only projects a Keynesian vision of the interdependencies that represent society as a matrix of relations rather than as a set of autonomous atoms, but also serves as a continual reminder of our nonimmediate relation to the world altogether, whether private or public, a world in which we are always belated because "'some medium of exchange'" (155)—some social mediation—is always required for anything to signify at all. Neither self nor world is in itself either independent or immediate; as a set of representations in the first instance, life is a secondary rather than a direct phenomenon from the start it can never be said properly to have (had). Foreshadowing Woolf's rather more overt vision of a world without a given self, Forster must conclude by implication that nothing exists autonomously, and that autonomy itself—the very token of the will to modernity whose typology and nature as a notion the novel elaborates—is a defensive reaction to its own impossibility within the semiotic grid of a culture to which we come belatedly and as a function of the bewildering overdeterminations of its signs and history. The novel's characters may try to act out the will to modernity in their various quests for the self-erasing ideal of "personal relations" that stands for a directness supposedly lost after an implied Eliotic "dissociation" divides modernity from tradition. As Forster's language shows, however, such acting out fails to work through the paradox of liberation that forever forbids the possibility of immediacy or of any kind of transcendent autonomy at all.

If the self-contamination of Forster's metaphors begins to emerge in the novel's habitual identification of psychic and real economy at the level of language—of "goods" and "goods," "worth" and "worth"—such an identity is even more trenchant and etymologically exacting in the movement of another of the novel's chief tropological systems, that of property. As we have seen in Pater's deconstruction of Arnold's selfsame ideals of originality and cleanliness, "property" is a figure etymologically bound to a series of what are, for Forster as well, epistemologically identical structures of desire: for property as such (as in Mrs. Wilcox's "property" [72] or in simple "possessions" [98]); for propriety in manners and sensibility (refinement and serenity); for the properness or integrity of a work of art; and for that self-possession or stability of ego that we equate with mental health. We should recall that *propre* also means what is clean or unspoiled, the graphic and/or tactile representation of the wishful desire for originality or autonomy central to the will to modernity in art and experience alike. Forster's use of the tropology of "property" is both exact in the novel's enduring deconstruction of its myth of the modern, and exacting in the strategic play of the figure throughout the text. Even one example suggests that behaving "'properly'" (9) and avoiding "impropriety" (13) will result in "self-possession" (17)—the possession of oneself is metaphorically akin to the solidity or ground of epistemological certainty and of plain real estate as well.

The figure's strategic vicissitudes organize the novel's language in a striking way. One wants one's "muddles" or dirt "tidied up" (69), for example, so as to let "self-possession," the propriety of one's own being, take on its apparently proper privacy (hence Bast's role as a grossly thematic reminder that the state of one's psyche and of one's economy are disastrously intertwined). Similarly, a "sloppy" soul (104) and the physically "untidy" (123) are figurations that epistemologically join what would otherwise be put asunder. Any "truth" is, as the Arnold to whom Forster sometimes alludes would have it, one of "clearness of vision" (182), freed from the haze or uncleanliness of outside influence. Thus Margaret's Arnoldean desire that Leonard "'wash out his brain and go to the real thing'" (145). We are in fact all in a "'mist'" (238), and therefore want our "vision cleared" (239)—we want to make a "clean breast" (247) of things. Even the apparently universal and nonliterary ideal of love is figured in the register of property and cleanliness, too: "She loved him," says Forster of Margaret's feeling for Henry, "with too clear a vision to fear his cloudiness" (220). The metaphorical chain is maintained when, for example, Jacky Bast's affair is described as "one new stain on the face of a love that had never been pure" (236). Of course, in a precise instance of Forster's wit, the last figuration again returns us, not to the will to modernity undiagnosed, but to the structure of modernism that produces its emergence. The origin or home—Jacky—to which Leonard wishes to return is, like Molly, already admittedly stained, the figure contaminating the origin as a precondition of the desire for it, its warmth a function of its distance.

With the categories and structure of modernism Forster's subject, then, *Howards End*, otherwise a proto-wastelander picture of London as full of "'rubbish'" (157, 161), "'slime'" (173), and "'heaps'" (175), is neither mimetic transcription nor a rehearsal of Eliot's anxiety about tradition as it will be projected in the ruinous landscape of *The Waste Land*. Instead, Forster's myth of the modern, with all its detailed characteristics, is, like Hardy's, an enormously prescient anticipation and prior critique of the ideology of a High Modernism yet to be misread. To say, then, that "the mind is overtaxed" (321) by the novel is to describe the effect of Forster's apparently flat prose as well as to cite still another example of its surprising spillage that scrambles the oppositions necessary to maintain a myth of the modern without being obvious about it. The privacy of the "mind" is troped as the form of a public system, "taxation." The sanctity of privacy itself—that "paradise within thee happier far" still sustaining English Romantic tradition as late as 1910—can, must be signified, alas, only in relation to that which it is not, the public, the traditional, the outside. Because property is, ironically, privacy, it is public enough for Forster to dub the age itself the "Age of Property" (149). Like "personal relations," "Age of Property" is, however, also an implicit contradiction, implying as it does a shared or communal belief in the kind of privacy such a public articulation forbids.

If, moreover, what is private is available only as a function of what is public, the belated status of modern experience and of the modern imagination are once again redoubled, too. Like literary language, the lineaments of being itself are already used, handed down—woven and rewoven, to recall Joyce. This is why Forster grows reflexive as a direct function of his realism rather than as a reaction against it. If the world itself is already taken to be a world of signs or representations from the start, it not only puts all its denizens in the belated role that the modern writer has toward tradition; it also makes the practice of writing about such a world an inherently reflexive procedure, since narrative representation must thereby be a representation of a world already understood to be a set of representations. As taxonomist and diagnostician of the ideology of modernism, then, Forster finds the lifelike objects of his fiction to be already fictions or representations in their own terms. As with his own burlesque pathetic fallacies, Forster will sometimes even provide us with clues as to just how equivalent life and letters (another version of the supposedly opposed public and private) can get to be, sometimes by affirmation, sometimes by negation. Helen, for example, writes to Margaret very early in the novel that though (as Meg has said) "'life is sometimes life and sometimes only a drama,'" "'it really does not seem life'" at all "'but a play'" (4–5). Tibby's sense of family life as scripted ("a scene behind footlights" [280]) is also in line with the novel's habitual systems of usage by which Forster's reflexive realism represents the real by representing the representations that compose it in the first place. Like his own mock-heroic allusions (e.g., 101), the terms by which everyone lives derive from quite discernible mythologies rather than from a natural expressiveness on Forster's own part. London is a "vast theatre" (129); Mrs. Munt "rehearse[s]" (13) for actual events, expecting her niece to "imitate" (14) her in turn; even Leonard's oaths are "learnt from older men" (49), a rather overt sign that the vocabulary of candor and earthiness, too, is belated because derivative or learned. Margaret's desire to have Ruth Wilcox as a friend is likewise figured in an overtly textual metaphor ("Desiring to book Mrs. Wilcox as a friend, she pressed on the ceremony, pencil, as it were, in hand" [79]), while the mourners surrounding Mrs. Wilcox's "grave" (another recurrent term that connotes writing and links it with death) are described as virtual letters in another writerly metaphor: they "moved between the graves, like drops of ink" (88). The life Forster represents in all its forms is, in other words, represented in the first instance as a system of texts or codes already in place when any new or original subject arrives on the scene.

Woolf and, more especially, Strachey will go on to show us, with even greater precision and far clearer intent, the world itself as a set of texts or representations like the textual representations that represent them. Even the various pastoral landscapes upon which *Howards End* dwells so fondly—and tries to separate from the "theatre" of the "Satanic" (84) city—are figured by Forster as "system after system" (167) in their own right, much as Charles and Dolly's newest child is, however humorously, "a third edition" (185). And while such vocabulary may be taken to suggest the dehumanization of life under technology, the measured repetition of Forster's strategic figurations should remind us instead that his focus is not on a world as such, but on the "reverberations" (23), as he puts it himself, of the dominant codes or discursive polarities by means of which the discourses of ideology produce rather than merely respond to the real.

What, however, is the point of the elaborate romance machinery at book's end? Does it mean to repress the contamination of its modernist categories in the hidden service of the kinds of ideals it otherwise puts in question? But while the book's modernist wishes may be summed up in Helen's rather Moorish remark that " 'One is certain of nothing but the truth of one's own emotions' " (170), we know that "one's own" is hardly certain as a category. Ironically, the aesthetic pleasure of the book's ending is its most enduring source of pain. The ending of *Howards End* is an overcompensatory romance whose desire to soothe despite the horrors involved is sociologically pathetic and, epistemologically, symptomatic of something else. Its attempted (or merely staged) dialectical resolution—the kind of structure made readily apparent in the tripartite shape of the later *Passage to India* (1924)— may or may not be but another programmed moment in a novel that is otherwise really a metatext that represents and interrogates the systematic self-representations of life itself rather than our chaotic experience of them. Not only must we ask why Bast dies, but also why it is Charles who kills him. In fact, Charles kills Bast as the function of a double Oedipal displacement. After all, Charles's father has not once but thrice slept with women Charles himself desires—his real mother (naturally), but also Jacky and Margaret, the latter he once fancies flirting with him early on in the story. Thus Bast, who has a sexual connection to Charles's father through his wife Jacky's affair with him, provides Charles with a reason for investing him with a son's displaced fury. Bast thereby becomes his ironic surrogate father as the husband of the

Jacky with whom his father has slept. As a subjective structure, it also has the effect of psychologizing away class differences in favor of personal ones, even though, as we shall see in a moment, Forster's psychoanalysis is political as well as poetical. Symbolically, Bast represents the father that Charles cannot in law kill, though he can—and almost does—ruin him by his attack upon the poorer man. More than that, however, Bast as displaced symbolic father substitutes not just for Mr. Wilcox himself, but, in the process, also suggests, by virtue of his own mobile symbolism, that even the real father is not an immediate origin either. The real father is real because he is a symbol, and a symbol of authority because he is a real father. The father actually represents, not himself, but the law that he serves by symbolizing or substituting for it in the eyes of the futurity that will organize itself retrospectively around his legacy. Even the ambiguity in the possible historical play of the Wilcoxes' Christian names, Charles and Henry (both kings of England, it is up to the reader to fashion a relation in accord with a given interpretation), encourages ambiguities as to whom it is that gains the ultimate, if sad, privilege, and encourages in turn the startling psychoanalytic ambiguities that Forster's Oedipal structure is designed to provoke. The father is himself the symbol or surrogate for something else even more primary than his own supposedly seminal authority. The original original—the father—is belated in relation to himself, ironically prior to himself as father since he can only stand for his purported natural authority by virtue of his symbolism. Even Freud himself (in James Strachey's translation) is momentarily explicit about it. Writing of the Wolf Man, Freud says, "He resisted God in order to be able to cling to his father; and in doing this he was really upholding the old father against the new" (1918:66). "The totem, I maintained, was the first father-surrogate, and the god was a later one, in which the father had regained his human shape" (1918:114).

What is repressed in the killing of Bast, then, is not just an expression of Charles's personal Oedipal rage, but the constitutive protest of subjectivity against its formation through categories that make its autonomy impossible. Thus Forster's machinery at novel's end performs double duty, framing Bast's murder in apparently suavely psychoanalytic terms so as to keep us away from the deeper problem to be repressed, not just in the static sociology of English life, but also in the epistemology of psychoanalytic reasoning (another instance of Forster's early scrutiny rather than expression of modernist ideologies): the failure of the notion of the Oedipus complex itself as a route to original truth. Hence Forster allows us to see just what Arnold has tried to hide more than anyone else: that origins, fathers central among their (ironic) figurations, are themselves but symbols or substitutes for something else absent but supposedly more primary, more original than the father even in the immediacy of his flesh.

Also a caution as to the ease or certainty with which we use the notion of authority at large, the novel's surprising psychoanalytic implications are at the same time at the hinge of the poetics of reflexive realism as a project in its own right. The original father's only symbolic power suggests that, in its narratological counterpart, the immediate—the thing represented—is also already a sign for something else at the very moment that it is what it is. A sign is what it is because it is, by the definition that allows it to signify in the first place, something different from itself to begin with. Hence, too, in both reflexive realism and in the transference that structures the analytic session (at least in the younger Strachey's formulation [1934]), the real is only symbolic, while only the symbolic is real. If Forster's text is reflexive because of its realism— because the world it refers to is already a tissue of signs—Forster's implicit notion of symbolism here suggests in turn that the real is precisely the symbolically authoritative.

Forster's reflexive realism in *Howards End*, then, is, like the later work of Woolf and Strachey (and of Conrad and Hardy before them, along with Ford), implicitly but efficiently pedagogical as well. Taking as his subject the systems by which we exist and the by-products or effects of them that make up our lives, Forster produces an allegory of reading in *Howards End* that asks its reader to decide—or not to—a mode of response within the wide spectrum of possibilities the book's complex operations may detonate reader to reader. If Joyce focuses on the minute *paroles* of life, forcing the reader to deduce from them the *langues* or codes that contextualize and so give each the meaning the reader requires them to have, Forster instead appeals directly, if invisibly, to the *langues* or ideological paradigms themselves in a cultural metafiction that sets the model for Bloomsbury prose to come. So organized are the components of the ideology of modernism in Forster's text that we can in the final instance only classify *Howards End* as a novel of classification that in turn asks us to classify it. Much, for example, as one may ask fruitlessly who one really is once the vagaries of "property" are exposed, so, too, may one read the book's famous "wych-elm" (the preeminent sign of fixity and established grace in the novel's myth of the modern) as the rather more transient sign to be found in reading it interrogatively—as a Joycean pun that asks instead, through an inversion of its normative meaning, the reflexive question "which elm?" that both frees the text from its denotative referents while simultaneously reaffirming their coherence by virtue of such educative transgression. The novel thereby demonstrates the ever-shifting possibilities produced by the play of both fixed codes and floating signifiers, enjoying just the kind of pleasure *The Waste Land* in particular cannot.

Like Helen's desire that Margaret " 'Burn' " (5–6) her letters at the novel's start, or like the Wilcoxes' decision to "tear the note up" (99) with which Mrs. Wilcox has bequeathed Howards End to Margaret, the novel itself functions—like the psychoanalytic transference—as a double operation that asks us both to absorb and destroy its variously incompatible messages at one and the same time. It wishes to leave "no traces behind" (102), even if its language continues to broadcast both its myth of the modern and the contamination of the dichotomies that sustain it. Such simultaneous absorption and cancellation—a structure also figurally identical with Freud's representation of the unconscious in the "Note upon the 'Mystic Writing-Pad' "(1925)is a strong and decisive response to the problematic of modernist belatedness. Like psychoanalysis, it secures the wishful primacies its representations of them habitually undercut.

Deferred Action in *To the Lighthouse*

With Virginia Woolf, we move to the middle ground—the switch or circuit—between Forster's taxonomic reflexive realism and Strachey's historiographical one. Before proceeding to our focus on Woolf's consummate achievement, *To the Lighthouse* (1927)—her *Lear* to the *Hamlet* of *Mrs. Dalloway* (1925), to which we shall briefly turn first—it is worth noting that Woolf is not only a literary corridor between Forster and Strachey, but also an exemplary—and reflexive—participant in Bloomsbury's collective sensibility by virtue of her outrageous borrowings (especially from *Howards End*) of phrases that become perhaps more familiar as tropes in her own prose ("rainbow bridge," "prose and passion"); even of organizing conceits such as Pointz Hall's doubling of Howards End in *Between the Acts* (1941). To call it borrowing or theft, however, is to maintain a sense of private property, literary or otherwise, that Bloomsbury itself rejects because it knows the notion is little more than an illusion and proper authority little more than a transpersonal function.

To speak of *Mrs. Dalloway* as we might wish—as the perfect whole it seems to be—is, of course, as critically problematic as it is to speak seriously of anything categorically autonomous. Like Pater and Forster, Woolf, too, submits the Arnoldean ideal of the proper to interrogation, clearest perhaps in the passage cited earlier from *Between the Acts*, in which the instance of music serves her, as it does Pater, as an especially clear example of the difference underlying all signification, and of the temporal or belated structure of its action. Like *Howards End, Mrs. Dalloway* is not an expression of the will to modernity, but a catalogue of the kinds of modernist ideals temporality or belatedness disallows, together with an enormously lucid account of the larger structure of modernism that produces such ideals symptomatically. The novel's own appearance of unity is therefore aligned with the customary ideal unities it presents in a number of registers (the pastoral nostalgia of Bourton, for example), chief among them the self. In perhaps the novel's most famous scene, Clarissa, (re)composing her selfhood before the mirror, thinks of herself as a "diamond" (1925:55). And yet—in a strategy like Forster's—the trope's identification elsewhere in the novel with precisely that public world to which it is opposed contaminates the privacy it otherwise signifies here. After all, "diamond" resonates with the novel's seemingly unrelated tropology of finance, empire, and the material resources of colonialism "where only spice winds blow" (143), a tropology into whose range "diamond" may vibrate so as to make it signify a specific type of imperial wealth, and that suggests Clarissa's personal wholeness to be dependent in turn upon the stability of her husband's money. The identification of psychic and real economy is as exact as Forster's: the language of privacy and that of common or public mythologies are once again the same. Woolf's like figuration of Clarissa as now "disinterested" (50) in Sally Seton resonates with the figure of Richard's apparently contrasting "deposit" (43) of affection for her, both terms conjoining in the tropology of imperial riches (116), and setting off a series of familiar Bloomsbury puns such as Clarissa's desire to "repay" or "pay back" sentiments (43), the crowd's "unspent" (27) emotions early in the novel, even the ironic "treasures" (211) of Septimus's psychosis. "Signs," in short, "were interchanged" (210). *Mrs. Dalloway* is little less than a textbook of the "shuffle" of "sunken meanings" in words, as Woolf herself presents it in "Craftsmanship" (1937), a strategic discourse of puns disguised (like Forster's, but unlike Joyce's overt ones) within the apparent semantic stability of common idioms.

Woolf's ambivalence about belief in the fiction of property, or, as she calls it in *Mrs. Dalloway*, "Proportion" (151)—Farfrae's machine now in the unabashedly antiseptic garb of the doctors Holmes and Bradshaw—is evident in Clarissa's own ambivalence about her social standing and consequent double values ("being part of it" on the one hand [6], being "outside, looking on" on the other [11]). It is even more evident in Woolf's (later) construction during the draftings of the novel of a "double" (1928:vi) for Clarissa who flaunts

Proportion with as much calculation as she cultivates it. Septimus, after all, is Clarissa's opposite, no longer shackled by the impossible desire for pure selfhood or "properness," since he gives in entirely to the public determinations that undermine any pure privacy in any case, allowing all Proportion to fall away. Clarissa instead represents just that citizenly contrast that produces ego over against the schizophrenia as displayed by Septimus himself. Hence both the advertising airplane and the motor-car early in the novel demonstrate not only the determinate reality of public languages in the world itself—now overtly a product of a political or ideological unconscious, a set of shared cultural presuppositions or representations—but also the ways in which such public symbols or languages send given spectators into distinct worlds of private thought. Like the various clocks that strike a few moments apart in relation to the central authority represented by Big Ben, the particularities that fashion privacy are each permutational instances of the dominant ideological arrangements of culture at large.

If *Mrs. Dalloway* recapitulates Forster's strategy of identifying private and public through the language of a text that reflexively enacts their interdependence at the level of the representations that form the world as such, *To the Lighthouse* goes on to identify the mechanism of belatedness with the mechanism of the text's own readability. As elegant an elegy as there is in English (its dialogical relations to *Lycidas*, *Adonais*, and *In Memoriam* are especially exorbitant), *To the Lighthouse* is Woolf's greatest novel if not her best one. The problems the novel sets out to address—the now-twinned thematic and dynamic of temporality or belatedness—are in fact just the kind that make a wholly perfect novel impossible. We have already seen rather briefly why such exact proportion is impossible in the apparently perfect *Mrs. Dalloway*; *To the Lighthouse*, published only two years later, takes the process logically further—to the summit, in fact, of Woolf's career as a novelist. Thus the reader of *To the Lighthouse* must technically experience the very kind of deferred action with which the book is thematically concerned, a consummate example of reflexive realism in which Woolf makes *récit* and *histoire* versions one of the other even as their differences are manifestly preserved. Linear though it may seem, the novel is done in what Pound would call "medallion" style, so that its three component parts may be shifted and rearranged in their relations to one another. Thus entirely different meanings may be inflected by the same parts depending upon the different relations among them one chooses to inflect. Do we read the novel as Mr. Ramsay reads—linearly, in the strictly chronological unfolding that characterizes his reading of Scott's *Antiquary* (as well as the alphabetical order by which he figures his career [1927:53–56])? Or do we read in the manner of Carmichael's "acrostics" (65), not unlike Mrs. Ramsay's equally contrasting way of reading "at random," "backwards, upwards" (178) instead? Which part of the novel, in other words, is early and which late? By the temporal schema of years, of course, part I obviously precedes part III by ten years; by the temporal schema of hours, however, part III precedes part I, since it begins in the morning and concludes at noon, while part I begins in the afternoon and ends in the evening.

If we follow the linear trajectory of years, consonant with Mr. Ramsay's linear mode of reading books, we follow the narrative as seems only natural, with part I coming first. By so taking part I as the origin it seems to be, however, the novel predictably enacts a myth of the modern—the fall from the plenitude of Mrs. Ramsay's Edenic presence that renders the later part III a fall into time and history. From this point of view, the priority of fathers oppresses sons and daughters alike; the sundering of "'subject'" and "'object'" leaves the question of "'the nature of reality'" in doubt (38); and the status of art remains one of recapturing secondarily some primariness forever behind it as both inspiration and inhibition. With the fiction of linear or chronological priority thus positing a myth of origins in Mrs. Ramsay from which all else is a fall or loss, we move, then, from a state of paradisiacal grace in part I (despite the twilight mood of its broody pastoral and the northerliness of its site in the Hebrides) to a state of wishful modernist redemption and resurrection in part III—Oedipal (James and Cam); philosophical (Mr. Ramsay); and aesthetic (Lily).

If, on the other hand, we follow both the diurnal schema as well as the models of reading offered by Carmichael and Mrs. Ramsay, part III may be put first instead. Part I remains, to be sure, a myth of origins, but now a self-conscious myth retroactively (re)produced by memory. This second reading or arrangement of the novel's parts gives us not only a nonlinear trajectory, but a trajectory rather exactly in accord with the structure of deferred action or belatedness that cautions the myth of the modern and even accounts for the sequence of normative modernist primacies it engenders in James's Oedipus, Mr. Ramsay's philosophical quiddity, and the autonomy of Lily's art. Such a rearrangement tells us, not that we have experienced an irreparable dissociation from Mrs. Ramsay's luminous sensibility, but rather that that which comes early is really a function of that which succeeds it. Belatedness is specified as the poetry of bereavement, as mourning, not just as its token but as its very type, and, in fact, as its very dynamic. Its paradigm is the narrative of memory, in which, as in all narrative, lost presence is produced as a deferred effect of its absence. Thus the novel's production of its world is the result of the remembrance or mourning that necessarily succeeds it, placing reader and narrator alike in an overlapping matrix of desire in which, biographically speaking, the most private of Woolf's writerly compulsions (must one allude to those famous *Diary* entries in which she confesses the book to be a form of mourning for her parents?) becomes a public mode of discourse instead—an elegy.

From this second point of view, then, the novel is no longer another myth of the modern, but an attempt to explain the emergence of such a myth by anatomizing its components, as does Forster, and by subsequently showing how a different shuffling of them may account for the myth they produce. By so reassessing the novel, it becomes a metacritical inquiry into the structure of the modernism that prompts its symptomatic will to modernity as it is concretized in almost everyone's attitude of desire toward Mrs. Ramsay herself.

To begin our reading with the otherwise neglected part II, then, is logical once we notice that "Time Passes" is at one and the same time the section in which Mrs. Ramsay dies and the one in which the narrator gives us the reflexive counterpart to her loss in the text's language. Much, after all, as Mrs. Ramsay's death flaws the subsequent lives of her family and friends, so the stylistic grumpiness and "reminiscent" landscape of part II flaws the novel itself as a literary instance of the belatedness that assails its remaining characters at the level of *histoire* in part III. Woolf willingly ruins her book in order to give us the ruined landscape of the late Romantic's tropological or imaginative (not mimetic) wasteland in part II, only, of course, to go on to invent a way of overcoming the loss it represents in the structure of the novel as a whole. The weakest sequence of the book, part II's awkwardness is about literary weakness itself as the literary-historical precondition under which Woolf must work, and which *To the Lighthouse* as "a whole structure of imagination" (258) will try to outwit and overcome. Unlike Hardy or Forster, however, Woolf does not oppose country and city in order to obtain an image of urban decay and a contrasting one of natural purity. Woolf's rural landscape in part II is no more a genuine pastoral retreat than any other such sequences in her fiction (Santa Marina in *The Voyage Out*, the frosty country interlude in *Night and Day*, the seaside in *Jacob's Room*, Bourton in *Mrs. Dalloway*, Pointz Hall in *Between the Acts*). Part II is instead (and like these other instances) actually a catalogue of the Romantic tropology of imaginative ruin and despair that is the precondition of belated or modern writing. As Maria DiBattista puts it, part II is "a Coleridgean nightmare" (1980:96). Recalling the common features of Romantic landscape from Blake to Shelley—

autumnal and twilight settings, ravaged natural scenes—Woolf's scholarship in "Time Passes" recapitulates the dark and destruction of, for example, the initial movement of *Alastor* or, more specifically, the imagery of *Adonais*; Coleridge's anxiety in the vale of Chamonix; even the failure of dawn at Snowdon in *The Prelude*. The figure of the "empty" house (194), too, once filled with life but now marked by Mrs. Ramsay's conspicuous absence, is in turn filiated to a tropological tradition from Bunyan and Keats to Emerson, Pater, and Stevens, in which the "House Beautiful" or "mansion" of literary imagination has become blasted thanks to the increasing burden of precedent by which the history of past usage has incrementally removed from it the possibility of newness or rehabilitation. Lily Briscoe's name alone should already alert us to the funereal status of all that is supposedly fresh and primary in the novel's northerly setting and September climate. For "Lily," after all, is the flower that signifies death, its customary symbolization already an instance of the reflexive rather than referential status of nature in a novel that, like *Howards End*, is really an account of the status of its representations rather than an expression by or of them.

If part II is a catalogue of the past literary usages that make belatedness the precondition of modern literary production, the movement to the lighthouse itself, deferred in part I but fulfilled in part III, is in turn the novel's summary figure for the extent to which it takes the notions of quest-closure and successful allegorization as objects of representation rather than as among its own goals. What are these exemplary quests of which the passage to the lighthouse—to the figure of the Romantic tower—is merely the generic structuring device in this metacritical fiction? Woolf is precise about them: (1) Mr. Ramsay's essentialist philosophical quest for Arnoldean "essences" (38); (2) James's and Cam's Oedipal drama; and (3) Lily's aesthetic quest. They are a trio of isomorphic allegories not unlike the catalogue of homologous ideals in *Howards End*, and their paradigmatic and distanced structuration in so exact a series of articulations shows them to be three tokens of modernist wish-fulfillment none sufficiently ironic to account for their merely symptomatic status as impossible desires of the Arnoldean or Eliotic type. The novel puts all three quests in question by adducing them as ideological formations of thought, each contained by the novel rather than recontaining it.

Chief among these overt symbolic quests is Mr. Ramsay's linguistically figured quest for knowledge, the famous attempt to reach beyond the letter Q (53–56), to reach the letter of one's own name, an ideal fusion, apparently, of knowledge as such and self-knowledge. Complicit with Mr. Ramsay's linear quest for philosophical knowledge is, of course, Woolf's plain adumbration of its terms, roundly considered ironic today, but historically as well as epistemo-logically faithful to the issues at hand. As a professional philosopher Mr. Ramsay is certain about his principal topics of contemplation. Though "'subject and object and the nature of reality'" (38)—Mr. Ramsay's concerns as his children see them—are joked about, these questions are not only to the point, but also have a double historical truth to them. Mr. Ramsay is, after all, continually described in the ebb tide images characteristic of the late Arnold, especially the Arnold of "Dover Beach" or "Calais Sands." Moreover, both his name and that of his protégé, Tansley, are the names of two Cambridge academics—Frank Ramsey the philosopher and Arthur Tansley the botanist—with closer personal ties to Bloomsbury than most during the time of the book's composition (Ramsey died in 1926; see Meisel and Kendrick 1985). Mr. Ramsay believes, of course, in "the thing itself" (287), and in the validity of questing for it in the usual positivist way. Like Leslie Stephen's empiricism, Mr. Ramsay's is a prime example of the Cambridge belief in fact—a fact that Woolf, in her enduring antipathy to Moore and his intellec-tual disciples (Poole 1978), is almost always at pains to include among her objects of scrutiny as surely (as we shall see) as she includes James and Alix Strachey's Freud.

The professional quest of philosophy in part I, then, becomes Mr. Ramsay's mournful journey to the lighthouse in part III, now a physical quest for the (ironically symbolic) reality of the thing itself supposedly embodied by the figure of the lighthouse. Woolf allows him his success in part III, the descrip-tion even tainted with Christian overtones that, as in Forster, are coterminous with the empiricist philosopher's search for primacy: "He sprang, lightly like a young man, holding his parcel, on to the rock" (308). The lighthouse is indeed as present as a "rock," although such epistemological surety can do nothing to bring Mrs. Ramsay back from the dead. Like the irony of Oedipus, the thing itself turns out to be what it is because it is no more than a symbol for something else, in this case for the type of truth for which its evidence is a mere token even when successful.

If Mr. Ramsay's Arnoldean quest for knowledge is given such exemplary status, so, too, is the overtly Freudian allegory surrounding Mr. Ramsay's son James and, somewhat less so, his daughter Cam. The self-consciousness of Woolf's use of a knowledge of the Oedipus complex—a patent case, though with a difference, of what she herself called, with some contempt, "Freudian Fiction" only seven years before (1920)—is so overt and clinically precise that we ought to be at least as suspicious of it as we traditionally are of Mr. Ramsay's own quest. Our very first look at James in part I, one recalls all too easily, shows him in the almost ludicrously Oedipal posture of brandishing, in his fancy, a poker with which he will kill the father before the father, at least in his fears, kills him (10). And much as Mr. Ramsay carries the name of a real contemporary philosopher, so, too, does the name James suggest that of Lytton Strachey's brother, James, translating Freud as Woolf wrote her novels. Part III resolves James's Oedipus complex so tidily as to suggest again its status as an ideological bundle rather than as a meaning, much as Mr. Ramsay's success is, at best, real because it is symbolic. The latter may also be symbolic because it is real, but, like the peculiar ironies of the Oedipus complex as *Howards End* details them, the mobility at work in the rhetoric of the establishment of the authority of either an unmediated real or authority itself belies the primacy their like idealities mean to have.

Accompanying both the epistemological and psychoanalytic quests, of course, is Lily's vaunted aesthetic quest, her attempt to conceive and execute her picture. Apparently the double or proving-ground of Woolf's own art, Lily's aesthetics are, however, like Mr. Ramsay's quest or James's, no more than the third and summary instance of a modernist myth subject to critique and correction (even recent attempts to adjust the picture fall short of taking Lily ironically; see Matro 1984). The nature of Lily's desire for Mrs. Ramsay's love in life in part I and for her memory, sanctified by art, after her death in part III is the same kind of modernist desire Woolf satirizes in philosophy and psychoanalysis. For Lily in part I, it is nothing less than a question of discovering the "secret" (79) of Mrs. Ramsay's being (as though, like the unconscious, it were already there):

> she imagined how in the chambers of the mind and heart
> of the woman who was, physically, touching her, were
> stood, like the treasures in the tombs of kings, tablets bearing
> sacred inscriptions, which if one could spell them out,
> would teach one everything, but they would never be offered
> openly, never made public. What art was there, known to
> love or cunning, by which one pressed through into those
> secret chambers? [79]

There is, implies Woolf, no such "art," and no such "secret chambers" into which it might penetrate. The figuration is ironic enough anyway. Like Trilling's characterization of the desire for a realm beyond culture to be a function of culture's own knowledge, here Lily uses a textual metaphor to represent what she proposes to be instinctual—beyond language or text—in Mrs. Ramsay herself. For Lily in part III, it is the same question, punctuated now by Mrs. Ramsay's actual loss: "What does it mean, then, what can it all mean?" (217). And despite the clarity with which the commemorative impetus for her painting suggests art to be recursive rather than direct or transcriptive, Lily's aesthetic ideals remain modernist, presuming, like Mr. Ramsay, that an essence or a primacy—an immediacy—lies behind it all: "But what she wished to get hold of was that very jar on the nerves, the thing itself before it has been made anything" (287). The next figure, however, frowns at the will to modernity just expressed: "Get that and start afresh," thinks Lily, "get that and start afresh" (287). Like Arnold's "again begin," the place of origin or singleness is itself one of repetition, already bifurcated as a function of its attempted apprehension. Lily also compounds the problem by recalling Mr. Ramsay's like empiricism in her belief that, "If only she could put [her impressions] together, she felt, write them out in some sentence, then she would have got at the truth of things" (219).

Taken together, this isomorphic trio of ideological or interpretative allegories—each as much a subject of the book as any of its characters—produces an overwhelmingly exact and dramatic closure that the mobile or dynamic structure of the novel at large disallows. Each of the three reaches a dialectical resolution within its own sphere (Mr. Ramsay's combination of success and resignation; James's parturition; Lily's completion of her picture) that together may be said to constitute sufficient unity through homologue for the novel as a whole. The recurrent form of the triangle, moreover, especially visible in the final shape of Lily's painting, stands in turn as a kind of diagram for the resolution or closure each of the dramas seems to produce, but which the novel epistemologically forbids in its simultaneous rejection of all three manifestly successful quests for quiddity, priority, immediacy. Such modernist resolutions are, in short, objects of interpretative reduction, subject as all notions of primacy are to the novel's structural dynamic of deferred action by means of which its own significant form is determined.

It is probably easiest of all to assume that Mrs. Ramsay's power or authority is a function of her enigmatic freshness both in life and in the tenacity with which she remains with her family and friends later on in death. But to trope Mrs. Ramsay as such a lost primacy is, especially given the book's enormous range of epistemological cautions, simply to sanctify another, if grander, myth of the modern to account for a novel whose aim is to thwart all such notions. As the history of Woolf's reception has long demonstrated, it is especially (and dangerously) comfortable to assume that Mrs. Ramsay's heroism is the result of her supposedly exemplary femininity, particularly her elevation to the role of urbane earth mother. And yet femininity, like authority (or, indeed, like any notion in the novel), is necessarily the result of a relation rather than the expression of an essence—masculinity or femininity, empiricism or art, it does not matter. Much as public and private are reciprocal in *Howards End* or *Mrs. Dalloway*, so Mrs. Ramsay's public authority in *To the Lighthouse* is a function of a privacy so profound as finally to have no ego at all by which to name it. Like the paradox of Romantic revelation represented by Septimus, Mrs. Ramsay's most solitary moments are precisely those when she descends so far within as to become part of a without (95)—a world without a self that is, as the self well knows, one of its greatest achievements.

Likewise, Mrs. Ramsay's nurturing femininity is in turn very often an effect of plainly masculine figurations instead. Here especially Woolf gets to impugn the primacy in question—an innate femininity—with decided linguistic zest. Few readers tend to forget the technically masculine potency that has passed over to Mrs. Ramsay's double-duty fertility given the "arid scimitar" (59) of the powerless male. Mrs. Ramsay has ejaculatory qualities as well, as though to confirm Woolf's strategic contamination of metaphorical attributions: "Standing between her knees, very stiff," for example, "James felt all her strength flaring up to be drunk" (59). Hence, too, Lily's characterization of Mrs. Ramsay that we remarked upon earlier is, when revisited, polluted by masculinist metaphors that are obviously, and humorously, out of apparent place. Lily imagines "the chambers of the mind and heart" of Mrs. Ramsay as "like the treasures in the tombs," not of queens, but "of kings." Even her desire to "press . . . through into those secret chambers" is an implicitly phallic figuration, though in the process the now-kingly Mrs. Ramsay is also implicitly switched back into a feminine posture insofar as the "secret chambers" must, in the unavoidably phallic role they assign to Lily, restore to Mrs. Ramsay herself the role of one who possesses an entrance for Lily's desired penetration.

Such interdependence by which all supposed primacies—immediacy, authority, femininity—are a product of exchange rather than of essences is a clear part, then, of the Bloomsbury design of replacing modernist ideals in all their registers with the real structures of desire that produce them as ideological defenses. To be sure, we may for a moment consider the argument that the contamination of masculine and feminine tropes in the representation of Mrs. Ramsay's authority is a clue to her status as a phallic mother not unlike Molly Bloom. Like Mrs. Wilcox, she is a bearer of patriarchal law perhaps even sterner than that born(e) by the father himself, and therefore no more an exemplar of an essential femininity than anyone else in the novel. We may also consider the possibility that the figural contaminations are also in the service of an underlying notion of all power or authority as masculine in its social representation in an ineluctably patriarchal ideology (hence "kings," for example, is not a slip but an inevitability).

What remains clear in any case is that Tansley need not drop his innumerable tomes upon the floor in order to impress Mrs. Ramsay with the weight of his erudition. Like everything else in Bloomsbury, knowledge or power is not a thing but a relation. It is, of course, the power of relations—or the relations that constitute power—that *To the Lighthouse* as a text dynamizes as well as thematizes. The power of the text lies in the overt mobility of its structure, allowing Mrs. Ramsay's presence in part I to be a retroactive function of her absence in part III if one reads the novel in the reverse sequence it suggestively recommends as a metacritical commentary rather than as a mere eruption of the will to modernity. Long recognized as a paradigm for loss and belatedness thematically, the elegiac *To the Lighthouse* is also a formal paradigm for the problematic of modernism as a whole. Temporality is not just an issue but an active part of its mechanism and effect, requiring a double mode of reception by which the book may produce the presence of its referents while simultaneously demonstrating their absent and only deferred emergence within a purely discursive or semiotic field.

Eminent Victorians: Strachey's Counterplot

Of all Bloomsbury, Lytton Strachey rouses little enduring interest beyond the pure pleasure of reading him—his reflexive realism is so refined as to go almost unnoticed. And yet Strachey's is likely Bloomsbury's consummate achievement in efficiency if not in size. In his three major texts, Strachey gives us no less than a summary of the problems the myth of the modern presents as well as a way of surmounting them by historicizing the aetiology of their (our) categories. In *Eminent Victorians* (1918), Strachey accounts for the power of his direct precursors, not as the result of the prescient Eriksonian methods for which he is customarily praised—such a project is, for Strachey, simply another expression of the will to modernity rather than a solution to it—but by means of identifying the discourse of historiography with the discourse of the history it (re)presents. In *Queen Victoria* (1921), Strachey goes on to show how the ideological oppositions that allow for the kind of power at work in *Eminent Victorians* were naturalized by the Victorians themselves so as to prevent the diagnosis of them that Strachey achieves. And in *Elizabeth and Essex* (1928), Strachey locates the historical origin of these oppositions in the Renaissance, thereby narrating the conditions of emergence of his own categories.

Current interest in Bloomsbury has done little, of course, to rescue *Eminent Victorians* from the neglect that threatens to depose it as a classic. Among the first direct expressions of revolt against the Victorian legacy, the book was greeted with immense enthusiasm by Strachey's young contemporaries when it appeared in 1918 (see Garnett 1956; Johnstone 1954). Whether one believes in objective history or not, however, the apparently polemical intentions of Strachey's narrative are likely what put us off a little today. Among the numerous causes that may be assigned to the book's declining credibility are our renewed interest in the Victorians themselves and our growing impatience with what seems to be Strachey's rather complacent diagnosis of hypocrisy and obsession in the four subjects of his biographical sketches. The text's irony now seems to inhere less in the portraits than in the portraiture. If Strachey meant to ridicule his Victorian forebears, it appears instead that the real victim was Strachey himself. But whatever reasons we may give for the book's decline in prestige, they are as much as anything else the consequence of our failure to attend to what Strachey himself has to say. *Eminent Victorians* is a far shrewder project than even its champions seem to realize, and a far more balanced text than its audacities would appear to suggest. To be sure, the book's initial aim is to throw into question the pious achievements of its eminent characters. But let us see what kinds of problems Strachey's polemical intentions manage to generate. Strachey sets himself up, of course, as a new sort of authority, one who can separate the reality from the sham of the Victorians and so adduce a "true history" (1918:164), as he puts it at one point in the Nightingale sketch, that will differ from the cover-ups written by the Victorians about themselves. Distinguishing himself from the standard Victorian biographer in the famous and problematical Preface to the narrative, Strachey makes claim to "a brevity which excludes everything that is redundant and nothing that is significant" (ix). And yet, a few sentences later on, he is himself the very model of redundancy: the biographer's "business," he says, is "to lay bare the facts of the case, as he understands them. That is what I have aimed at in this book—to lay bare the facts of some cases, as I understand them" (14). Not only does Strachey's narrator seem wittingly to violate one of his own principles. He also claims for himself a ground of factual accuracy that his cautious modesty earlier in the Preface ("I have attempted, through the medium of biography, to present some Victorian visions to the modern eye " [vii]) has largely eschewed.

These manifest inconsistencies in the Preface carry the suggestiveness of a clue. Although Michael Holroyd has made apologies for whatever contradictions may appear in the text (1968), it is probably more accurate to say that the text's condition is one of contradiction. In fact, Strachey's attempt to set himself up as an authority capable of separating fact from fiction embroils him in a series of paradoxes so overt as to seem almost intentional. Indeed, Strachey appears to burlesque those distinctions between truth and legend that have always been taken as the cornerstone of his fame. Consider, for example, the portrait of Florence Nightingale. "Everyone knows the popular conception," says the narrator at the start of the sketch. "But the truth was different. The Miss Nightingale of fact was not as facile fancy painted her" (135). What, then, is Strachey's version of the truth? "A Demon," he says, "possessed her" (135). Somehow the seriousness of the psychological assertion—if that is what it is—is reduced by the absurdity with which it is expressed. Strachey's peculiar version of "fact" displays an astonishing capacity for hyperbole, one that even rivals Miss Nightingale's for a melodramatic understanding of her life and mission—the understanding, at least, that we get through Strachey's loaded version of what the facts of her biography seem to be. Moreover, the ambiguous keyword "vision" appears throughout the Nightingale portrait, sometimes as a cipher for fancy, myth, and legend, and sometimes as a cipher for the narrator's refutations and counterclaims. The distinctions are necessarily hard to grasp, and Strachey's use of the same word on both sides of the imaginary boundary line between the world of fact and the world of fiction makes it no easier to be clear about his categories. Strachey's "fact," after all, is just as fanciful as the legends it seeks to overturn. Indeed, our present uneasiness about the book's simpleminded distinctions between truth and myth may even help to point us in the direction of what seems to be the narrative's hidden strategy of intent.

As it turns out, fact and fiction are simply rival interpretations of the same evidence. *Eminent Victorians* is everywhere concerned with interpretation, and the relentlessness with which it discerns its presence in all aspects of the stories it tells elevates interpretation to the status of a major theme in the narrative. The narrator, of course, is an interpreter par excellence, working only from other books, as Holroyd reminds us, hence pursuing his personal indictment of the fathers more or less strictly within the confines of an exegesis—he even lists his sources, all of them published, at the end of each chapter. "It is only possible to discern with clearness," says the narrator of Manning's story in an exemplary aside, "amid a vast cloud of official documents and unofficial correspondences in English, Italian, and Latin, of Papal decrees and voluminous *scritture*, of confidential reports of episcopal whispers and the secret agitations of Cardinals"—the subject of all this has yet to appear—"the form of Manning, restless and indomitable, scouring like a stormy petrel the angry ocean of debate" (69–70). It is a rather dramatic and detailed picture that emerges despite the "cloud" of evidence that Strachey has found to obscure the subject of his search. Like the army telegraphist in the Nightingale portrait, it is his job "to compress the messages which pass . . . through his hands" (168).

Strachey's concern with the labor of reading evidence and writing evaluations of it is clearest in the choices he makes to describe and motivate his characters. Like the narrator, all four subjects read and write habitually, even obsessively. Manning, for example, uses his diary to examine "with relentless searchings . . . the depths of his heart" (45), since his whole life, piety and politics alike, resolves itself, in Strachey's words, into the question of "how . . . to judge" (48). Miss Nightingale, meanwhile, pours out her frustrations during the Crimean campaign in an endless series of letters, and produces later in the story a massive volume of analysis about the British army little different in form and method from the constant decipherment of the Bible and other religious tracts that absorbs both Dr Arnold and General Gordon in the second pair of Strachey's four portraits. Moreover, if there is a common factor that explains why Strachey's characters appear so preposterous to us, it is because they find huge significance in absurd portents and clear answers to issues shrouded in ambiguity—much, in fact, the way Strachey himself does. Strachey's description of the kinds of theological hermeneutics that engage Manning and Newman in the first, and probably the best, portrait, might well be (mis)taken for a description of his own activity in the narrative: "But directly someone found it important to give them a new and untraditional interpretation"—Strachey is at this point discussing the Thirty-nine Articles of the Anglican Church—"it appeared that they were a mass of ambiguity, and might be twisted into meaning very nearly anything that anybody liked" (31).

Hence Strachey sets himself up in the same position of blatant and often criminal authority for which he derides the subjects of his sketches. The adventures of his characters resemble nothing so much as the adventures of their narrator in his attempt to render their lives. The style of his own power over history tends in fact to mirror the style and power of his Victorian protagonists since, like them, he threads his way through the evidence with a singlemindedness of intent that begins to focus as much abuse on his own enterprise as on the material it is intended to indict. Indeed, Strachey's hyperbolic demeanor seems so much like the comportment of his subjects that he appears almost to have learned his methods from them. The narrator's prose is often no less starched and affected than the targets of its invectives are supposed to be, with the result that Dr. Arnold's Rugby and Strachey's Bloomsbury tend to seem far more alike than they are different. Cyril Connolly later on pointed out the "Mandarin" quality of Strachey's prose, although he maintains it is meant to "lull" the mandarin ear into "revolutionary" conclusions rather than to double mandarin procedures (1948:47).

This reflexive strategy establishes a kind of retrograde movement or counterplot that tempers the narrative's otherwise uninhibited polemic. It even accounts for the degree of attention the narrator lavishes on the nuances of biblical interpretation and theological dispute throughout the book. Except for the usual reasons of humorous scorn and slander, there seems little cause for the atheistic Strachey to write about four religious fanatics and to dwell so long and with such relish on the intricacies of the various religious questions that assail them. Even stranger is the fact that all this proceeds with little of Strachey's customary vituperation and even less of the languid yawning that one expects the Bloomsbury attitude toward theological questions to be. The reason, though, is clear enough: Strachey is downright fascinated by interpretation in whatever form it appears.

The intrigues of religious interpretation generate the whole drama of Strachey's portrait of Manning, and if we are to ascribe the uniqueness of the sketch to something more than its simple psychologizing, the cause must be the narrator's constant attentiveness to the specific hermeneutic dramas that lead both Manning and Newman—the latter the real hero of the sketch— along the intertwining paths of their respective careers. Strachey's interest in these debates is, of course, more a function of his interest in interpretation itself than in the fatuous religious dilemmas that Manning and Newman both try to resolve. Indeed, both men are interpreters before they are anything else, with Newman's aestheticism and Manning's political schemes both functions of their shared propensity for the reading of signs.

Dr. Arnold is above all a theological interpreter, too. According to Strachey's citation from a description of Arnold by "one of his contemporaries," the headmaster's "religious doubts" are the result of his confusion about "'the proof and the interpretation of the textual authority'" (208). (The Higher Criticism and its effects on a figure like Clough provide still another reflection on Strachey's hidden theme.) Despite his puzzlement, however, Arnold envisions Rugby as a "theocracy" because he is an obsessive reader of the Bible, deciding to "treat the boys at Rugby as Jehovah had treated the Chosen People" (214). Even his commitment to the study of Greek and Latin comprises a model insistence on the interpretation of documents. Moreover, his conviction that the aim of education " 'is,' " in his own words, " 'not knowledge, but the means of gaining knowledge' " (219) establishes a clear ground of identity between himself and Strachey's narration, the latter's focus almost always on the instrument of interpretation rather than its particular conclusions.

Like Arnold, General Gordon is almost always studying his Bible, and like Manning and Florence Nightingale, he is almost always to be seen scribbling in his diary in an attempt to purge his frustrations and to find in them some meaning or secret that will elucidate and compose the conflicting messages presented by his experience. Of course, the melodramatic visions of both Gordon and the Mahdi resemble nothing so much as Strachey's own melodramatic caricatures of these brother visionaries, and both kinds of melodrama proceed according to the same style of hermeneutic search. Like the exegetical Strachey, Gordon hunts "for prophetic texts" and tends to "dally with omens" (260), trying always "to discover what were the Bible's instructions, and to act accordingly" (258). "A day never passed," says Strachey, "on which he neglected the voice of eternal wisdom as it spoke through the words of Paul or Solomon, of Jonah or Habakkuk. He opened his Bible, he read, and then he noted down his reflections upon scraps of paper" (261). Meanwhile, of course, all the Sudan hangs on the question of another interpretation, one that stands at another center of Gordon's story: "There were signs by which the true Mahdi might be recognised—unmistakable signs, if one could but read them aright" (273).

In this concluding portrait, it is the problem of Gladstone's character that provides Strachey with a summary account of the medium in which both characters and narrator come to take their existence in *Eminent Victorians*, the medium of ciphers and interpretation. Stalking the length of the book like a nimbus, Gladstone overarches the narrative, playing major roles in the first and last portraits and now bespeaking the pervasiveness of the book's hidden design at its close:

What, then, was the truth? In the physical universe there
are no chimeras. But man is more various than nature; was
Mr. Gladstone, perhaps, a chimera of the spirit? Did his

> very essence lie in the confusion of incompatibles? His very
> essence? It eludes the hand that seems to grasp it. . . .
> Speech was the fibre of his being; and, when he spoke, the
> ambiguity of ambiguity was revealed. The long, winding, in-
> tricate sentences, with their vast burden of subtle and compli-
> cated qualifications, befogged the mind like clouds, and like
> clouds, too, dropped thunderbolts. [308]

Eminent Victorians, then, is a self-accounting book since it is a text about texts, an interpretation of interpretations, a piece of writing about writing. From this point of view, its missionary anti-Victorianism is in many ways a vehicle for its meditation on the nature of signs and their configuration. Strachey's counterplot collapses the distance his manifest intentions wish to draw between the narrator's present and his subjects' past, turning this modern-ist history into an allegory of repetition in which all subjects—including Strachey himself—are the fools of interpretation. Even the certitude of a clear finale is shattered, since the narrative offers a double ending to Gordon's story whose intentional ambiguity distinguishes itself radically from the clear termi-nations common to the usual discourse of positivist true history.

That the book is a meditation specifically on the nature of (writing) history goes, of course, without saying. We have now only to take Strachey at his word to understand just how specific an identity he means to draw between himself and his subjects when he makes the famous claim in the Preface that "it is perhaps as difficult to write a good life as to live one" (viii). Strachey suggests that there is less difference than we like to assume between discourse and adventure, and that writing and acting, reading and scheming, are more similar than they are different. Hence part of Strachey's achievement in *Eminent Victorians* may well be to destroy our cherished distinctions between art and action by means of an interpretation of life that sees the world itself as a text or a complex of languages, and that exacts from all human endeavor the single and enduring feature of reading and interpreting signs. Strachey thereby calls into question the usual modernist faith in immediacy and the truth of one's impressions by inserting the mediating and distancing factor of interpre-tation between the subject and his objects of knowledge and desire. Such a strategy also explodes the difference between legend and reality that is the narrative's fictional starting point and its predominant working myth. That Strachey should destroy these customary dichotomies under the pretence of asserting them makes of his famous irony a far weightier tool than we may have expected it to be.

Strachey's counterplot finally suggests that we should take the polemical dimension of modernism a little less seriously than we used to. Strachey's attempt to map out a new perception of the past (and, by implication, a new literary and historical period in the present) turns out to be made on the model of the objects and events from which it wants to distinguish itself—it claims a difference by means of a resemblance or repetition. *Eminent Victorians* makes overt the paradoxical nature of modernism as a whole in its dependence on the models from which it wants to be freed. The rift in question is not between modernity and the past, but within the will to modernity itself. Like Strachey's Gladstone, its "very essence" lies in the "incompatible." To invoke history and to deny it are its twin and irreconcilable imperatives.

Victor/Victoria

Recapitulating the reflexive realism of *Eminent Victorians* in which the world the text represents is itself a tissue of texts, *Queen Victoria* also takes as its subject the very category that organizes *Eminent Victorians*—psychic interiority—charting the nature of its emergence as a function of the oppositions between private and public fashioned by Victoria's reign. While retaining the stance of the psychobiographer, Strachey now begins to account even more fully for the categories he seems only to use, showing us again how the writing of history is the history of the form it writes. Like *Eminent Victorians*, *Queen Victoria* is as much, then, a historiography of historiography as it is (or never can be) a history itself. As in *Eminent Victorians*, its central characters— Albert and Victoria—are equally enwreathed in a monumental enterprise of reading and writing, especially government documents and other texts of power, but also distinctly private texts, especially Victoria's letters.

The real power behind the throne, of course, Prince Albert is, most characteristically, "to be seen seated at his writing-table, working" (1921:179), producing endless memoranda. "It was always found that the Prince had made a memorandum" (156–57). "Side by side" with him is Victoria at "her own writing-table" (179). "Treasuring every word, preserving every letter," Victoria herself "was all breathless attention and eager obedience" (179), a premonition, too, of her later widowly habits of collecting and mummifying all the texts of both their lives in an orgy of record-keeping that makes of history itself the kind of document it reflexively produces in its own turn. In their "happiest days" at Balmoral, for example, whatever stirs Victoria requires her to fly "to her journal to note [it] down" (187). Of life there: "it was more like something in a story than real life" (188). But what, after all, is the difference in a world of texts? When Albert's mood is unclear, he is a "cipher" (107). After Albert's death, Victoria is more than ever "reading and writing at her desk" (217); "unceasingly the pen moved over the black-edged paper" (221). The examples are almost as ceaseless as what they describe: "The mere effort of grappling with the mass of documents which poured in upon her in an ever-growing flood was terribly exhausting" (235), but "she had to do her duty" and "make notes" (235). Well after Disraeli, the old queen is, still "with unstinting industry, carrying on an enormous correspondence" (259). In her late years, "it was through her writings that she touched the heart of the public" (293).

Thus, too, are we early, but only casually, reminded that Mr. Creevey keeps a "diary" (11), a text that will in fact become one of Strachey's own principal sources even as it is also an overt element within the story proper. Like Victoria's letters (73, 86–87, 142, 214) or like Strachey's casting of her as "the royal critic" (70) prior to a performance of *Hamlet*, such textualizations remind us that the story itself is, ironically, put into place in the first place by documents such as those it will belatedly interpret. The princess Victoria's first knowledge of her future place comes in plainly textual terms as her mother subtly brings her to a "final realisation of the facts" by giving her a "history lesson" centered upon "the genealogical table of the Kings of England slipped beforehand by the governess into the book" (31). Victoria, in short, finds her place in a web of determinations not only already prepared, but also materially displayed before her as a text. Indeed, as though to strengthen both the metaphor and the actual role of documents throughout the tale, "the Princess's main achievement," says Strachey of her private particularities, is in fact "linguistic" (32), since she is "virtually trilingual" (32) despite an enduringly weak "mastery of English grammar" (32), as her letters notoriously demonstrate.

Though her relation to her uncle, King Leopold of Belgium, has been reduced to "the cold channel of correspondence" (33), it is nonetheless only through one such channel or another that Victoria can be said to exist at all. When her uncle comes to England for a visit, to hear him speak, writes Victoria in her diary, "'is like reading a highly instructive book'" (42). Virtue and benign comportment, it seems, are, in life itself, best expressed (and in this case doubly so) by the metaphor of the text, a metaphor necessarily reflexive even when—especially when—found in the stuff of history itself. And not only does Uncle Leopold talk like a book; the "organisation" of his

Belgium— of its "industry" and "prosperity"—is "a pattern"(42), says the narrator, to which all Western governments should aspire. And power, it follows, is a shrewd negotiation of that web of organization.

With less illustrious personages such as Lord Melbourne, the figures of reading and interpretation are also exemplary: "Nobody had ever been able quite to gauge the shifting, emotional complexities of his married life" (63), says Strachey. Indeed, while Melbourne's wife "whirled with Byron," he stayed home "and occupied his solitude with reading," with "habits of study" and a "love of learning" whose "wide and accurate knowledge of ancient and modern literature . . . formed so unexpected a part of his mental equipment." His passion for reading, insists Strachey "never deserted him," especially a love of biblical "exegesis" (61). Statecraft and reading are again procedurally matched. As Melbourne grows older—and as the chain of Strachey's characteristic metaphors does, too—"he wrote long memoranda in utterly indecipherable handwriting" (135). But if Melbourne gives us an early instance of the power of the textual metaphor in elucidating the mechanism of statecraft, it is the figure of Disraeli whom historical circumstance itself has prepared almost perfectly for Strachey's hand. As a novelist in his own right, he is already not just an exemplar of the textual status of historical referents at large, but also a reflexive instance of the production of the real by writing as an actual activity. Textual and real power are not only likened in Strachey's narration; they are also often one and the same.

No wonder, then, that the politics of the English court are almost always a question of interpretation and negotiation, even before Victoria's rise. After the princess Charlotte's untimely death, the "royal kaleidoscope had suddenly shifted, and nobody could tell how the new pattern would arrange itself" (7). Given the opportunity for the willful taking and exercise of power, enter Stockmar, the book's shadow-hero and surrogate narrator second only to Disraeli (and to whom Melbourne is a pale third). "The satisfaction of his essential being," says Strachey of Albert's German tutor, "lay in obscurity, in invisibility—in passing, unobserved, through a hidden entrance, into the very central chamber of power, and in sitting there, quietly, pulling the subtle strings that set the wheels of the whole world in motion" (57–58). And yet the "invisibility" of Stockmar's power over power (much like that which Lily desires from Mrs. Ramsay) shares, of course, in the pervasive medium of texts and interpretation, too. Hence Albert's (and Stockmar's) "work" (126) of rule lies in distinctly interpretative regimens that hardly need the embellishment of metaphor to make them reflexive: Albert's Germanic propensity for "dividing the subjects to be considered into 'categories'" (127), for example, or the exemplary coordination, in Albert's earliest organizational act as prince, of household systems hitherto uncoordinated, but eventually arranged by "memorandum" (128). While before, "Her Majesty's guests . . . were often left, having utterly lost their way in the [palace's] complicated passages, to wander helpless by the hour" (129), now all is put in relation to a central authority.

But now, too, a new element is added to the reflexive realism of *Eminent Victorians* recapitulated here, one that will become Strachey's overweening preoccupation both in *Queen Victoria* itself and in his masterpiece, *Elizabeth and Essex*—the new preoccupation with historicizing the categories by which his own narration customarily proceeds, chief among them the distinction between public and private. The precise ground of Strachey's representation of the operational distinction between public and private at the level of *récit* is in fact the overt focus of his *histoire* in *Queen Victoria*. Hence the book's key irony begins to emerge in its premise even before Victoria's birth once we realize that (as will occur again and again) the private world of marriage and childbearing is at the center of the enormous coils of public statecraft and diplomatic negotiation ordinarily opposed to it categorically. Unlike Forster and Woolf, for whom such contamination is instead carried out at the level of metaphor (not that Strachey's text is free from it either, as we shall see, too), Strachey boldly locates such contamination where it properly should be seen from the point of view of the history he (re)presents: in the constitutive rhetorical irony by which publicity distinguishes the private houses of European power in their very articulation. Thus, "to marry as a public duty" (11)—the announced intention of the Duke of Kent after Charlotte's death—is an exemplary interplay of private and public in the real history that is Strachey's actual subject—the Victorian scenario that reifies the terms of psychic interiority by which it gets narrated. Such intriguing irony is, moreover, central to Strachey's account of Victoria's own power and of the categorical or ideological power it bequeaths to his own generation as the measure of a truth already behind it.

Not through the back gate of rhetoric but by the front door of direct representation, then, Strachey makes the curious blend of Victoria's privacy and publicity the ultimately organizing categories of his memorable portrait. As soon as we are introduced to Victoria's figure as a child, the emphasis is placed immediately upon her personal qualities. Commendable in the nursery, they are also, as we shall see, full of premonition. "Passionate and naughty" the little "Drina" may be, but—in a joke that echoes Wilde's jest about the mythology of Washington's honesty in "The Decay of Lying" (1891)—she is also "extraordinarily truthful": "she never told a lie" (25). Praiseworthy as such a quality is for private persons, Strachey's insistence upon the depth and reliability of Victoria's personality is more than mere psychohistory, a clue that his historiography is another kind of fiction entirely. It is a fiction centered on the ironically productive nature of the terms by which the raw materials of his referents come down to him.

To be sure, Strachey exploits the resources of his language so as to call attention to connotations that may easily topple his project's own self-representations despite the assurance with which his protagonists wield them and live by them. As with Forster and Woolf, one strand of Strachey's tropology programmatically identifies psychic and real economy as the epistemological buttress for his more playful but similar argument. Thus the public language of " 'the value of money' " (13) spills into the language of personal relations. "The interest increased" (23) in the princess, for example, once her probable succession becomes apparent. Or, with a change in government power and public mood, the Duchess of Kent and her daughter "became assets of the official majority of the nation" (28). Likewise, the aged Melbourne, allowed to write letters privately to the queen, "could not resist taking advantage of the opening they afforded" (117); similarly, too, even Theodore Martin, one of Victoria's earlier biographers, describes the queen's " 'brain,' " Strachey tells us in a figuration reminiscent of Forster, as " 'constantly overtaxed' " (222).

The characteristic array of such figures is predictable in both intent and specificities. Thus the young Victoria's "sense of propriety was keen" (26), both personally ("naturally simple and orderly . . . pious without difficulty" [26]), and in public (Victoria replies, for example, to George IV that her favorite tune is " 'God save the King, sir' " [27]). Bringing perilous scrupulosity to bear on the status of Victoria's paradoxically private and public "propriety" (what is proper to what?), Strachey even appeals to the notion of sincerity—to what Victoria privately feels—in order to frame the question of the truth of public record in history: "The Princess's reply has been praised as an early example of a tact which was afterwards famous. But she was a very truthful child, and perhaps it was her genuine opinion" (27–28).

Assuming that it is, Victoria's behavior as she grows older also grows more understandable. It is precisely Victoria's early personal perfection—her "irresistible sincerity" (293), as Strachey will call it later on—that mars her, leads her into direct conflict with the publicity to which it is normally opposed, but which will also turn out to solve the problem by exploiting its terms:

> One seems to hold in one's hand a small smooth crystal pebble, without a flaw and without a scintillation, and so transparent that one can see through it at a glance.
> Yet perhaps, after all, to the discerning eye, the purity would not be absolute. The careful searcher might detect, in the virgin soil, the first faint traces of an unexpected vein. [35]

And what is that "unexpected vein"? Why, Victoria's insistence upon the primacy of her private and often tempestuous emotions, an insistence that will allow her her success as well as her failure, and that allows Strachey himself to decipher rule or power in an astonishingly efficient way, the measure of Strachey's art the distance it draws between itself and the ideology by which its terms are already captured.

After all, the historical period depicted and the nature of its monarch endure hand-in-hand because of their remarkable identity. With the passage of the Reform Bill in 1832, England's passage into the world of the bourgeoisie—of domesticity and the virtues of private life held (ironically) secure by public policy—not only means that "the centre of gravity in the constitution shifted towards the middle classes" (28). It also means that the flamboyantly private Princess Victoria "was henceforward the living symbol of the victory of the middle classes" (29). The reasons are both logical and (self-)contradictory. For it is exactly the strength of Victoria's private emotions—of her "personality" (274)—that so endears her to the country even through—perhaps even aided by—the entr'acte between Albert's death and her reemergence from extended mourning. After all, Victoria's "proper footing" (39) or "propriety" (43) is, as her look during her coronation shows, "strangely mingled" (50)—"mingled" not just because of the confluence "of innocence, of gravity, of youth, and of composure" (50), but also because her reign will mingle, with unsurpassed success, the private and the public in a mode of ideological calculation designed to repress the reciprocal dynamic between them that the text at large uncovers.

Hence the moment at which Victoria is unveiled as queen may be a public one, but its force derives almost entirely—at least as Strachey tells it—from her personality and the contrast it provides with the brutal past of the Georges: "they had vanished like the snows of winter, and here at last, crowned and radiant, was the spring" (52). The fulfillment of Romantic desire by means of the conventional tropes (winter melts to springtime freshness, Victoria becomes a symbol of the warm south) is also reinforced, Strachey reminds us, now that "sentiment and romance were coming into fashion" (51), too. Whether Victoria is cause or effect is left manifestly open, although the trajectory of Strachey's argument suggests the Victorian ideology of power to be itself productive of a world it fashions in its own image.

What is "ominous" (52) about Victoria as she first emerges as monarch is, not surprisingly, a direct result of what makes her attractive in the first place: the radiance—and reality—of her personal feelings. And it is Victoria's early sequestration from any real "power" (53) that brings out not just the flaw—the contrasting privacy—in her constitution, but the flaw that will also be the key to her later success. "Surrounded, indeed, by all the outward signs of respect and consideration," the "inward truth" (53) that Victoria is without any real authority early in her reign, before the appearance of Albert, is itself a formulation that betokens the means by which Victoria will go on to exercise what power she will in fact come to have. Indeed, as the change begins, the deadpan Strachey is quite overt about the categories that are at issue: "No doubt it was true," says Strachey of the young queen's first inroads at taking real power in the government, "that technically she took no part in public business; but the distinction between what is public and what is private is always a subtle one; and in the case of a reigning sovereign—as the next few years were to show—it is often imaginary" (55). What requires Forster a network of puns Strachey delivers straightforwardly.

Even before Albert, Victoria's first real political bond—her relation with Lord Melbourne—is already a perfect example (at least in Strachey's rendering) of both the personal nature of the queen's public power as well as the almost equally personal manner of the public servant with whom it meshes. Though Melbourne's "behaviour was from the first moment impeccable," its nature is as personal as Victoria's own: "He was at once reverential and affectionate, at once the servant and the guide" (64). In a premonition of Albert's effect upon her, it is Melbourne's ability to relate to the queen in an exceedingly intimate, if respectful, manner that wins her over. Almost rehearsing Victoria's response to meeting Albert later on is "the enchantment" of Melbourne's "presence and his conversation" (89), one that makes up Victoria's new "paradise," now "peopled by two persons" (67), herself and her prime minister, and a relation securely grounded in the personal bond between them.

Despite the intimacy that brings Melbourne and Victoria together, Melbourne's primary lesson in statecraft is one that Victoria will first remember and then—with the entrance of Albert—forget. It is the lesson to be understood perfectly by Elizabeth and to be ignored by Essex, the lesson in diplomatic skill that Melbourne teaches Victoria in another real instance of the direct use of reading and writing in statecraft as such. Thus Melbourne—in a retrospectively ironic effort to neutralize Uncle Leopold's desire that Victoria marry Albert—rewrites Victoria's letter to the king and bids her copy it (76), a letter filled with an "elaborate formula" (76) whose lesson is to delay and defer, and to do so in order to make the private and public appear strictly separate even when the question—that of royal marriage—necessarily and obviously mixes the two. She learns no less than Melbourne's lesson of a strict dichotomy between private and public when one exercises power—indeed, as the price of its exercise.

The drama of the appointment of the court's ladies is exemplary, exacerbating as it does Victoria's native difficulty in separating private and public, feeling and policy. On the one hand, she will not allow what she takes to be the privacy of the royal chambers to be influenced by a public change in government (she does not wish to dismiss her Whig ladies even with a Tory government due). And yet, on the other hand—as Melbourne persuades her—she comes to see that it is not in fact a private question at all despite its effect upon her personal surroundings. It is, rather, a purely political, and therefore purely public, question which ought not to have the slightest shadow of personal feeling about it at all. Now Melbourne's lessons will again be apparently heeded, at least if Victoria is to ride out the crisis. And yet despite what looks like Victoria's understanding of the distinctions that have hitherto escaped her, the delicate compromise she seems to reach is still—despite her self-restraint—"a matter which concerned her personally" (84–85), even though the household is clearly a question of public policy. The queen comes to insist completely on her personal feelings no matter their public bearing, with the ironic result that a change in public policy itself results directly from her private obstinacy. For "if she insisted upon retaining all her Ladies," then Peel—whose party had, by rights, won the election—"could not form a Government" (87). Victoria's private "passionate urgency" (87) produces a sudden "wave of enthusiasm" (87) among the old Whig ministers, who, "swept . . . headlong down the stream of her desire" (87), could not "'abandon'" (87) such a woman by resigning in the due course set for them by the public sphere alone. Melbourne ends up retaining his post and his cabinet, and Victoria her ladies. By finally flaunting Melbourne's instruction to separate private and public, Victoria's purely personal feelings end up winning the public day. Even Melbourne realizes "that he had allowed his judgment to be overruled and his conduct to be swayed by private feelings and the impetuosity of Victoria" (89).

No sooner does the bedchamber crisis pass, however, than another, far more dangerous one arises: her uncle's desire that she marry her German cousin Albert. If the personal has happily become the fulcrum of public power in the first affair, now another affair that mixes private and public far more plainly—marriage and statecraft—will present the same difficulty compounded. And yet again, as luck would have it, Victoria's by-now utterly personal style of existence—one that has altogether forgotten Melbourne's early lesson—will again succeed in providing for the zenith of her public success as a married queen, the latter a direct function of her genuinely private preference for Albert as a man. For when Albert arrives, Victoria—prepared to be politic, deferring in her decisions—caves in completely, and, as Strachey tells it, from the heart rather than the brain:

> Albert arrived; and the whole structure of her existence
> crumbled into nothingness like a house of cards. He was
> beautiful—she gasped—she knew no more. Then, in a flash,
> a thousand mysteries were revealed to her; the past, the pres-
> ent, rushed upon her with a new significance; the delusions
> of years were abolished, and an extraordinary, an irresistible
> certitude leapt into being in the light of those blue eyes, the
> smile of that lovely mouth. The succeeding hours passed in
> a rapture. [93]

Victoria has fallen in love (now we can see, too, that all her successful relations with men both before Albert—Melbourne—and after him—Disraeli—are patterned on this exemplary moment). Like the "enchantment" of Melbourne's "presence" before, Albert's mere presence now decides her immediately and irrevocably: "She had no shadow of a doubt" (93). Again the purely private determines Victoria's course of public action—to marry the lustrous Albert for love. As anybody's history attests, it produces an enormous, if paradoxical, success.

While Albert is, in Strachey's usual psychobiographical portraiture, as self-willed as Victoria as a child and a young man (96ff.), he will learn and keep the lesson that Victoria forgets. Old confidant of Leopold, Albert's tutor, Stockmar, is as distressed with his pupil, even as late as the occasion of his marriage, as Melbourne is with the queen's behavior during the affair of the bedchamber. Like Victoria, the young Albert, too, has no interest in "politics" (he "never read a newspaper") and has distinct "room for improvement" in his "manners" (101). Stockmar's task is a rugged one indeed, especially since Albert "was not in love with her" (102) despite Victoria's feelings for him. And yet in the absence of "reciprocal passion" (102) lies Albert's inadvertent opportunity, and the means by which—and by the rule of Melbourne and Stockmar alike—he can himself seize public power as a direct function of his private position. Unlike Victoria's, however, it is an openly political decision, and one designed to endure. He will, in short, reverse the structure of his wife's relation to authority by heeding both Stockmar and, by implication, Melbourne in their like admonition that power may have its private causes but is resolutely public in structure and nature.

As Albert begins to dominate the scene, Victoria herself can be made to return, when necessary, to the Melbournean admonition, too. As early as the marriage invitations, "she was induced to conceal the bitterness of her feelings" (104), for example, toward the Duke of Wellington. Nonetheless, her "temper grew steadily sharper and more arbitrary" (104) as the wedding approaches; Victoria, in short, still lets private emotion almost fully rule her thoughts and actions even in affairs of state. Though she has a momentary epiphany when her "agitation" makes her "feverish" (106) just before the wedding—"No doubt, she loved Albert; but she loved power too" (107)—the dominion of feeling characteristically wins the day, especially when she sees her beloved prince: "He reappeared, in an exquisite uniform, and her hesitations melted in his presence like mist before the sun" (107). Even the royal epithet, the radiance, has already shifted to the implicit king rather than remaining with the explicit queen.

Albert's leeway—and Stockmar's peculiar advantage—in building a position of power lies in the hazy legal domain of his political status as the queen's husband, "an entity unknown to the British Constitution" (107). At first "not master in his own house" (108) either politically or domestically—public or private—Albert is still more than capable of separating the two spheres and ruling them both. He is strong in each, and knows, unlike his wife, their differences. Despite the "stiffness and formality" (109) that put off his new English compatriots in public, "in strict privacy, he could be natural and charming" (110). In short, what fails to endear him to others—too rigid a distinction between ceremony and solicitude—is what will come to be his means of taking charge in a structure of power the reverse of Victoria's own. And Albert's and Stockmar's "undertaking" (111) is, of course, aimed at the "tremendous prize" (111) of Albert's becoming, in effect, King of England. Whether Albert is aware of it or not, psychologically Stockmar knows that it is best to harness the potency of Albert's "personal pride" (111) in order to insure the proper exercise of his public "duty" (111). Albert's only obstacle is Victoria herself. And, to be sure, there is at first "a struggle of angry wills" (113). But Victoria, we must remember, is "in love" (113), and acquiesces, entirely now, to the enchantment of her husband's blue eyes: "she fought at a disadvantage; she was, in very truth, no longer her own mistress; a profound preoccupation dominated her, seizing upon her inmost purposes for its own extraordinary ends" (113). Solidifying—indeed, rectifying—relations with Peel is Albert's first real act of public success, adjudicating the Tories' eventually genuine arrival into power by agreeing with Peel (unlike his wife) upon a shift in the bedchamber equivalent to that in the government itself (115–16). A "turning point" for the prince, it not only gives him legitimate public authority, but also, and ironically, renders Victoria herself "much impressed and deeply grateful" (116). By a strict separation of them, then, Albert now comes to rule both the public and the private spheres of his ambition. Even the queen's beloved governess Lehzen is banished, this time by Albert himself, and, all in all, concludes Strachey, "Albert was," at last, "supreme" (119). In short, Victoria's private space is taken away from her by the marriage that secures it.

Albert succeeds, then, as both ruler and bourgeois by relegating the queen to the role of "the little *Hausfrau*" (123), so "happy" that "she wanted everyone to know it" (121). Albert's public success is the result of his private success, his private success the result of his public. "He was the real centre . . .—the actual controller of the forces and the functions of the Crown" (133). "Albert had, in effect, become King" (133). It is in fact just their public image of private bliss that provides for the population of England as a whole a "resplendent looking-glass, the ideal image of the very lives they led themselves" (137). No wonder, then, that Victoria will later on make the otherwise private estate of widowhood a public symbol. Forever emotional, Victoria's reaction to Albert's death is purely personal, too (213). Her habit of collecting and cataloguing everything ("in her old age almost an obsession" [280]) is itself a reified repetition of Albert's classificatory inclinations, Victoria's archive a kind of reflexive monument to a husband whose sensibility she pathologically maintains in the routine by which her mourning structures her later life.

What political action Victoria again begins to take is done in the public name of Albert, though still fueled entirely by her private grief: " '*no human power* will make me swerve from *what he* decided and wished,' " writes Victoria in her diary. "She grew fierce, she grew furious, at the thought of any possible intrusion between her and her desire" (214)—Albert has her infantilized even after his death. The realm itself is no less than "the Queen's protracted privacy" (220). Changes in government now are accepted, too, but in doggedly private ways. "'I am,'" writes an appropriately Arnoldean Victoria, "'on a dreary sad pinnacle of solitary grandeur,'" an utter seclusion ironically designed to honor the "sacred trust" of Albert's still "mysterious presence" (216) even in absence. Though the realization comes slowly that "responsibility rested upon her alone" (217), she exercises it in the only way she knows how—by becoming the dashing Disraeli's beloved while remaining the collector of Albert's memorabilia. Watching the emergence of Gladstone and Disraeli alike with the characteristic "passionate and personal interest which she invariably imported into politics" (231)—Strachey is now entirely overt about it—it is the equally passionate (or so he seems) Disraeli who wins the queen all over again, and, like Albert, wins the reality of rule as well. Disraeli, she is convinced, alone "had understood" (231) her feelings upon Albert's death. His "place in her affections" was therefore "assured" (232). As for Gladstone, she dislikes him for the same reasons she likes his counterpart: "She disliked his personal demeanour towards herself" (237). With Disraeli, however, "romance" returns (242), and for it she pays the price paid once before: infantilization at the skillful hands of a man to whom "women's hearts"—even a queen's—are "an open book" (242).

Far more than even Albert, Disraeli, the consummate statesman, is fully aware of the mechanism for power now at his disposal, and even more discerning and successful in his understanding of it than Stockmar. "The Faery"—as he calls the queen in their symbolic romance—"should henceforward wave her wand for him alone" (243). Again the private will be made the crucible of the public because Disraeli holds the same key to Victoria as Albert did:

> He was nothing if not personal; and he had perceived
> that personality was the key that opened the Faery's heart.
> Accordingly, he never for a moment allowed his intercourse
> with her to lose the personal tone; he invested all the transac-
> tions of State with the charms of familiar conversation; she
> was always the royal lady, the adored and revered mistress,
> he the devoted and respectful friend. When once the per-
> sonal relation was firmly established, every difficulty disap-
> peared. But to maintain that relation uninterruptedly in a
> smooth and even course a particular care was necessary:
> the bearings had to be most assiduously oiled. [244]

And so again Victoria is "entranced" (248). "For him she would do anything" (248). And when Disraeli is at last worn-out and retired, Victoria has no choice but to become the only thing she is without a proper male companion: "a woman and nothing more" (258).

Though by 1886 the nation again acclaims a more forthcoming Victoria, this time it is because the personality and privacy she represents have themselves at last become a public institution. No wonder, then, that "her being, revolving for so many years round an external object, now changed its motion and found its centre in itself" (271). Her "passion" (275) is rooted, of course, in "the irresistible potency of her personality" (274). "The need for a symbol" (291) has made her privacy identical with the publicity to which it is otherwise opposed. What has inhibited Victoria's power throughout her life becomes its fulcrum as she reaches old age.

Despite Strachey's earlier judgments, Victoria has never really changed:

> Yet in truth it is difficult to trace any fundamental change
> either in her theory or her practice in constitutional matters
> throughout her life. The same despotic and personal spirit
> which led her to break off the negotiations with Peel is
> equally visible in her animosity towards Palmerston, in her
> threats of abdication to Disraeli, and in her desire to prose-
> cute the Duke of Westminster for attending a meeting upon
> Bulgarian atrocities. [288]

Necessarily, however, Victoria's success ends, as it began with Albert, with its self-erasure:

> Yet, at the end of her reign, the Crown was weaker than at
> any other time in English history. Paradoxically enough, Vic-
> toria received the highest eulogisms for assenting to a politi-
> cal evolution, which, had she completely realised its import,
> would have filled her with supreme displeasure. [289]

Ironically, of course, Strachey as narrator follows precisely the style of thought against which his own texts inveigh. For his judgments are almost always, as usual, based on an extreme psychologism, much as his descriptions are almost always purely personal as well. Indeed, the priority Strachey gives to personal letters and diaries (e.g., 92) as opposed to the implied falsity of public statements made at the same time pivots on precisely the distinction between public and private that the book itself, like its powerful protagonists, knows to be rhetorically interdependent but functionally effective when maintained as separate. Strachey's discoveries, in short, are of the same structure of error as Victoria's own, residing as they do in flamboyantly private categories as problematic as the queen's. Though, to be sure, the distinction between public and private is, "in the case of a reigning sovereign," "often imaginary" (55), says Strachey, it is on the basis of this "imaginary"—and discredited— distinction that the narrative itself is apparently structured. As in *Eminent Victorians*, the form of Strachey's narration is a reflex of what it narrates, implicated in the very system from which it claims to break away. Like the "double process" (132) of Albert's power, the power of Strachey's reflexive realism is "double," too. At once a representation of its story while at the same time a representation of its own procedures as a narrative, *Queen Victoria* is an attempt to account for the mythology of its own organizing terms, especially when it begins to detail the items within the story that will come to form the actual components of its belated narration of them. Hence the latter part of the narrative (and large portions of its early sequences) directly describes the production of those relics and archives out of which the narrative itself will be made—the radiant "monument" (225ff.), the archival house, perhaps especially Strachey's quiet cataloguing of the actual composition of his own source-documents as the story unfolds.

But while the point of Victoria's collecting is that all "should be immutably fixed" (281), the point of Strachey's collecting is rather different. Read as psychobiography, of course, Strachey not only remains trapped in the categories whose play his narrative charts rather than transcribes or expresses; he also reduplicates at the level of psychology, surely ironically, the desire for the "immutably fixed"—an Arnoldean or Eliotic desire—on the part of Victoria herself. As though knowing the dubieties of the psychobiography his texts already account for rather than simply produce, Strachey's especially outrageous reduction of the political to the psychological in discussing Albert's differences in policy with Palmerston is so plainly absurd—and so deaf toward all the cautionary voices in the text—that it is a patent example of the kind of Victorian misreading that the book as a whole would have us make an object of scrutiny in its own right instead: "But his disagreement with the details of Palmerston's policy was in reality merely a symptom of the fundamental differences between the characters of the two men" (156). A "fixed" or inherent notion of a truth universally resident in personality would make irrelevant the focus on history by which Strachey defines himself as a writer. With the composition of *Elizabeth and Essex*, however, Strachey will not only again make his narrative reflexive and his terms ironically self-accounting and even self-erasing; he will also narrate the history of their origination as categories of knowledge in the ideology of the English Renaissance.

The Earl of Essence

If *Queen Victoria* recapitulates and refines the aesthetic of *Eminent Victorians*, *Elizabeth and Essex* recapitulates both in turn and in turn refines their unfolding program to produce a consummate reflexive realism that reduplicates its subjects in its forms and its forms in its subjects. It is, of course, hardly unusual to find virtually everyone in a Strachey novel reading and writing as the very sign of the power character itself may wield in the world. As in *Eminent Victorians* and *Queen Victoria*, in *Elizabeth and Essex* the world of the real is again rendered as a set of already prepared texts into which a given subject is inscribed even before birth (especially noble ones), with political power in particular a function of the cunning of one's hermeneutic abilities within such a vortex of signs. Elizabeth herself has extensive linguistic skills, "mistress of six languages besides her own, a student of Greek, a superb calligraphist" (1928:18). Combined with her "protean mind" (18), such verbal prowess produces surpassing strength "in the elaborate confection of studied ambiguities" (18) whose discursive exactitudes are often the motive force of her enormously effective statecraft. If Essex is in his own turn a "literary General" (107), the trope is not simply rhetorical ornament on Strachey's part, but part of the now-familiar Stracheyesque strategy of identifying the play of texts with the nature of the real. Perez, instigator of the horrible Lopez affair, provides an example that goes beyond metaphor to the actual identification of real and discursive power as Strachey figures Renaissance politics as itself an exercise in the day's literary modes: "How delightful to weave plots, change policies, and direct the fate of Europe in learned antitheses and elegant classical allusions!" (95).

Much, then, as Albert controls empire from his desk in *Queen Victoria*, so *Elizabeth and Essex* gives us the powerful Cecil, equally characteristically, "at his table writing" (109). Fully displaying statecraft as a direct function of textuality, Cecil's exercise of power on the part of the Crown consists in sending a letter, for example, filled with "words" of "such a diplomatic mixture of flattering devotion and ornate self-confidence" that they "were, apparently, exactly what were required" (104). So central is Cecil's exemplary figure that Strachey even closes the narrative with a portrait of him alone in his chamber, scribbling away like an immortal Albert, ending the story while simultaneously mirroring the means of its production:

> But meanwhile, in an inner chamber, at his table,
> the Secretary sat writing. All eventualities had been
> foreseen, everything was arranged, only the last soft touches
> remained to be given. The momentous transition would
> come now with exquisite facility. As the hand moved, the
> mind moved too, ranging sadly over the vicissitudes of mor-
> tal beings, reflecting upon the revolutions of kingdoms, and
> dreaming, with quiet clarity, of what the hours, even then,
> were bringing. [286]

And despite the obvious national and religious differences, King Philip of Spain is Cecil's exact counterpart, "controlling from his desk" in the Escorial "a vast empire" (138) as "his hand moved over the paper from morning till night," "withdrawn into" an "inner room of his palace" (138) and surrounded by the signs of Catholic iconography (139).

The Lopez affair is the novel's most extended instance of the identity of the interpretation of texts and the machinations of political power. Indeed, the juridical context allows the reflexive identification even more plainly than does the exegetical context of *Eminent Victorians*. Lopez's statements are described in terms almost identical to those by which the question of the truth of Gladstone's character is described in the earlier novel: "Who could disentangle," asks the narrator, "among his statements the parts of veracity and fear, the desire to placate his questioners, the instinct to incriminate others, the impulse to avoid, by some random affirmation, the dislocation of an arm or a leg?" (81–82). The conclusion is obvious enough: "Only one thing was plain about such evidence:—it would always be possible to give to it whatever interpretation the prosecutors might desire" (82). Hence "Judges, as well as prisoners, were victims of the rack" (82), both implicated—the former for rule, the latter for victimization to assure it—in "the machinery" (82) of power at large. Even more—and in an extension of *Queen Victoria's* penchant for narrating the composition of some of its own sources as part of the story it tells—*Elizabeth and Essex* is also predictably rich with references to the actual contemporary production of England's founding literary texts. *Henry V*, for example, is played at the Globe during the course of the book (207–08), while Strachey also remarks on the newness of the word "essay" and Bacon's early skill at handling one kind of form that Strachey himself inherits and that authorizes the text that represents its emergence (129). Meanwhile, Essex—good courtier and chivalric hero—composes, in proper fashion, "verses"

(143), while Elizabeth, too, is "busy with literary composition" (103), translating "the *Ars Poetica* into English prose" (195).

If the equivalence of power and the interpretation of texts recapitulates *Eminent Victorians*, Strachey's deeper focus on the nature and history of the narrative's overtly enabling categories of the private and the public recapitulates *Queen Victoria*. Again appearing to write a kind of psychohistory based on the stability of subjective categories, Strachey again turns out to be writing a metacommentary on the status of such categories even as he uses them without apparent duplicity. As in *Eminent Victorians* and *Queen Victoria* alike, however, he takes the manifest stance of the modern psychologist in *Elizabeth and Essex* as well, separating fact from fiction with confidence and ease. Much, for example, as Cecil can, in his own words, see Essex " 'pass from dissimulation to verity' " (191), so, too, can Strachey himself assure us (whatever ironies attend the affirmation by negation) when "a certainty" on the part of his actors is "in fact . . . baseless" (83). Nor is there any apparent hesitation in distinguishing between "what was fancy and what was fact" (205) or between "a sentimental novelette" and "history" proper (265). Indeed, Strachey appears to use the familiar psychohistorical stance to account for Elizabeth's "image—magnificent, portentous, self-created" (10)—a narrative stance based on the usual distinction between "the real and the apparent" (10) that the book will, like his others, ultimately overthrow, but that, as usual, it also needs as its enabling fiction. To clear away, then, that Arnoldean "deceit of vision" (10) that has forged a deceptively mighty image of Elizabeth rather than a supposedly more human one, Strachey will, it seems, "look below the robes" (11) to find a crack. As if to signify the plainly Freudian context, Strachey quotes the lines from Virgil that are Freud's epigraph to *The Interpretation of Dreams* (96). We now know, too, the care with which Strachey tried to detail the hysterical nature of Elizabeth's enigmatic sexuality and its ironically helpful role in her larger—and peerless—designs as a politician: his brother and sister-in-law, the psychoanalysts James and Alix Strachey (to whom the book is dedicated), provided him with an almost clinical definition of vaginismus incorporated into the description of Elizabeth's "sexual organisation" (20) early in the novel (see Meisel and Kendrick 1985:Epilogue).

What is pathological from a personal point of view, however, nonetheless has its public compensations, and Elizabeth trades in the former for the latter—a classic case, it seems, of exemplary sublimation. "For years," Strachey assures us, "she made her mysterious organism the pivot upon which the fate of Europe turned" (25). Hence, too, the book's apparently resolute allegory of psychoanalytic closure. Elizabeth's successful procurement of power with the beheading of Essex is in fact the successful resolution of her own Oedipus complex. For if her father, Henry VIII, has beheaded her mother, she in turn beheads her own lover, Essex, and in so doing at last becomes her father both psychologically and politically: "Yes, indeed, she felt her father's spirit within her; and an extraordinary passion moved the obscure profundities of her being, as she condemned her lover to her mother's death. In all that had happened there was a dark inevitability, a ghastly satisfaction; her father's destiny, by some intimate dispensation, was repeated in hers" (263). Especially noteworthy is that Strachey gives the later Elizabeth rather than the earlier Henry the priority: "her father's destiny . . . was repeated in hers," not hers in her father's.

Such extreme psychological reductionism or individualizing of historical events is, however, just what Strachey will also put in question even as he puts it in place. As in *Eminent Victorians* and *Queen Victoria*—and in *To the Lighthouse* as well—the book's psychoanalytic project is its beginning, not its end. As we shall see, Strachey all at once utilizes such categories, scrutinizes their epistemological status, and, with Essex in particular, also describes the history of their emergence. These are, of course, the terms of Strachey's own enablement as an English writer, and, as a historian, he retains the directly dutiful power to rewrite a past that might otherwise oppress him. Now, however, he will rewrite the past not just to collapse the difference between "modernity" and Victorianism, but also to account for the origin of the category of originality itself—of modernity in all its registers, chief among them the desire for the proper, the private, "one's own"—by historicizing its origination in what is an ultimately pedagogical relation between Elizabeth and Essex themselves, and one in which the distinction between private and public is painfully produced in directly human terms. The structure of the relation bespeaks not just the nature of the categories it virtually invents, but also frustrates the will to modernity's wish for origins by representing the origin of the origin as itself a historical category, thereby rendering us preconditionally incapable of producing the newness—the originality, the proper, the private—the will to modernity always demands. In the process, too, Strachey will find in Elizabeth's power an exact counterpart to his own.

More than psychohistory, then, *Elizabeth and Essex* is, like *Eminent Victorians* and *Queen Victoria*, a primer in the way the real gets produced as a function of the power of the categories that articulate it ideologically. Elizabeth's image may well be a "deceit of vision" to posterity, but it is also the intentional means of self-presentation and (self-)governance that Elizabeth herself creates and uses for the purposes of consolidating her reign. Thus the

"inconsistency" of the age finds a likeness in its ruler: "In reality, she succeeded by virtue of all the qualities which every hero should be without—
dissimulation, pliability, indecision, procrastination, parsimony" (11). She is
in short a mistress of "cunning and prevarication" (12). "Entangled in the
forces that surrounded her" (13), deferment and delay are her only weapons.
And her private temperament ("A deep instinct made it almost impossible for
her to come to a fixed determination upon any subject whatever" [12–13])
lends itself perfectly to the hesitant style of statecraft in which she so successfully engages: "Her only object" is "to put the day of decision off—and off—
and off"; she has "a passion of postponement" (15). And while this may serve a
psychoanalytic interpretation well by suggesting Elizabeth's unconscious and
metaphorical revulsion both to the closure of orgasm and the teleology of
procreation, it is less symptomatic than it is illustrative. It is an exercise in how
to take power and maintain it. It is no less than a policy of "beautiful negotiation" (98), by means of which Elizabeth herself not only makes the nonimmediate, the nonimpulsive, the nonpersonal the engine of her worldly power,
but in the process also provides a model for the power of the text that so
represents her.

Despite a natural "amorousness so irrepressible" as to be almost "scandalous" (23), Elizabeth is—even with Essex—extremely clear and strict about
drawing precisely those boundaries that escape Victoria, and, as we shall see,
Essex as well. Throughout her reign, there are in any case "no transitions—
only opposites, juxtaposed" (27). And while the appearance of Essex carries
with it all the seductiveness of Albert's appearance to Victoria, it is just here
that Elizabeth differs so strikingly from her future counterpart—and so instruc-
tively. Rather than surrender her public role to her private, admittedly tempestuous emotions, the rule of prevarication and delay—of policy—intervenes
even when it comes to the otherwise irrepressible Essex himself and the
temptations into which Elizabeth is led. Essex "swept Elizabeth off her feet"
with "his boyish fascinations" (31), and, "young as he was, he could upbraid
the great Queen with impunity" (33). Nonetheless—and in an ominous premonition of the climax to come—Elizabeth is sharp with him even early on
despite the "lavish . . . protestations of his worship—his adoration—his love"
(37). To be sure, Elizabeth has her fits of "fury" (144) in public. And yet, as in
the case of the Polish ambassador, the "fury," private as it may be, is rendered
in public terms of such cool domination that the personal is blunted and
channeled as Elizabeth delivers her tirade in "a rolling flood of vituperative
Latin" (144). Elizabeth thereby maintains a strict difference between her
"public duties" and her "private delights" (38) as the very precondition of

maintaining the power of her realm. It requires, in other words, the simultaneous maintenance and cancellation of two registers of experience virtually invented, at least in Strachey's historiography (and, perhaps, in Shakespeare's as well), by Elizabeth herself. While the "complicated contrasts" (19) of Elizabeth's mind and actions might appear to be simply contradictory, the double process at work is in fact highly strategic, Elizabeth entertaining as she does a double relation with Essex—her lover from the point of view of her privacy, her liege from the point of view of her public reign.

If Elizabeth, like Albert, is strict in separating the public from the private, Essex, by contrast, is like Victoria in his constitutional inability to do so, living entirely in the private. He has an "open manner" "plain to all" (5), a properly feudal or chivalric virtue in which word and deed are, or must be, one and the same in order that honor and propriety be observed and preserved. If the "new spirit was resounding . . . in the glorious rhythms of Tamburlaine" (itself an odd metaphor, since Tamburlaine, exemplary of chivalric rather than courtly virtue, represents a pre-Elizabethan kind of power), then "its living embodiment was Essex" (70). And yet Strachey's seemingly problematic analogue to Tamburlaine is actually more accurate than it appears, since Essex must obviously make some mistake that puts him out of step with an age that he, too, customarily represents. It is perhaps because his chivalric feudalism or openness—the ground of his resemblance to Marlowe's hero—makes him "rash and impetuous" (64). His "superb self-confidence" (70) both rules and ruins him. "His restless and romantic temperament urged him irresistibly to the great adventure of war; thus only could his true nature express itself" (70). Even at his trial late in the book, "Essex could never distinguish very clearly between a personality and an argument" (256). As with Victoria, in other words, all is private for him. The distinction between public and private does not (yet) exist, even though, as we shall see, it will become the pivotal dichotomy of the new age and the precise thing he fails to understand. While Elizabeth's prevarication is her enduring mien as she maintains throughout the story a clear though muted separation between her private relations, including those with Essex, and the public policy upon which she must decide, Essex himself, by contrast, plays the chivalric nobleman from an earlier age from start to finish. "Romantic to the last," imbued quite plainly with the spirit of "ancient chivalry" (40), he even kisses the blade of his sword on returning to his native soil after a diplomatic expedition to France. And when rebuffs from the queen drive him into contemplation, his self-sequestration in "the tapestried inner chamber of Essex House" (48) represents a full retreat to the "inner" or private that betokens his error in his dealings with the queen.

Essex's headstrong sincerity in wishing to prosecute Lopez is probably the most acute example of his inability to separate realms as Elizabeth does. Though the Cecils tell the queen they believe the doctor to be innocent (77), Essex "was still unshaken" (77). He takes the affair very personally indeed. "*His* honour, no less than the Queen's was at stake" (78). Once prosecution begins, of course, guilt is inevitable (81ff.), and so Essex's pride predominates. Elizabeth's "instinctive perception," however, remains one of Lopez's "innocence" (91), and yet, though she hesitates "even more than usual" (91), she allows the execution to be carried out. Even Essex's great victory at Cadiz (really a sneak attack) is primarily a personal event, too. "Flinging his hat into the sea" (105), Essex is praised by the defeated Spaniards as one who shows "chivalry" (106). Composing verses to celebrate the event, he uses "a play upon his own name" (107), a "play" that may also authorize our calling him by the fatal name the Earl of Essence instead. Though it is Francis Bacon who is Essex's chief counsel in politics, their growing inability to understand one another shows us both Bacon's knowledge of the particularities of Elizabeth's statecraft and Essex's final incapacity to participate in this new or modern system that requires a surrender of the chivalric belief in the primacy of temperament and the supposed expression of essences that justifies it: "the actual steps which he urged Essex to take in order to preserve the Queen's favour were totally unfitted to the temperament of the Earl. Bacon wished his patron to behave with the Machiavellian calculation that was natural to his own mind. Essex was to enter into an elaborate course of flattery, dissimulation, and reserve" (121). But, asks Strachey, could "the frank impetuosity of Essex . . . ever bend itself to these crooked ways?" (122). The answer is simple, since the earl is a medieval, not a modern, man: unlike either Bacon or Elizabeth, "the Earl was incapable of dissembling" (123). "Was it not clear that his nature would assert itself in spite of all his efforts?" (123). Essex in short cannot produce the separation between appearance and meaning, public and private that are central to holding power in the new Elizabethan or modern ideology. "His very honesty," says Strachey, "would display his falsehood" (124).

Essex's "lot," then, "seemed to lead him irrevocably along the paths of action and power" (127), even though—and here especially lies Essex's flaw—"he could not determine whether that was indeed the true direction of his destiny" (127). Trapped in a personalization so extreme ("his destiny"), Essex doubly confounds his problems as a chivalric man facing a new world of distinctions between public and private, policy and love, that are as unreal to him as they are real—and effective—for Elizabeth. The queen's decision to divide command among Essex, Raleigh, and Thomas Howard throws Essex into the paroxysms of a courtly lover ("Essex took to his bed" [131]), a characteristically personal reaction to Elizabeth's public policy decision based erroneously on his private relation to the monarch. Elizabeth goes so far as to visit him by his bed (131), but then—in an augury of what is to come—decides to "'break him of his will . . . and pull down his great heart'" (131). Reconcilement with Elizabeth only reinforces the reality of Essex's purely personal world: "The Queen wished him back; very well, she might have her wish—but she must pay for it" (154). All too often, in other words, "politics gave way to love-making" (166). Essex even turns his back upon the queen in a session at court (172) and proceeds to lose "his temper," clasping "his hand to his sword" "with a resounding oath" (172). With the chivalric gesture complete, the Earl of Essence at last stands isolated, dramatically doomed on the stage of the court itself.

Already there is talk of the Tower, but for now the queen "did nothing" (172). The greater misunderstanding is yet to come. After the dangerous incident at court, Essex "could not—he would not—think that he had been in the wrong; she had treated him with an indignity that was unbearable; and then as he brooded over what had happened, anger flamed up in his heart" (176). Chivalric throughout, Essex still believes Elizabeth to be his peer rather than ruler—and that she reacts to him as personally as he does to her—by the law of a now-outdated feudalism that makes all aristocrats equal. With the amorous element adding to the problem, for Essex as a feudal lord, any context is the same. The prerogatives of rank—public though they may be—are also always and only personal, since they derive from his sole and particular person. In a letter to the queen, he says as much quite directly, hardly noticing the distinction he fails to make, but one that Elizabeth is sure to see: "'I do confess that, as a man, I have been more subject to your natural beauty than as a subject to the power of a king'" (178).

The flattery is, however, misplaced. Despite her own private feelings, Elizabeth responds by reminding Essex of their double relation and of his refusal to admit the distinction it involves: "'submit to your sovereign,'" she writes back, "'between whom and you there can be no proportion of duty'" (178–79). Duty is, according to Elizabeth, both absolute and nonprivate. Essex's rebuttal centers on his insistence that she has "'driven him into a private kind of life'" (179), but, then again, Essex's public life has been private all along. For him—as he writes again to the queen—"'the duty of attendance is no indissoluble duty'" (179). And therein lies the misimpression that leads to his fatal destiny. Now, of course, Strachey must go on to note the clear fact that Essex is really "the last extravagance of the Middle Ages flickering through the high Renaissance nobleman" (181). His heated and continuing criticism of the queen is not only personal, but also calls into question the intention of Elizabeth's new notion of centralized political authority. "Not a realist " but a "romantic" (181), Essex will not accept the lesson Elizabeth has to offer. He prefers a fight to the finish. Though for the private Elizabeth, "the withdrawal of that radiant presence was becoming insupportable" (185), the public Elizabeth can keep the private one at bay by leaning on her "innate predisposition to hedge," to prevaricate—to "put it off, and put it off" (186). The next reconciliation is therefore "not a complete one" (186), even though "it appeared that the past had been obliterated" (187). Again it is a public affair that sets the problems in motion, and again it is Essex's predisposition to treat things privately that causes the real difficulty. With the new need to appoint a lord deputy of Ireland, Essex's name is advanced, and Cecil prudently hesitates because of a knowledge of public affairs—and of Essex's character— shared by his equally politic antagonist, the Irish Tyrone, who diagnoses Essex's political troubles in a swift and efficient thought: "Personal animosities had been added to public feuds" (200).

Essex is certainly no Albert, and is already headed for treason, beginning to murmur threats in Ireland to start what would be nothing less than a "civil war" (212). After achieving a truce with Tyrone, Essex, still feeling "impotent" (214), does indeed ride to London with a possible "attack" in mind (215), but, in a display of his intimate relation with the queen, bursts into her bedroom instead. Giving expression to benign personal feeling rather than to hostile political ones, the act is nonetheless a disastrous one. The embarrassment— the invasion of Elizabeth's private space no matter the level of her relation to Essex—is extreme and exemplary, and probably more decisive than any overtly political difficulty the two may have: "And there, quite close to him, was Elizabeth among her ladies, in a dressing-gown, unpainted, without her wig, her grey hair hanging in wisps about her face, and her eyes starting from her head" (216). Only a valet may have such liberties—or a husband. Essex is neither.

Elizabeth's reaction runs the spectrum of feeling until she discovers the bottom one—"she was afraid" (217). "Was it possible that at this very moment she was in his power? Completely in the dark, she at once sought refuge in the dissimulation which was her second nature" (217). Guessing at last "that she was in no immediate danger" (217), Elizabeth has finally recognized the truth about Essex, and, even more, why he is also dangerous beyond the realm of her private concerns. If Essex understood such distinctions, he would pose no threat. But since he does not, Elizabeth commands him "to keep to his chamber" (218). "Now completely at her mercy . . . she could decide at her leisure what she would do with him" (219). Enter Bacon, and the romantic Essex's tragic fate is sealed as Strachey reveals the exact nature of the problem by pointing out the implicit difference between them:

> As for Bacon, he was in his element. He felt that he could thread his way through the intricacies that surrounded him with perfect propriety. To adjust the claims of personal in-debtedness and public duty, to combine the feelings of the statesman and the friend, to hold the balance true between honour and ambition—other men might find such problems difficult, if not insoluble; but he was not frightened by them; his intellect was capable of more than that. As he talked to Elizabeth, he played upon the complex theme with the pro-found relish of a virtuoso. [222]

Avowedly selfish—and manifestly the tale's villain—in condemning Essex from a political point of view ("it was essential to win the good graces of Robert Cecil" [223]), Bacon is nonetheless clear about the newly operative Elizabe-than distinctions, presaging as they do the bitter world of the modern corpora-tion: "Essex was," according to Bacon, "a mischievous person, whose activities were dangerous to the State. While he was clearly bound to give him what help he could as a private individual, he was certainly under no obligation to forward the return of such a man to power" (223). For all his chill, Bacon understands the categories exactly, better than Elizabeth herself and certainly better than Essex. "Was this," asks a disingenuous Strachey, "still a lovers' quarrel?" (228).

Despite another reconciliation, however, once Elizabeth cuts off Essex's income from wine-growing, he reacts still more violently. His remarks be-come "insane" (237) and reach the queen with a new effect. Elizabeth now worries that her habitual strategy of prevarication and delay will no longer work with Essex in so extreme a state. She enters a momentary "paralysis" (237), unaware of impending public events. Now desperate, Essex at last takes the leap, no matter his residual hesitations and ambivalence, plunging into the streets in plain civil insurrection. But despite a performance of *Richard II* (241–42), "there was no sign of any popular movement" (244) in his support, only a vacuum in which, to the general population, "the Earl was their hero; but they were loyal subjects of the Queen" (244). It is this quite elementary fact that Essex himself has not been able to grasp. It is again the figure of Bacon who summarily elucidates the problems at hand:

> He had no hesitations or doubts. Other minds might have
> been confused in such a circumstance; but he could discrimi-
> nate with perfect clarity between the claims of the Earl and
> the claims of the Law. Private friendship and private benefits
> were one thing; the public duty of taking the part required of
> him by the State in bringing to justice a dangerous criminal
> was another. It was not for him to sit in judgment: he would
> merely act as a lawyer—merely put the case for the Crown,
> to the best of his ability, before the Peers. His own opinions,
> his own feelings, were irrelevant. [248]

And because Bacon's "own opinions, . . . own feelings" are "irrelevant," he demonstrates b, his frigid impartiality the truth of the argument he presents. Bacon's is, necessarily, a "double tongue" (258), its two registers the private and the public, friendship and the law.

As for Elizabeth, she, too—like the heroine of a Victorian novel—"rec-ognised the truth—the whole truth—at last" (262). Accordingly, her relation to her own private being suffers a tremendous shock, including the recogni-tion that the prerogatives of rule and the pleasures of privacy are so distinct that rulers may be forced to rule out a private life altogether:

> Her tremendous vanity—the citadel of her repressed
> romanticism—was shattered, and rage and hatred planted
> their flag upon its ruins. The animosity which for so long
> had been fluctuating within her now flared up in triumph
> and rushed out upon the author of her agony and her dis-
> grace. He had betrayed her in every possible way—mentally,
> emotionally, materially—as a Queen and as a woman—
> before the world and in the sweetest privacies of the heart.
> [262–63]

Even Essex "at last . . . understood," but too late, and, symptomatically, in only personal terms: "He had utterly misjudged her nature, that there had never been the slightest possibility of dominating her, that the enormous apparatus of her hesitations and collapses was merely an incredibly elaborate facade, and that all within was iron" (265). Essex fails because, like Victoria, he cannot separate private and public even in his final recognition. With Elizabeth, by contrast, the modern or protobourgeois age is born, since she codifies, both in her demeanor and her actions, a strict separation between power and love not unlike the one Albert will inherit in the later history of ideology.

If Elizabeth, unlike Essex, maintains power as a function of her ability to maintain simultaneously two opposed states in her own person—the private and the public, the lover and the monarch, the friend and the law—the text of *Elizabeth and Essex* is itself double in a like fashion. On the one hand, Strachey's language seems, as it usually does, almost as flat and scoured as Forster's despite the superadded irony and more severe wit. On the other hand, however, Strachey's language is, in an extension of the Bloomsbury strategy of reverberation we have already seen in Forster and Woolf, also a language of strategic puns designed to identify the differences between public and private that the coherence of his tale seems to depend upon. Strachey's literary power, in other words, is like Eliabeth's political power in its ability to operate in two contradictory registers at the same time. It is, moreover, by means of the transgressions of Strachey's language that the law it means to account for historically is articulated. A double process, its dual registers do indeed have a strategic relation, and one that summarizes not only the Blooms-bury imagination, but also the solution to the larger problematic of modern-ism we have seen variously negotiated throughout the present study. On the one hand, Strachey's text is fully serious in its belief in the psychological opposition between private and public that structures and strains its protago-nists' love and that issues in the lessons of power. On the other hand, how-ever, the novel is also fully accounting as to both the nature and the history of the categories so used in its modernist allegory, one in which the psychobio-graphical supposedly uncovers a primal truth.

The linguistic spillage that identifies psychic and real economy is, as in Forster and Woolf, at work throughout *Elizabeth and Essex* as well. The young Elizabeth decides that her lovers will be "a paying concern" (27), much as Essex himself declares the opposite in a like figuration: "'I have been free from taxation of incontinency with any woman that lives'" (125–26). Hence, too, the plain identification of the economic with government: "the new Lord Deputy," for example, is "to be invested" with his "authority" (193). Bacon's profound statecraft is almost predictably figured as "a beautiful economy" (272), while Elizabeth's "thrift" is "spiritual as well as material" (14). There is, however, in addition to the habitual tropological identification by Bloomsbury of the public and private, the more precise identification of the private in *Essex* as the sexual. Though at first sight in the service of the book's psychobiographical project, such Stracheyesque identification erodes the sta-bility of its subjective terms perhaps more than the larger project of the identification of psychic and real economy of which it is a part. " 'I will spend all my power' " (59), remarks Essex in the usual colloquialism, though, by virtue of Strachey's systematic arrangements of such idioms, the phrase becomes part of the book's programmatic focus on the tropological link, not just between private and public, but between sexuality and power. Already evident in Elizabeth's plain equation of her lovers with "economic concern" or in Essex's figuration of "incontinence" by "taxation," such a program here centers most especially on the overdeterminations that stem from the repetitive figure "head," radiating as it does into the now-twin spheres of authority and sexuality at once.

The figure already has a history in Strachey's own texts. In *Eminent Victorians*, access to power is construed, in the exegetical metaphor by which Strachey figures it there, as access to "Godhead" (1918:19). In *Queen Victoria*, we have a married woman who is without both a maidenhead (the "membrana" [1928:24] that Elizabeth, by contrast, always has), and without the reality of her role as head of state either, again in contrast to Elizabeth. It is Albert, therefore, who is the "natural head" of the family (1921:176). Without a head in either sense, then, Victoria allows us to see how power is still a question of what she lacks, a question of the "head," in Albert's case in an especially phallic sense. In *Elizabeth and Essex*, by contrast, Elizabeth has a head (three, actually), though all of them invisible—a maidenhead, a stable head on her shoulders, and supreme command as head of state. Unlike Victoria, Elizabeth's supreme wisdom lies in not marrying. By keeping her maidenhead, she can keep her head, both in the sense of self-possession and of public rule.

Strachey in fact elevates the spillage of such a figure to the level of one of the text's most pervasive tropological systems. Thus the terms by which Strachey recalls that Elizabeth's father, Henry VIII, had executed her mother, Anne Boleyn: "When she was two years and eight months old, her father had cut off her mother's head" (20). Moments later, we are told that, by implicit contrast, the young Elizabeth, despite crisis, "kept her head" (21). (The Lord Admiral, not so fortunate, was "beheaded," too [22].) We have already noted, meanwhile, how the impenetrability of Elizabeth's maidenhead or "membrana" (24) is—like her ability to keep her figurative head even as her mother loses her literal one—the "pivot upon which the fate of Europe turned" (25). Elizabeth's ability to keep her head, then, is overdeterminedly—at the level of both language and plot—the source of her power as "head" of state. (King Philip is, in both a figurative and literal sense, quite correct: " 'the cause is the sex of the sovereign' "[162].) Not surprisingly, Essex's impetuosity is in turn often the result of his having "lost his head" (88) or of his tendency to "lose his head" (192)—a merely figurative usage early in the story perhaps, but one that documents a movement toward its real enactment at the story's climax. In a premonitory gesture, Elizabeth's annoyance after the Cadiz success leads her to decide that, had Essex failed, "she would have cut off his head" (160). By tale's end, the movement from connotation to denotation is complete after Essex's overt treason: "It would be enough if she cut off his head" (264).

Of course, whatever further suggestions to which we may be led (e.g., the relation of authority and castration) would likely end up in psychoanalytic burlesque, reminding us that Strachey deploys such terms as "head" in order to account for them as well as to use them. In *Essex*, such accounting is historical as well as rhetorical. The book is an account of the invention of a distinctly private or psychological space—Elizabeth's epistemology as opposed to Essex's, the book's chief subject in the history it narrates as well as the discursive creation that allows the text its ability to speak the way it does. Like private and public, the book's subject and the categories that describe it/that it describes are parallel to the verge of identity. In fact, it is fair to say that *Elizabeth and Essex* articulates its own articulation as a function of what it articulates. It narrates no less than its own conditions of emergence, the origin of precisely those distinctions between public and private, particularly between power and sexuality, that put the protopsychological categories that enable it into place for the first time in Strachey's history of English ideology. He seeks the origin of the originary opposition between public and private that authorizes his own manifest categories of representation. Hence the ultimate achievement of describing the origin as a direct function of one's historical belatedness from it. If Essex's transgressions lead to Elizabeth's establishment of the lawful distinction between public and private (and, of course, the other way around), it is, similarly, Strachey's transgressions as a writer—particularly the double process of using psychological categories while also putting them into question—that allows him to satisfy both modernist projects at once, offering the appearance of primal discovery or explanation while also understanding—and therefore exposing— the means of production of such a return to the past. On the one hand, Strachey's history is in possession of the origin it seeks to recuperate ("It is very possible that you have succeeded," wrote Freud to Strachey, "in making a correct reconstruction of what actually occurred" [Meisel and Kendrick 1985:Appendix I]). On the other hand—and like the deferred action proper by which Elizabeth herself remembers the primal scene of her father's killing of her mother—Strachey's history is in possession of its origins only by virtue of the belatedness that impels his desire to find them.

EPILOGUE

Conrad as a Pedagogy

of Reading

Things are because we see them, and
what we see, and how we see it,
depends on the Arts that have
influenced us.

> —Wilde, "The Decay of Lying"

When, finally, on the afternoon after
our arrival, I stood on the Acropolis
and cast my eyes around upon the landscape,
a surprising thought suddenly entered
my mind: "So all this really does
exist, just as we learnt at school!"

> —Freud, "A Disturbance of
> Memory on the Acropolis"

The Myth of *Heart of Darkness*

What all our writers share, then, is not only the fact of coming late, but of knowing it all too well. What distinguishes them is whether they repress or account for such a precondition in art and experience alike. If there is a recurrent structure to our modernist problematic, it is the structure of the retroactive production of lost primacy by means of evidence belatedly gathered to signify the presence of its absence. Whether or not to admit that any myth of the modern is a defense against belatedness is the real crisis that helps to define each of our writers in turn. Their own choices provide us with new evaluative opportunities in canon-formation and with some implicit rearrangement in our assumptions about what modernism is. Those writers who take temporality into account both as subject and mechanism are those whose fictions (continue to) have greater power and persuasion than do those of our writers who do not—Hardy, Pater, Joyce, Forster, Woolf, Strachey. Those who repress temporality and try to repress their equal imprisonment within a late Romantic episteme by invoking a classicist and/or theological escape are, by contrast, those with less life today, perhaps because they wrote for eternity instead—in particular, Arnold and Eliot. Modernism as a problematic is finally a question of whether one gets trapped in a paradox of liberation ironically structured to set one free only in the language of capture, or whether one recognizes the myth of the modern for what it is—a reaction-formation that provides as many advantages as it does restrictions.

If any reflexive realist—the most prudent negotiators of our problematic—gathers up all that we have seen in a single, canonical text, it is Conrad in *Heart of Darkness* (1902). As exemplary and enduring a modern classic as we have, Conrad's novel creates the terms of its appeal by challenging us to specify the meaning Marlow tries to find in the character of Kurtz. Those readers who write about what they discover in Marlow's tracks pursue what Marlow himself says he is unable to disclose: the substance, the essence, the details of what it is that Kurtz has done, and what it is that he represents. Answers to the enigma usually reveal a common predisposition to assign highly concrete meanings to the tale, and to take the multiplicity of clues provided by the narrative as indices of a significance to be found beyond the margins of the text. Much as Lawrence influentially privileges the will to modernity in Hardy despite his precursor's recursive irony, *Heart of Darkness* is also the recipient of an enormously influential canonical reading that similarly privileges, in the scandalously implicit name of Freud, those same, outworn modernist oppositions reified by Lawrence and deconstructed by Hardy. Albert J. Guerard's classic interpretation of the novel as "a journey within the self" (1958) renders *Heart of Darkness* no less than the myth of the modern par excellence. For Guerard, Kurtz's admittedly "unspoken" conduct succeeds in becoming the token of a struggle with the instincts: "[W]hen the external restraints of society and work are removed," says Guerard, "we must meet the challenge and temptation of savage reversion" (1958:36). Like Hardy's myth of the modern, in other words, the oppositions that seem to structure *Heart of Darkness* are, at least according to Guerard and his heritage (including even Watt 1979), precisely those of restraint and passion, repression and desire—natural energy, in short, struggling against the incivilities of civilization.

Especially representative of the extensive influence of the canonical reading is Francis Coppola's like desire for the (really absent) "unspeakable rites" (84) in which Kurtz supposedly engages, a darkness Coppola renders visible in the closing sequence of *Apocalypse Now* (1979) by supplying us with the actual presence of the grotesqueries of Kurtz/Brando never authorized by the tale upon which the film is based. Not surprisingly, the film willingly implicates itself in an Eliotic genealogy of modernism by placing volumes of Jessie Weston, Frazer, and Eliot's poems by Kurtz's bedside. In so doing, Coppola supplementarily provides precisely what the tale's readers have always wanted, but which Conrad himself—despite Guerard, or the more rhetorically sophisticated hedging in the equal service of the reality of the "unspeakable" in James Guetti (1965)—quite intentionally withholds. For the novel's reader, as for Marlow himself, a visible presence for the reported evils of Kurtz seems absolutely required, although it remains the central wit of the novel not to present it. " 'The inner truth,' " Marlow assures us—and so ironically assures us, by negation, that there really is such a primacy in the first place—" 'is hidden' " (93). Even so—and as if to assure us once again that there is indeed a center to his quest—Marlow asserts, too, that, despite the landscape's silence and inchoateness, " 'there you could look at a thing monstrous and free' " (96), and so be reminded " 'of your remote kinship with this wild and passionate uproar' " (96). Hence the core or truth to be extracted is, like Arnold's or Eliot's, fixed, immutable, eternal; it is apparently boldly natural in an almost Lawrentian way—" 'truth stripped of its cloak of time' " (97), the myth of the modern in its plainest form. The native cannibals, of course, belong in turn to the "'beginnings of time'" (103), since, despite all anthropological common sense, they "'had'"—or seem to have—"'no inherited experience to teach them as it were'" (103). They are, in short, an almost pure eruption of nature in what we would today call Marlow's Orientalizing primitivism (Said 1978). Thus too—if we are to pluck more Guerardian instances from the text in order to enforce such a reading—the natives are "'as natural and true as the surf'" (61) perhaps because the coast on which it breaks is "'featureless'" (60). European civilization is on the rampage, however, and so regresses into the savage freshness to which it is customarily opposed, even though its real, and now unrepressed, desire to scorn the law for nature's own sake is at last revealed or expressed. It is, ironically, civilization itself, especially in the form of Kurtz, that will revert instead to the savage, the cannibals' contrasting and unexpected restraint a paradox usually left unexplored except in its political ramifications. Like the celebrated clerk, immaculately starched even in the jungle (67–68), civilization is a question of believing in the supreme fictions one imposes on natural chaos (J. H. Miller 1965). "'What was in there?'" (81) stands as a summary emblem for the book's, or at least its reader's, apparent desire, searching as it seems to be for "'the amazing reality of its concealed life'" (80).

If we inquire into the details of Guerard's own critical language, however, problems begin to occur almost immediately. Guerard's untenable assumption that African culture is without "society" is necessary, of course, if his psychological symbolism is to hold. If the novel's landscape is to be read as the terrain of the id, then its native inhabitants have to be cast as primitives. Guerard's assumptions thereby conflict with subsequent contentions in anthropology that there are no such qualitative differences as he supposes between European and "savage" cultures (Lévi-Strauss 1962) as well as with Conrad's own attempt to call such differences into question within the tale itself. Although the cannibal crewmen aboard Marlow's riverboat display, to his own surprise, a greater restraint than the novel's rapacious Europeans (104–05), and although Kurtz's "savage" woman stages a stately ballet of farewell for her departing lover (135–36), Guerard nonetheless insists on his primitivism in order to ground the tale's meaning in the psychological categories he discerns as principal in Conrad's text.

Little different epistemologically from the structure of Lawrence's canonical reading of Hardy, Guerard's reading of Conrad requires us to bring to Conrad as well the same kind of late Romantic oppositions at work in a normative reading of Hardy. Here their almost visible struggle—Marlow as repressive culture, Kurtz as instinctual id—seems to usurp center stage altogether, though leaving us with no more than the usual battle between Eros and civilization, natural instinct and social repression. We are customarily inclined to shape Conrad's entire career in such terms as well, particularly if we simply equate *Heart of Darkness* as a whole with the desire to secure a modernist primacy beyond culture whose simultaneous dangers and attractions are well represented by Kurtz. It is, of course, the satanic visionary who is the constant danger throughout Conrad's fiction, even if he is also the focus of its fascination. In his debased version—Almayer, Willems, Jim—the softheaded romantic visionary threatens the community the way Wait threatens the life of the ship in *The Nigger of the "Narcissus"* (1897). Martin Decoud in *Nostromo* (1904) is, by contrast, the type's high exponent, with Nostromo and Charles Gould active versions of the same noble, if also solipsistic, impulses, and hence greater, if ironic, threats to the community than Decoud himself. A character like Marlow mediates between the poles (like Conrad himself), an isolatoe and a captain at once, with the nature of such mediation the very subject of *Youth* (1902). Indeed, the mediation there suggests, in the difference between the older and the younger Marlow, that the later Conrad himself comes to look more cautiously upon the visionary stance endemic to youth, even if his enduring attraction to it as a surrogate or spectator—like the captain in *The Secret Sharer* (1912)—is the apparent motive force behind *Lord Jim* (1900) as well as *Nostromo*, and, arguably, aspects of the late phase such as *Victory* (1915). Thus Conrad's early infatuation with the solitary visionary in *Heart of Darkness* and *Lord Jim* eventually gives way in later years to the necessity of social control and authority in *The Shadow Line* (1917) and *A Personal Record* (1912; see Thorburn 1974).

Whether or not Conrad's texts really behave like the stages of an Eriksonian psychodrama, however, it is still worth asking whether Conrad's own prose affirms the validity of the kinds of oppositions that structure the normative reading of his career at large and of novels such as *Heart of Darkness* in particular. Let us compare the conclusions to which Conrad apparently comes here with those of *The Secret Sharer* (1912), an exemplary exercise since both works take as their overt topic one of the myth of the modern's principal primacies, the presumably natural status of the self.

The Secret Sharer: "Something against Nature"

If the canonical reading of *Heart of Darkness* imagines the seat of selfhood as a brute, primitive unconscious struggling against the repressions of ego and civilization, *The Secret Sharer*, by contrast, regards even the unconscious determinations that structure the ego as social rather than instinctual or biological. At the start of the tale, Conrad's narrator is, not unusually, lost in what Jameson calls a "sensorium" (1981:230), looking for an object upon which to rest his "eye" (1912:91), and, by implication, his "I" as well. But how is the discourse of the I, this individuality, to be constituted? As in *Heart of Darkness*, it is, of course, dramatized through the use of the titular secret sharer, but now the enigmatic nature of Marlow's secret identity with Kurtz as culture's representative of a realm "beyond culture" has been reversed by the entirely different structure of the bond between Conrad's nameless captain-narrator here and Leggatt, his outlaw double. For in *The Secret Sharer*, the unconscious other we harbor within is not something inherent, natural, and timeless, but, rather, something already social, temporal, and historical to begin with. No representative of instinct as is Kurtz, Leggatt signifies a different kind of unconscious with which the captain-narrator of the later text will have to come to terms: an unconscious that is constituted by law and circumstance rather than by instinct or brute reflex. Hence the opening line of the novel situates—or as yet fails to—the captain-speaker in a series of unexpected ways: he is not only unpositioned sensorially; he is also unpositioned rhetorically, since there is, curiously, no "other hand" ready to match the opening phrase "On my right hand" (91) with which the tale begins. All we find in the second sentence is the remark that "to the left" (not even a balancing "my" "left" to match the "my right") were "a group of barren islets, suggesting ruins of stone walls, towers" (91). There is, in short, no "other" yet, except in the premonitory form of a landscape that evokes images of ruins and blasted towers—the precise tropological notations for belatedness—that already suggest the "other" to be the burdens of tradition and law rather than the eruption of an atemporal nature (the familiar landscape figurations also include twilight [92] and the Coleridgean "mountain gorge" [141] of Koh-ring at the book's climax). The young captain is therefore in fact positioned in the opening paragraph within a "mysterious" but symbolic "system of half-submerged bamboo fences, incomprehensible in its division of the domain" (91). Unlike Marlow in *Heart of Darkness*, here the speaker pays little attention to the Egdonesque abandon of nature. Instead, his gaze is riveted upon the "half-submerged" "system" of as-yet indecipherable but clearly regulatory power.

Unlike Marlow, too (for whom we are given, even in *Heart of Darkness*, enough of a history to motivate his voyage), our nameless captain in *The Secret Sharer* assures us that the circumstances of his being newly assigned to his first command are "of no particular significance" (93). It is, apparently, a purely paradigmatic operation that is about to transpire. Perhaps the captain's "strangeness" to his ship and shipmates (93–96) is basic to the novel's plainly allegorical project of designating the operations that constitute selfhood. That the captain is in the exact position of coming late in both the tradition of command in general and of his vessel in particular is to insist, moreover, that the precondition of command or self-possession is one of overt belatedness, and one that in turn identifies the role of the new captain with the role of the belated writer.

What is to occur, then, is an account of the self as social and linguistic, and, as we shall see, also juridical—psychic and real economy are functionally interdependent rather than at odds. In *The Secret Sharer*, selfhood is directly articulated not as an instinctual pulsation, but as "that ideal conception of one's own personality every man sets up for himself secretly" (94). A representation of the other as id, we might say, has given way to one of the id as other, or of the other as superego. Thus while Marlow's instinctual secret sharer Kurtz is rarely and hardly visible, the captain's sociological secret sharer here appears, ghostly though he may be, early, enduringly, and at close range throughout. Almost everything is sparely but exactly shown rather than hidden. The ship itself, for example, is initially "littered like any ship in port with a tangle of unrelated things" (95). The job, of course, is to untangle the "tangle" so as to see "properly" (95)—the emergence of the self or the "proper" the function of a narrative ordering in relation to the laws and instruments that come before it and constitute it. The structural identity of the coherence of memory that formally links selfhood and narrative alike is punningly remarked upon when the narrator tells us of "my mind picturing to myself the coming passage" (96), or, even more, when he calls his new assignment "the novel responsibility of command" (96).

Above all, Leggatt is, unlike Kurtz, a cold mirror, a play of surfaces and appearances rather than of lush depth. Though Leggatt emerges from the sea (the latter replete with temptingly Jungian symbols of natural plenitude and a universal motherhood), Conrad almost immediately casts the situation in the terms of a Lacanian mirror stage rather than as the captain's Marlovian confrontation with something naturally hidden within himself. The structure of self—of the "proper," of "command"—now emerges as a play between form and formlessness, imagistic wholeness and imagistic "litter." Thus when the captain first discovers Leggatt alongside his ship, he peers over to look into the "darkling glassy shimmer of the sea" (97) and "the shape of his black-haired head" (98) "upturned exactly under mine" (98). Immediately taken with Leggatt's own "self-possession" (99), our otherwise unprepossessing captain suddenly feels a "corresponding state in myself" (99). "Self-possession"—the surety of the proper, of command—is, ironically, the function of identifying with the image of another's wholeness or self-possession (hence the captain soon learns how to dominate his crew as well as himself by scrutinizing "the face of every . . . man" [113]). "It was," says the captain, "as though I had been faced by my own reflection in the depths of a sombre and immense mirror" (101). Like his "ideal conception" of himself, then, the captain's "double" (101) is, ironically, the "other" place in which he finds his "proper" self. Just the reverse of Guerard's natural conception of the self in *Heart of Darkness*, selfhood in *The Secret Sharer* is, in the novel's own words, "like something against nature," virtually "inhuman" despite its being the basis of being human at all (136). Always speaking in whispers, neither Leggatt nor the captain will ever "hear each other's natural voice" (137).

Much as selfhood thereby requires the simultaneous belief in two contradictory notions—the self is what it is because it is the function of another—so, too, does the captain's willingness to aid Leggatt rest upon his like understanding of a double process in the law of the sea that Leggatt's own captain, Archbold, is not wise enough to understand. No wonder Archbold is physically incoherent in Conrad's description—"smeary" "eyes" (116) accompanied by a "muddle . . . as to . . . bearings" (117). Leggatt's killing of a rebellious crewman during a storm may well be a crime from a single-minded point of view; from the point of view of the double process of command, however, it is no crime at all, especially since Leggatt is first mate. Leggatt kills his crewman so as to preserve the entire ship's company: "It was all very simple. The same strung-up force which had given twenty-four men a chance, at least, for their lives, had, in a sort of recoil, crushed an unworthy mutinous existence" (124–25). Like the captain's two sleeping suits both "simultaneously in use" (104), or like his "confused sensation of being in two places at once" (111), the logical operation required to contextualize Leggatt's crime is identical with the structure of subjectivity itself once both are articulated as double or simultaneously contradictory operations.

Decentering *Heart of Darkness:*
Modernism as Metacriticism

Is *Heart of Darkness* as different from *The Secret Sharer* as it seems? Does the earlier work, as Guerard's influence suggests, render Kurtz a primitive in order to produce a lost primacy? Or does it, like the later *Secret Sharer*, articulate such primacy in secondary and therefore ironic terms? If we return to *Heart of Darkness* after *The Secret Sharer*, it becomes clear that, as with Hardy's *Mayor*, Conrad has in fact planted a myth of the modern as but one of a number of elements in his text. "The greatest authors," an almost Althusserian Ian Watt reminds us in his book on Conrad, "are rarely representative of the ideology of their periods; they tend rather to expose its internal contradictions" (1979:147). Indeed, Conrad gives us his myth with even more severe cunning than Hardy does, since to recognize it as such opens up, as the book's ultimate subject, the structure of reader-response by which our modern classics are customarily assessed. Conrad's text is a pedagogy of reading, an instance of reflexive realism almost unparalleled in its period.

Let us look first at the immediate consequences of Guerard's method of interpretation by noting the problematic texture of the critical language it produces. What Guerard means by "the evil of vacancy" to which the "hollow" Kurtz "succumbs" (1958:36) is a little difficult to tell in the light of his first argument. Surely "the temptation of savage reversion" carries with it some fecundity, some fullness of instinct that Guerard's insistence on hollowness and vacancy, like Conrad's own, seems to call into question. Guerard falls into these same rhetorical contradictions time and again in his reading of the novel. "Marlow's temptation," he writes, "is made concrete through his exposure to Kurtz" (39), despite his remark later on that Conrad is always "deferring what we most want to know and see" (41). Similarly, says Guerard, the novel symbolizes "the night journey into the unconscious, and confrontation of an entity within the self" (39), even though Kurtz's vanishing act late in the story means, according to Guerard, that "a part of [Marlow, too] has vanished" (41). This is critical language somehow divided against itself, stipulating the presence of meaning on the one hand while noting the withdrawal of its ground on the other. The tale's apparently organizing categories are already put in some question when, for example, we learn that the cannibals working as crewmen aboard Marlow's steamer are not vessels of raw instinct, but rather, " 'men one could work with' " (94). Far more than the rapacious—and supposedly civilizing—Europeans, the cannibals are unexcelled in the kind of restraint that distinguishes civilization from the nature they supposedly represent. In fact, the state of the Europeans, whether of Kurtz himself or the others, already puts in question the tale's operative distinctions. The twist or boomerang in the notion that Western imperialism equals repression and African savagery natural passion is that it is precisely the European rather than the African who has no restraint, a formulation that exactly reverses or contaminates the opposition out of which the original and normative distinction arises. Despite Marlow's—and Guerard's—insistence on a natural core secreted within Kurtz, there is finally "'no sign'" whatever—nothing to be read—"'on the face of nature'" (129) itself even late in the journey.

Guerard's contradictions derive from undue assumptions about Conrad's text, and his reading falls prey to the same epistemological temptations that Marlow, by contrast, is forced to overcome by the end of the tale. It is Conrad's radical understanding of how language itself creates and controls the kind of knowledge we have that leads to Marlow's deepest realization, one that he finds, in Conrad's words, "'altogether monstrous, intolerable to thought and odious to the soul'" (141). It is, moreover, Marlow's crisis in knowledge that allows us to see why Kurtz's "vacancy" in the story is necessary and inevitable, and that tends to supplant our usual sense of the psychological terror the novel evokes with a horror perhaps even more difficult to face.

Let us focus, then, on Marlow's key conclusion about Kurtz, one based upon the evidence of the shrunken heads displayed before the Inner Station: "'They only showed that Mr. Kurtz lacked restraint in the gratification of his various lusts, that there was something wanting in him—some small matter which, when the pressing need arose, could not be found under his magnificent eloquence'" (131). Marlow takes the heads as evidence of Kurtz's lack of restraint ("showed"). Like Guerard, Marlow draws his conclusion by taking such evidence as a token of what is not really present ("We feel cheated," says Watt, "at not being given a ringside seat at one of Kurtz's orgies" [1979:233]). Such inference leads to conclusions about absence in another sense, too. What is present through the evidence is Kurtz's absence of morality—"that there was something wanting in him." Kurtz has such a lack because he seems to be a lustful creature, full of desire—that is, "wanting," like Bellow's Henderson, in another sense. In fact, "wanting" taken as the presence of desire depends upon "wanting" taken as the absence of gratification. In the middle of Marlow's assertive claim, in other words, we find ourselves thrown back upon the kind of riddles that baffle Marlow himself elsewhere in the novel. What Kurtz has depends on what he has not; what he has not depends on what he has. We seem trapped in a play of language at the very moment of Marlow's attempt to disclose some discovery about Kurtz.

The mutually interdependent relation between the two senses of "wanting," though, suggests that meaning is a lateral event within language. The canonical reading of the novel, however, appears to have a view of language that, by contrast, presupposes some kind of direct link between words and things, not only in Conrad, but also, for Guerard at least, in Freud as well. It is Freud, however, who draws our attention to language as an oppositional or differential mechanism as early as 1910, well before the notion receives its official introduction into linguistics proper with the publication in 1916 of Ferdinand de Saussure's *Cours de linguistique générale*, and only eleven years after the first publication of *Heart of Darkness*. In his brief essay on Karl Abel's pamphlet "The Antithetical Meaning of Primal Words" (1884), Freud discovers an "astonishing" (1910:11:10) philological explanation for contradictions in the language of dreams, and delights in its transformation by Abel into a synchronic rule about the mechanism of meaning in language as a whole (see also Empson 1930:193ff.). "Our concepts," writes Freud, "owe their existence to comparisons" (11:156). Quoting from Abel's pamphlet, Freud provides us with the following account of why language and its conceptions are relational structures rather than transparent vehicles for the expression of essences:

> "If it were always light we should not be able to distinguish
> light from dark, and consequently we should not be able to
> have either the concept of light or the word for it. . . ." "It is
> clear that everything on this planet is relative and has an
> independent existence only in so far as it is differentiated in
> respect of its relations to other things. . . ." "Since every con-
> cept is in this way the twin of its contrary, how could it be first
> thought of and how could it be communicated to other people
> who were trying to conceive it, other than by being measured
> against its contrary. . . ?" "Since the concept of strength could
> not be formed except as a contrary to weakness, the word
> denoting 'strong' contained a simultaneous recollection of
> 'weak,' as the thing by means of which it first came into
> existence. In reality this word denoted neither 'strong' nor
> 'weak,' but the relation and difference between the two, which
> created both of them equally." [1910:11:157–58]

Thus it is the conditions of human usage as a whole that stipulate the kind of problem that Marlow confronts in the next section of the sentence we have been examining: "some small matter which, when the pressing need arose, could not be found." It is the possibility of finding "some . . . matter," in the sense of substance, that Marlow claims "could not be found," even in its effect of producing nothing concrete to go by in the case of Kurtz. Of course, the double meaning of "wanting" has already suggested what Marlow here makes explicit: that language—the inevitable medium of his interpretation of Kurtz—is in no position to discover the "matter" or ground that Marlow, like all interpreters, wishes to assign to the elusive object of his quest.

But lest this recessive quality of "matter" seem merely fanciful, let us turn for a moment to the start of the tale, where Conrad discusses just these difficulties in broad terms. Marlow's parable of the Roman official who came to Britain long ago is a caution he brings to bear on his own notions about the centrality of the (never properly named) Congo. To the Roman, Britain is the periphery of a circle whose center is Rome. And yet now, centuries later, Britain is itself the center of another circle whose periphery includes the African colonies. By implication, the Congo will perforce become the center of still another, newer circle, whose periphery will in turn become the center of still another new circle, and so on, ad infinitum. The model, in other words, is epistemological as well as political. Every discovery of a center or an origin is subject to a decentering, or, to put it another way, every disclosure of a ground is subject to the recession of that ground. Conrad's formulation helps to explain, and may even govern, the problem of Marlow's quest for Kurtz and the forever recessive object or center that Kurtz is.

It is just this shift or recession of centers that makes up the drama of Marlow's search. Pursuing Kurtz to the Central Station, Marlow finds that there is still another center, the Inner Station. And having found Kurtz there, Marlow finds the essential Kurtz to escape him again, since the object of his quest is a "'shadow'" (134), "'unsteady . . . pale, indistinct, like a vapour'" (142). All Marlow has to work with is "'a voice'" (135), "'discoursing'" (113)—nothing, that is, but language. In this way, Kurtz has "'kicked himself loose of the earth'" (144). In fact, Kurtz has "'kicked the very earth to pieces'" (144). As a piece of language, Kurtz is "wanting" the "earth" or "matter" that Marlow wishes him to consist of so as to make him an object concrete enough to seize upon. But because the recessive Kurtz is a mere series of contradictory or differential utterances (*kurtz*, for example, is twice described as "'long'" [134, 142]), his ground—his objecthood—cannot be located. "'There was nothing either above or below him,'" says Marlow, "'and I knew it. . . . I . . . did not know whether I stood on the ground or floated in the air'" (144). Indeed, Conrad's notoriously playful rhetoric programmatically puts its enabling oppositions into question throughout the text, redoubling, for example, the oscillation of plenitude and lack in the figure "wanting" in its dual figurations of the novel's landscape. Thus the jungle is by turns a "'network of paths'" (70) and a "'secret'" lurking in a "'nothing'" (74), the latter prompting a "'waiting— . . . for something'" (77) that the earlier figuration already cancels as a possibility. Hence, too, Marlow feels, as late as the moments preceding Kurtz's death, that he is "'also . . . buried in a vast grave full of unspeakable secrets'" (138), a condition repeated in the figure of the dead Kurtz's "'unseen presence of victorious corruption'" (138). As the journey home begins, Marlow's rhetoric maintains its duality when he speaks of the "crowd" of natives ready to see them off. "'Of [their] presence behind the curtain of trees,'" says a rhetorically licentious Marlow, "'I had been acutely conscious all the time'" (145). Even Conrad's apparently decisive designation of the jungle as the primeval and eternal core of nature—"'truth stripped of its cloak of time'" (97)—falls into a self-contamination or self-questioning as the result, for example, of the subsequent idiomatic plural that implies, quite contrary to the phrase's manifest intent, that the natural core or origin in question is not single or fixed but a (possible) plurality of such origination: "'Going up that river,'" says the questing Marlow, "'was like travelling back to the earliest beginnings of the world'" (92). Even the origin of the world, that is, is not a single beginning, but a set of possible "beginnings" none of which can be said to have priority over another.

What is true of Marlow's search for Kurtz is true also of Marlow's presence in the Congo. Notice, for example, that the "'insoluble problem'" (126) of the harlequin, "'covered with patches all over, with bright patches, blue, red, and yellow'" (122), resembles the map Marlow has seen in Brussels, with its "'blue, a little green, smears of orange, and . . . a purple patch'" (55). No wonder the harlequin's "'aspect'" reminds Marlow of "'something funny [he] had seen somewhere'" (122). Here at the real site to which the map's representations refer, Marlow finds simply another version of the (same) representation. That is, the grounded reality of what the map represents withdraws from Marlow even as he stands upon it, turning as it does into a representation of itself much in the same way that Kurtz, too, is (only) language or representation.

This recession of presence, this decentering, is in evidence throughout the novel and is the book's active epistemological principle. In fact, it well accords with the famous definition of meaning attributed to Marlow at the start of the tale: "the meaning of an episode was not inside like a kernel but outside, enveloping the tale which brought it out only as a glow brings out a haze, in the likeness of one of these misty halos that sometimes are made visible by the spectral illumination of moonshine" (48). Conrad's anonymous narrator discards the notion of meaning as a core or "kernel" without reservation, setting up instead a more problematic definition that plays upon the meanings of "spectral illumination." "Spectral" signifies "prismatic" and "phantom-like" at once, thereby defining meaning as without substance (in the sense of "specter"), multiple and prismatic (in the sense of "spectrum"), and at a distance from an original source of illumination ("moonshine"). All of these requirements are met, of course, in the tale itself, though they are by no means met in the tale Guerard tells. What is more, it is these requirements that Marlow meets again at the close of the sentence we have been examining: "some . . . matter which . . . could not be found under his magnificent eloquence." Just as there is no "kernel" inside, so there is nothing to "be found under" Kurtz's "eloquence." The reason has nothing to do, of course, with Kurtz's being any more of a liar than anyone else, but with the inescapable conditions of meaning itself. The "matter" of Kurtz's meaning escapes Marlow not because his wishful essence is difficult to locate or, as a psychoanalytic critic might argue, because it must remain repressed, but because it simply does not exist. The geology of surface/depth meaning must give way, in Marlow's understanding as well as in our own, to a surface topography—a map perhaps—of relations within a system of representations or signs.

Conrad, of course, is concerned with representations throughout the text. Even in our focus sentence, Kurtz's eloquence is figured implicitly as a fabric or raiment ("under" makes "eloquence" a covering of some kind), while elsewhere in the text it is described as "'folds of eloquence'" (147), similar to the "'diaphanous folds'" (46) of the narrator's own discourse. Like the book's images of maps, documents, dress, ciphers, and so on, the numerous images of fabric or text-ile are representations of representations, each one suggesting a weave or a network of relations much like the one presented by the text itself. These are Conrad's alternative and interchangeable metaphors for the structure of language that we, like Marlow, interpret in the pursuit of a grail-object unavailable to us as such.

Thus the "horror" that assails Marlow has to do with the impossibility of disclosing a central core, an essence, a ground to what Kurtz has done and what he is. There is no central thread in the weave of the evidences that contribute to his character, much less no deep center to his existence as a surface of signs. So when we puzzle over Kurtz's absence when Marlow finds him gone from his cabin, we may offer the conclusion that Kurtz's absence is itself a sign for his meaning, one which is "short" or "wanting." Hence Marlow's own puzzlement at Kurtz's absence takes on a direct meaning within our present perspective:

> "I think I would have raised an outcry if I had believed my
> eyes. But I didn't believe them at first—the thing seemed so
> impossible. The fact is I was completely unnerved by a sheer
> blank fright, pure abstract terror, unconnected with any dis-
> tinct shape of physical danger. What made this emotion so
> overpowering was—how shall I define it?—the moral shock I

> received, as if something altogether monstrous, intolerable to thought and odious to the soul, had been thrust upon me unexpectedly. This lasted of course the merest fraction of a second, and then the usual sense of commonplace, deadly danger, the possibility of a sudden onslaught and massacre, or something of the kind, which I saw impending, was positively welcome and composing. It pacified me, in fact, so much, that I did not raise an alarm." [141]

Marlow's "fright" and "terror" are responses to the "sheer blank" and "pure abstract[ion]" of Kurtz's self-evident absence, even though—or rather, because—it is "unconnected with any distinct shape," especially the "physical." Thus the promise of presence, no matter in how terrible a form—"a sudden onslaught or massacre, or something of the kind"—is "positively welcome" and pacifying to Marlow's "altogether monstrous" realization that presence itself is a fiction.

Marlow, however, plays little tricks on himself to instill a sense of ground in the absence he sees in presence, where there is " 'nothing underfoot' " (150). When the harlequin, for example, tells him that the text he thinks is cipher is really Russian, Marlow feels a momentary relief, as though Russian were a more natural, or grounded, code than cipher. Indeed, Marlow grants such a reassuring, and fictive, priority to Russian much as he prefers to accent the plain sense of a word like " 'degradation' " (144) in order to make Kurtz apprehensible to him. Like "wanting" or like "short," "degradation"—which seems only to mean besotted or dirty, with all its echoes of soil and ground—has a second layer of meaning, too. This alternative meaning has the sense of "not even 'spectral,' " of a "gradation" that has been neutralized (de-graded) or decomposed, rendering even the prismatic grades of light promised by the narrator's "spectral" definition of meaning early in the tale absent in Kurtz's radical case. Thus Marlow is almost literal when he says, " 'I could not appeal in the name of anything high or low' " (144), since Conrad finally drains Kurtz of all distinguishing, discriminating, nameable qualities, leaving him the " 'blank' " (52, 141) that scares Marlow most of all.

Now perhaps we can be more precise about why *Heart of Darkness* is Marlow's story. It is the narrative of a consciousness at odds with itself in an exemplary way. The tension Marlow represents is one between two notions of the world—one present, one absent; "wanting" or *kurtz* in both senses—with two grammars or vocabularies to match. This is also the unspoken tension we have seen in Guerard's critical language, with its oscillation between contradictory rhetorics, an oscillation that now appears to be a response to the self-divided discourse of the narrative itself. No wonder, then, that, like all the places in the novel, Kurtz's ostentatiously named " 'Intended' " (152 ff.) has no proper name either. Like the tale's own "intended" meaning, what Kurtz himself is " 'Intended' " to mean has no more proper a referent than contextualization alone can supply. The " 'great and saving illusion' " (159) that Marlow will give her by saying that Kurtz's last words were her elusive name is in fact analogous to the "saving illusion" of Guerard's canonical reading, a will to · modernity that restores or recuperates the presence of an absence about whose fluctuation the tale as a whole quivers or vibrates in its delicate negotiation of the structure of modernism at large.

The problematic meaning of Marlow's quest, then, finally issues from Conrad's concern with the problematic of all meaning in *Heart of Darkness*. Rather than a psychological work, *Heart of Darkness* is a text that interrogates the epistemological status of the language in which it inheres. We are left with nothing less than a critique of our normal stipulation that being is presence, and, within the sphere of criticism, with a critique of our belief that literary texts entertain a subject/object relation to states in the world and to their own meanings. Even the title of Conrad's text is a paradox or riddle designed to tempt its interpreters rather than to locate for us a heart or center that does not exist. It is not Guerard's "psychic need" or "literary tact" (1958:40)—nor is it Guetti's "alinguistic" truth (1965)—that keeps the details of Kurtz's experiences or their meaning at a remove from us in the story. Instead, it *is* the meaning of the story that keeps Kurtz's meaning absent and that makes of absence the ground of presence itself.

To read the novel otherwise is to succumb to the myth of the modern that Conrad installs as an instructive trap in a text that seduces its readers into the surety of a meaning that its larger structure simultaneously undercuts. *Heart of Darkness* is finally about the terms of its own reading—a pedagogy of reading, since the various meanings by which we recuperate the text are finally mirrors of a wishful rather than expressive " 'Intended,' " of the categories by which our customary mode of reading a text proceeds. In so doing, the text finally interrogates its readers, or at least the frames of expectation and desire in which its interpretative community is customarily situated. For Conrad, as for Hardy, the myth of the modern is the supreme test of one's poetics and politics alike. Does one accept such a myth directly, literally, or does one treat it with suspicion, as do the strong texts in which it appears instead as an item of inquiry? To suspect it, of course, is to caution the will to modernity with which modernism as a whole has too long been simply identified. To characterize modernism as metacriticism instead, then, is to join in its spirit of self-interrogation rather than to submit to a wishful transcendence that is, except in Arnold and Eliot, an index of temptation rather than a measure of truth. Conrad quells our perpetual will to modernity by pointing out the dubious implications to which the desire that impels it defensively too often leads, thereby confronting us with a mirror of our reading rather than with a meaning beyond it.

To call modernism itself metacriticism also provides us with a rather exact link to the postmodern, a term we continue to use despite our hesitations because its products tend largely to be continuous with those metacritical modernist texts to which they are often in direct, and sometimes flamboyantly obvious, relation (besides, any "modernist" project is always postmodern anyway, since the "now" or "modern" it seeks is already behind it). To characterize postmodernism as a negation of the negation (see Stone 1984) is to say that art and literature after modernism are simply overt about the metacritical status that all strong modernist texts already exhibit. What modernism negates, of course, is the tradition it begins to minimalize, whether in Eliotic fragments or Joycean metonymies. Nor does such a view of the postmodern require the maintenance of the problematic notion of an authentic avant-garde (Poggioli 1968), or of the kind of dogmatically reflexive texts that aggravate the old modernist problem rather than solve it by continuing to oppose reflexivity and realism, art and society, self and world—in short, all the customary oppositions our strongest modernists have themselves put in question. To be sure, if it is agreed that modernist art at large takes among its principal concerns the status and means of production of the text itself (see Krauss 1985), then a notion of an avant-garde that is truly postmodern must go a step beyond metacriticism by calling attention not only to the means of production of a given work, but also (as with Kurt Schwitters) to the status of "art" itself as an "institution" (Bürger 1984:49; see also Foster, ed., 1983).

Satisfactory as such a view may be momentarily, however, especially outside literature, we must remember that the usual postmodernism is a mere "imitation modernism" of the kind practiced by, say, the later John Barth, Gilbert Sorrentino, or William Gass (Meisel 1982). It is not, then, surprising to say that it is the strongest vein in High Modernism proper—reflexive realism—that remains the most reliable current in the wake of fiction following Joyce. Reflexive realism alone formalizes and extends the strong modernist adequation between reflexivity and representation that was invented in the first place to evacuate from both art and criticism the ideological oppositions between form and content, abstraction and representationalism, metafiction and realism. If modernism proper is a mode of metacriticism designed to overcome the burden of past forms, then a thriving postmodern aesthetic must, of necessity, be not only an elaboration of it, but also the gain of its loss. Quoting Barth, John Updike sums up the situation of the successful postmodernist in quite recognizable terms: "'He has the first half of our century under his belt,'" writes Updike, "'but not on his back.'" "The moderns digested," Updike concludes, "he looks relatively plump" (1984: 142). Though this may be a different image from that of the gaunt Schwitters, in spirit it is in fact similar, and in practice far richer in potential and even fresh power.

Of course, to discuss in any detail the fate of modernism, especially the transatlantic displacement it undergoes by the 1930s, is beyond the bounds of the present study. Still, we may suggest in conclusion that reflexive realism remains the most durable fictive stance after modernism because its ability to insinuate the ironies of art into the configurations of ideology is so ready to hand. Indeed, such a focus is at times the overt finale of such a project, as in Mailer's *Executioner's Song* (1979), in which the end of the novel, in Stracheyesque fashion, narrates the emergence of the documents from which its own beginnings are retroactively made. The latter can be charted by the text only by virtue of an implicitly backward or recursive movement, its reflexive intention simultaneous with—indeed, a function of—the scenes it represents. While even Robbe-Grillet or Brecht may wish to maintain the difference between reflexivity and representationalism in order to call attention to the means of text-production, reflexive realism collapses the distinction in favor of a more strategic intent. By implicating itself in the ideological systems it takes as its subject, and by narrating itself as a function of narrating them—whether in Updike or Mailer at one extreme or Manuel Puig at the other—reflexive realism solves the problem engendered by the postmodern paradox of how one can presume to know ideology if it can be known only through its terms. To narrate the world as already a representation of itself is to have skirted the lower ironies that assail any attempt to produce purely reflexive art, and to have welcomed the higher ironies of nonescape that strong modernism already puts into practice.

Works Cited

PRIMARY SOURCES

Arnold, Matthew. 1849. *The Strayed Reveller, and Other Poems.* All references and citations from Arnold, unless otherwise indicated, are from the Edition de Luxe of the *Works*, 15 vols., London: Macmillan, 1903–04. Arnold's poems are distributed throughout vols. 1 and 2 (*Poems*), although without line numbers. Volume and page numbers for the prose are included in the text.

———. 1852. *Empedocles on Etna, and Other Poems.*

———. 1853a. *Poems.*

———. 1853b. "Preface to First Edition of *Poems.*" In *Irish Essays*, vol. 11.

———. 1854. *Poems, Second Edition.* "A Farewell" is the only new poem added to the *Poems* of 1853.

———. 1857. "On the Modern Element in Literature." Not included in the Edition de Luxe. Rpt. in *The Complete Prose Works of Matthew Arnold*, 11 vols. Ed. R. H. Super. Vol. 1 (*On the Classical Tradition*).

———. 1861. *On Translating Homer.* In the Edition de Luxe, vol. 5.

———. 1865. *Essays in Criticism, First Series*, vol. 3.

———. 1867. *New Poems.*

———. 1869. *Culture and Anarchy*, vol. 6.

———. 1877. *Last Essays on Church and Religion*, vol. 9.

———. 1879. *Mixed Essays*, vol. 10.

———. 1888. *Essays in Criticism, Second Series*, vol. 4.

Conrad, Joseph. 1897. Preface to *The Nigger of the Narcissus*, vol. 23. All references and citations from Conrad are from the Canterbury Edition of *The Complete Works*, 24 vols., Garden City: Doubleday & Page, 1924.

———. 1902. *Heart of Darkness.* In *Youth*, vol. 16.

———. 1912. *The Secret Sharer.* In *'Twixt Land and Sea*, vol. 19.

Eliot, T. S. 1919. "Tradition and the Individual Talent." Rpt. in *Selected Essays.* London: Faber, 1951.

———. 1920. *The Sacred Wood.* Rpt. London: Methuen, 1960.

———. 1921. "The Metaphysical Poets." Rpt. in *Selected Essays.* London: Faber, 1951.

———. 1922, 1930, 1944. All references and citations from Eliot's verse are from the *Collected Poems* (1963). Rpt. New York: Harcourt, Brace & World, 1970.

Citations from the drafts of *The Waste Land* are from the facsimile edition, ed. Valerie Eliot. New York: Harcourt Brace Jovanovich, 1971.

―――. 1923a. "The Function of Criticism." Rpt. in *Selected Essays*. London: Faber, 1951.

―――. 1923b. "*Ulysses*, Order and Myth." *The Dial* 75 (November 1923): 480–83. Rpt. in *James Joyce: The Critical Heritage*, vol. 1. Ed. Robert H. Deming. New York: Barnes and Noble, 1970, 268–71.

―――. 1930. "Arnold and Pater." Rpt. in *Selected Essays*. London: Faber, 1951.

―――. 1933/1964. *The Use of Poetry and the Use of Criticism*. Rpt. London: Faber, 1970.

―――. 1934. *After Strange Gods: A Primer of Modern Heresy*. Rpt. New York: Harcourt, Brace & Co., n.d.

Forster, E. M. 1910. *Howards End*. Rpt. New York: Vintage, n.d.

―――. 1949. "Art for Art's Sake." Rpt. in *Two Cheers for Democracy*. New York: Harcourt, Brace, 1951.

Freud, Sigmund, and Josef Breuer. 1895. *Studies on Hysteria*, vol. 2. All references and citations from Freud are from *The Standard Edition of the Complete Psychological Works of Sigmund Freud*, 24 vols. Ed. James Strachey. London: The Hogarth Press and the Institute of Psycho-Analysis, 1953–74.

―――. 1900. *The Interpretation of Dreams*. *Standard Edition*, vols. 4 and 5.

―――. 1910. "The Antithetical Meaning of Primal Words." *Standard Edition*, 11:153–61.

―――. 1918. "From the History of an Infantile Neurosis." *Standard Edition*, 17:7–122.

―――. 1925. "A Note upon the 'Mystic Writing-Pad.'" *Standard Edition*, 19:227–32.

Hardy, Thomas. 1878. *The Return of the Native*. All references and citations from Hardy are from the Anniversary Edition of *The Writings of Thomas Hardy*, New York and London: Harper and Brothers, 1920.

―――. 1886. *The Mayor of Casterbridge*.

―――. 1891. *Tess of the d'Urbervilles*.

Joyce, James. 1914. *Dubliners*. Ed. Robert Scholes and Richard Ellmann. Rpt. New York: Viking, 1967.

―――. 1916. *A Portrait of the Artist as a Young Man*. Ed. Chester G. Anderson and Richard Ellmann. Rpt. New York: Viking, 1974.

―――. 1922. *Ulysses*. Rpt. New York: Modern Library, 1961. Reset and corrected edition of the 1934 Random House text.

―――. 1984. *Ulysses: A Critical and Synoptic Edition*. Ed. Gabler, Steppe, and Melchior. New York: Garland.

Lawrence, D. H. 1914. Quoted in *Selected Literary Criticism*. Ed. Anthony Beal. Rpt. New York: Viking, 1969.

―――. 1936. "Study of Thomas Hardy." In *Phoenix: The Posthumous Papers, 1936*. Ed. Edward D. McDonald. Rpt. Harmondsworth: Penguin, 1980, 398–516.

Lewis, Wyndham. 1929. "D. H. Lawrence." Rpt. in *Enemy Salvoes: Selected Literary Criticism*. Ed. C. J. Fox. London: Vision Press, 1975.

Pater, Walter. 1873. Originally published as *Studies in the History of the Renais-*

sance. "The School of Giorgione" (1877) was added to the third edition of 1888 (*The Renaissance*). All references and citations from Pater are from the Library Edition, 10 vols. London: Macmillan, 1910.

————. 1885. *Marius the Epicurean.*

————. 1887. "A Prince of Court Painters." In *Imaginary Portraits.*

————. 1889. "Style." In *Appreciations.*

————. 1893. *Plato and Platonism.*

————. 1895a. *Greek Studies.*

————. 1895b. "The Child in the House." In *Miscellaneous Studies.*

————. 1895c. "Emerald Uthwart." In *Miscellaneous Studies.*

————. 1896. *Gaston De Latour: An Unfinished Romance.*

Strachey, James. 1934. "The Nature of the Therapeutic Action of Psycho-Analysis." *International Journal of Psycho-Analysis* 15 (1934): 127–59.

Strachey, Lytton. 1914. "A Victorian Critic." Rpt. in *Literary Essays*. New York: Harcourt, Brace & World, n.d., 209–14.

————. 1918. *Eminent Victorians*. Rpt. New York: Harcourt, Brace & World, n.d.

————. 1921. *Queen Victoria*. Rpt. New York: Harcourt, Brace & World, 1949.

————. 1928. *Elizabeth and Essex*. Rpt. New York: Harcourt, Brace & World, 1956.

Woolf, Virginia. 1920. "Freudian Fiction." Rpt. in *Contemporary Writers*. London: The Hogarth Press, 1965.

————. 1925. *Mrs. Dalloway*. Rpt. New York: Harcourt, Brace & World, 1953.

————. 1927. *To the Lighthouse*. Rpt. New York: Harcourt, Brace & World, 1955.

————. 1928. "Introduction." *Mrs. Dalloway*. New York: Modern Library.

————. 1937. "Craftsmanship." Rpt. in *Collected Essays*, 4 vols. New York: Harcourt, Brace & World, 1967, 2:245–51.

————. 1939. "A Sketch of the Past." Rpt. in *Moments of Being*. Ed. Jeanne Schulkind. New York: Harcourt Brace Jovanovich, 1976.

————. 1941. *Between the Acts*. Rpt. New York: Harcourt Brace Jovanovich, 1969.

Yeats, W. B. 1936. *The Oxford Book of Modern Verse*. Ed. Yeats. Rpt. New York: Oxford University Press, 1937.

SECONDARY SOURCES

Aiken, Conrad. 1923. "An Anatomy of Melancholy." Rpt. in *A Collection of Critical Essays on "The Waste Land."* Ed. Jay Martin. Englewood Cliffs: Prentice-Hall, 1968, 52–58.

Althusser, Louis. 1964. "Freud and Lacan." Rpt. in *Lenin and Philosophy*. Trans. Ben Brewster. New York: Monthly Review Press, 1971, 195–219.

Arendt, Hannah. 1951. *The Origins of Totalitarianism*. Rpt. New York: Harcourt Brace Jovanovich, 1973.

Bate, Walter Jackson. 1970. *The Burden of the Past and the English Poet*. Rpt. New York: Norton, 1972.

Bersani, Leo. 1976. *A Future for Astyanax: Character and Desire in Literature.* Boston: Little, Brown.

Blackmur, R. P. 1952. *Form and Value in Modern Poetry.* Rpt. New York: Anchor, 1957.

———. 1967. *A Primer of Ignorance.* Ed. Joseph Frank. New York: Harcourt, Brace & World.

Blamires, Harry. 1966. *The Bloomsday Book.* Rpt. London: Methuen, 1972.

Bloom, Harold. 1967. "The Place of Pater." In *The Ringers in the Tower: Studies in Romantic Tradition.* Rpt. Chicago: University of Chicago Press, 1973, 184–94.

———. 1969. "Browning's *Childe Roland*: All Things Deformed and Broken." In *The Ringers in the Tower.* Rpt. Chicago: University of Chicago Press, 1973, 156–67.

———. 1970. *Yeats.* New York: Oxford University Press.

———. 1973. *The Anxiety of Influence.* New York: Oxford University Press.

———. 1974. "The Crystal Man." *Selected Writings of Walter Pater.* Ed. Bloom. New York: New American Library.

———. 1975. *A Map of Misreading.* New York: Oxford University Press.

———. 1982. *The Breaking of the Vessels.* Chicago: University of Chicago Press.

Brisman, Leslie. 1977. "Swinburne's Semiotics." *The Georgia Review* 31 (Fall 1977): 578–97.

Brooks, Cleanth. 1939. *Modern Poetry and the Tradition.* Chapel Hill: University of North Carolina Press.

Budgen, Frank. 1934. *James Joyce and the Making of "Ulysses."* Rpt. Bloomington: Indiana University Press, 1964.

Bürger, Peter. 1984. *Theory of the Avant-Garde.* Trans. Michael Shaw. Minneapolis: University of Minnesota Press.

Bush, Ronald. 1984. *T. S. Eliot: A Study in Character and Style.* New York: Oxford University Press.

Cixous, Hélène. 1968. *The Exile of James Joyce.* Trans. Sally A. J. Purcell. New York: David Lewis, 1972.

Cohn, Dorritt. 1978. *Transparent Minds: Narrative Modes for Presenting Consciousness in Fiction.* Princeton: Princeton University Press.

Connolly, Cyril. 1948. *Enemies of Promise.* Rev. ed. New York: Macmillan.

Cope, Jackson. 1981. *Joyce's Cities: Archaeologies of the Soul.* Baltimore: Johns Hopkins University Press.

De Man, Paul. 1971. *Blindness and Insight.* New York: Oxford University Press.

———. 1984. *The Rhetoric of Romanticism.* New York: Columbia University Press.

Derrida, Jacques. 1967. *Of Grammatology.* Trans. Gayatri Chakravorty Spivak. Baltimore: Johns Hopkins University Press, 1976.

DiBattista, Maria. 1980. *Virginia Woolf's Major Novels: The Fables of Anon.* New Haven and London: Yale University Press.

Donoghue, Denis. 1974. "'The Word Within a Word.'" In *The Sovereign Ghost: Studies in Imagination.* Berkeley and Los Angeles: University of California Press, 1976, 183–206.

————. 1981. "Leavis and Eliot." *Raritan Review* 1 (Summer 1981): 68–87.

Dowling, David. 1985. *Bloomsbury Aesthetics and the Novels of Forster and Woolf.* New York: St. Martin's.

Drew, Elizabeth. 1949. *T. S. Eliot: The Design of His Poetry.* New York: Scribner's.

Eagleton, Terry. 1981. *Walter Benjamin.* London: Verso.

Eisenstein, Sergei. 1947. *The Film Sense.* Trans. Jay Leyda. Rpt. New York: Harcourt, Brace & World, 1970.

Ellmann, Maud. 1981. "Disremembering Dedalus: A *Portrait of the Artist as a Young Man.*" In *Untying the Text.* Ed. Robert Young. London: Routledge & Kegan Paul, 189–206.

————. 1982. "Polytropic Man: Paternity, Identity and Naming in *The Odyssey* and *A Portrait of the Artist as a Young Man.*" In *James Joyce: New Perspectives.* Ed. Colin MacCabe. Brighton: Harvester, 73–104.

Ellmann, Richard. 1972. *Ulysses on the Liffey.* New York: Oxford University Press.

————. 1977. *The Consciousness of Joyce.* London: Faber.

Empson, William. 1930. *Seven Types of Ambiguity.* Rpt. New York: New Directions, 1966.

————. 1982. "The Ultimate Novel." Rpt. in *Using Biography.* Cambridge: Harvard University Press, 1984, 217–59.

Epstein, E. L. 1982. "James Joyce and the Body." In *A Starchamber Quiry.* Ed. Epstein. London: Methuen, 73–106.

Fineman, Joel. 1980. "The Structure of Allegorical Desire." *October* 12 (Spring 1980): 47–66.

————. 1985. *Shakespeare's Perjured Eye: The Invention of Poetic Subjectivity in the Sonnets.* Berkeley and Los Angeles: University of California Press.

Fletcher, Pauline. 1983. *Gardens and Grim Ravines: The Language of Landscape in Victorian Poetry.* Princeton: Princeton University Press.

Foster, Hal, ed. 1983. *The Anti-Aesthetic: Essays on Postmodern Culture.* Port Townsend, Wash.: Bay Press.

Frye, Northrop. 1963. *T. S. Eliot.* Rpt. New York: Capricorn, 1972.

————. 1967. *The Modern Century.* Rpt. New York: Oxford University Press, 1969.

————. 1969. Introduction to *The Tempest.* In William Shakespeare, *The Complete Works.* Ed. Alfred Harbage. Baltimore: Penguin, 1369–72.

Gardner, Helen. 1950. *The Art of T. S. Eliot.* New York: Dutton.

Garnett, David. 1956. *The Flowers of the Forest.* New York: Harcourt, Brace.

Giamatti, A. Bartlett. 1984. *Exile and Change in Renaissance Literature.* New Haven and London: Yale University Press.

Gilbert, Stuart. 1930. *James Joyce's "Ulysses."* Rpt. New York: Knopf, 1952.

Goldberg, S. L. 1961. *The Classical Temper: A Study of James Joyce's "Ulysses."* Rpt. London: Chatto and Windus, 1963.

Gregor, Ian. 1970. "Eliot and Matthew Arnold." In *Eliot in Perspective.* Ed. Graham Martin. New York: Humanities Press, 267–78.

Guerard, Albert J. 1958. *Conrad the Novelist.* Rpt. New York: Atheneum, 1967.

Guetti, James. 1965. "*Heart of Darkness* and the Failure of the Imagination." *Sewanee Review* 83 (Summer 1965): 488–504.

Hartman, Geoffrey. 1962. "Romanticism and Anti-Self-Consciousness." In *Beyond Formalism*. New Haven and London: Yale University Press, 1970, 298–310.

———. 1972. "Reflections on the Evening Star: Akenside to Coleridge." In *New Perspectives on Coleridge and Wordsworth*. Ed. Hartman. New York: Columbia University Press, 85–131.

———. 1975. "Evening Star and Evening Land." In *The Fate of Reading*. Chicago: University of Chicago Press, 147–78.

Hayman, David. 1970. "The Empirical Molly." In *Approaches to "Ulysses."* Ed. Thomas Staley and Bernard Benstock. Pittsburgh: University of Pittsburgh Press, 103–35.

Hollander, John. 1981. *The Figure of Echo: A Mode of Allusion in Milton and After*. Berkeley and Los Angeles: University of California Press.

Holroyd, Michael. 1968. *Lytton Strachey: A Critical Biography*. 2 vols. New York: Holt, Rinehart and Winston.

Howe, Irving. 1967. *Thomas Hardy*. New York: Macmillan.

———. 1970. "The Culture of Modernism." In *Decline of the New*. Rpt. New York: Horizon, 1970, 3–33.

Jameson, Fredric. 1979. *Fables of Aggression: Wyndham Lewis, the Modernist as Fascist*. Berkeley and Los Angeles: University of California Press.

———. 1981. *The Political Unconscious*. Ithaca: Cornell University Press.

Javitch, Daniel. 1978. *Poetry and Courtliness in Renaissance England*. Princeton: Princeton University Press.

Jay, Gregory. 1983. *T. S. Eliot and the Poetics of Literary History*. Baton Rouge: Louisiana State University Press.

Jay, Paul. 1984. *Being in the Text: Self-Representation from Wordsworth to Roland Barthes*. Ithaca: Cornell University Press.

Johnstone, J. K. 1954. *The Bloomsbury Group*. New York: Noonday.

Kain, Richard. 1947. *Fabulous Voyager: James Joyce's "Ulysses."* Rpt. Chicago: University of Chicago Press, 1959.

Kellogg, Robert. 1974. "Scylla and Charybdis." In *James Joyce's "Ulysses."* Ed. Clive Hart and David Hayman. Berkeley and Los Angeles: University of California Press, 147–79.

Kendrick, Walter. 1977. "The Sensationalism of *The Woman in White*." *Nineteenth-Century Fiction* 32:1 (June 1977): 18–35.

Kenner, Hugh. 1956. *Dublin's Joyce*. Rpt. Gloucester, Mass.: Peter Smith, 1969.

———. 1971. *The Pound Era*. Berkeley and Los Angeles: University of California Press.

———. 1978. *Joyce's Voices*. Berkeley and Los Angeles: University of California Press.

Kermode, Frank. 1957. *Romantic Image*. Rpt. New York: Vintage, 1964.

Krauss, Rosalind. 1985. *The Originality of the Avant-Garde and Other Modernist Myths*. Cambridge: MIT Press.

Langbaum, Robert. 1957. *The Poetry of Experience*. Rpt. New York: Norton, 1963.

Leavis, F. R. 1930. *Mass Civilisation and Minority Culture*. Cambridge: Minority Press.

———. 1932. *New Bearings in English Poetry*. Rpt. Harmondsworth: Penguin, 1967.

———. 1958. "T. S. Eliot as Critic." Rpt. in *Anna Karenina and Other Essays*. New York: Clarion, 1969, 177–96.

Levenson, Michael. 1984. *A Genealogy of Modernism: A Study of English Literary Doctrine, 1908–1922*. Cambridge: Cambridge University Press.

Levin, Harry. 1941. *James Joyce*. Rpt. New York: New Directions, 1960.

———. 1960. "What Was Modernism?" In *Refractions*. New York: Oxford University Press, 1966, 271–95.

Levine, George. 1981. *The Realistic Imagination: English Fiction from Frankenstein to Lady Chatterley*. Chicago: University of Chicago Press.

Lévi-Strauss, Claude. 1962. *The Savage Mind*. Rpt. Chicago: University of Chicago Press, 1966.

Lukács, Georg. 1920. *The Theory of the Novel*. Trans. Anna Bostock. Rpt. Cambridge: MIT Press, 1971.

Materer, Timothy. 1979. *Vortex: Pound, Eliot, and Lewis*. Ithaca: Cornell University Press.

Matro, Thomas G. 1984. "Vision and Achievement in *To the Lighthouse*." *PMLA* 99:2 (March 1984): 212–24.

McFarland, Thomas. 1985. *Originality and Imagination*. Baltimore: Johns Hopkins University Press.

Meisel, Perry. 1972. *Thomas Hardy: The Return of the Repressed*. New Haven and London: Yale University Press.

———. 1980. *The Absent Father: Virginia Woolf and Walter Pater*. New Haven and London: Yale University Press.

———. 1982. "Imitation Modernism." *The Atlantic*, March 1982, 86–88.

———. 1984. "Freud's Reflexive Realism." *October* 28 (Spring 1984): 43–57.

Meisel, Perry, and Walter Kendrick, eds. 1985. *Bloomsbury/Freud: The Letters of James and Alix Strachey, 1924–25*. New York: Basic Books.

Michaels, Walter Benn. 1981. "Philosophy in Kinkanja: Eliot's Pragmatism." In *Glyph 8*. Ed. Michaels. Baltimore: Johns Hopkins University Press, 170–202.

Miller, D. A. 1983. "Discipline in Different Voices: Bureaucracy, Police, Family, and *Bleak House*." *Representations* 1:1 (February 1983): 59–89.

Miller, J. Hillis. 1965. *Poets of Reality*. Cambridge: Harvard University Press.

———. 1970. "Virginia Woolf's All Souls' Day." Revised as "*Mrs. Dalloway*: Repetition as a Raising of the Dead." In *Fiction and Repetition: Seven English Novels*. Cambridge: Harvard University Press, 1982, 176–202.

Naremore, James. 1973. *The World Without a Self: Virginia Woolf and the Novel*. New Haven and London: Yale University Press.

Parker, Andrew. 1982–83. "Ezra Pound and the 'Economy' of Anti-Semitism." *Boundary 2*, 11:1–2 (Fall/Winter 1982–83): 103–28.

Parrinder, Patrick. 1984. *James Joyce*. Cambridge: Cambridge University Press.

Paul, Herbert. 1902. *Matthew Arnold*. Rpt. New York: Macmillan, 1920.

Perkins, David. 1976. *A History of Modern Poetry*. Cambridge: Harvard University Press.

Poggioli, Renato. 1968. *The Theory of the Avant-Garde*. Trans. Gerald Fitzgerald. Cambridge: Harvard University Press.

Poirier, Richard. 1967/1971. "The Literature of Waste: Eliot, Joyce, and Others." Rpt. in *The Performing Self*. New York: Oxford University Press, 1971, 45–61.

Poole, Roger. 1978. *The Unknown Virginia Woolf*. Cambridge: Cambridge University Press.

Quillian, William H. 1983. *Hamlet and the New Poetic: James Joyce and T. S. Eliot*. Ann Arbor: UMI Research Press.

Reiss, Timothy J. 1982. *The Discourse of Modernism*. Ithaca: Cornell University Press.

Riddel, Joseph. 1978. "The Elliptical Poem." *Genre* 11:4 (Winter 1978): 459–78.

Riquelme, John Paul. 1983. *Teller and Tale in Joyce's Fiction*. Baltimore: Johns Hopkins University Press.

Said, Edward. 1978. *Orientalism*. New York: Pantheon.

Senn, Fritz. 1984. *Joyce's Dislocutions*. Ed. John Paul Riquelme. Baltimore: Johns Hopkins University Press.

Spanos, William V. 1978. "Hermeneutics and Memory: Destroying T. S. Eliot's *Four Quartets*." *Genre* 11:4 (Winter 1978): 523–74.

Spender, Stephen. 1953. *The Destructive Element*. Rpt. Philadelphia: Albert Saifer, 1983.

Steiner, George. 1978. *On Difficulty and Other Essays*. New York: Oxford University Press.

Stone, Jennifer. 1984. "Gramsci's Archetexture." *Italian Quarterly* 97–98 (Summer 1984–Fall 1984): 65–80.

Sultan, Stanley. 1977. *"Ulysses," "The Waste Land," and Modernism*. Port Washington: Kennikat Press.

Thorburn, David. 1974. *Conrad's Romanticism*. New Haven and London: Yale University Press.

Tillotson, Geoffrey. 1968. "Matthew Arnold's Prose: Theory and Practice." In *The Art of Victorian Prose*. Ed. George Levine and William Madden. New York: Oxford University Press, 73–100.

Trilling, Lionel. 1939. *Matthew Arnold*. Rpt. in *The Works of Lionel Trilling*. New York: Harcourt Brace Jovanovich, 1979.

———. 1955. Originally published as *Freud and the Crisis of Our Culture*. Boston: Beacon. Subsequently revised and reprinted as "Freud: Within and Beyond Culture" (1965). All citations are from *Beyond Culture* (1965). Rpt. in *Beyond Culture: The Works of Lionel Trilling*. New York: Harcourt Brace Jovanovich, n.d., 77–102.

Unkeless, Elaine. 1982. "The Conventional Molly Bloom." In *Women in Joyce*. Eds. Suzette Henke and Elaine Unkeless. Urbana: University of Illinois Press, 150–68.

Updike, John. 1984. "Modernist, Postmodernist, What Will They Think of Next?" *The New Yorker*. September 10, 1984, 136–42.

Van Ghent, Dorothy. 1953. "On *A Portrait of the Artist as a Young Man*." In *The English Novel: Form and Function*. Rpt. New York: Harper & Row, 1967, 316–32.

Walzl, Florence. 1966. "Gabriel and Michael: The Conclusion of 'The Dead.'" *James Joyce Quarterly* 4 (Fall 1966): 17–31.

Watt, Ian. 1957. *The Rise of the Novel*. Rpt. Berkeley and Los Angeles: University of California Press, 1965.

———. 1979. *Conrad in the Nineteenth Century*. Berkeley and Los Angeles: University of California Press.

Weber, Samuel. 1982. *The Legend of Freud*. Minneapolis: University of Minnesota Press.

Williams, Raymond. 1958. *Culture and Society, 1780–1950*. Rpt. New York: Harper Torchbook, 1966.

———. 1973. *The Country and the City*. Rpt. New York: Oxford University Press, 1975.

Wilson, Edmund. 1931. *Axel's Castle*. Rpt. New York: Scribner's, 1969.

Index

FR Rev = equality
creates the { leadership
problem of { community
{ judgement

in short — the
problem of judgement

see p. 53